It's Only Business!

'...offers a wealth of essential information, analysis, and insight for all those who are prepared to proactively unite the power of markets with the authority of universal ideals.'
—*Fred Dubee, Senior Adviser, Global Compact, United Nations*

'The book displays considerable scholarship and effort...must be read by all serious business leaders and managers.'
—*The Hindu*

'...this anthology of interesting cases on CSR is commendable, highlighting...the existence of pockets of focused effort in the Indian business landscape.'
—*Business World*

'Mitra believes corporate responsibility assumes great worth in a country like India...comments on the worldwide transition under way and the approaches and efforts in CSR.'
—*Business India*

'Meera Mitra's book is...not just timely, but a valuable addition to the growing body of work in this area.'
—*Business Today*

It's Only Business!

India's Corporate
Social Responsiveness in
a Globalized World

with a Foreword by
N.R. Narayana Murthy

MEERA MITRA

OXFORD
UNIVERSITY PRESS

OXFORD
UNIVERSITY PRESS

Oxford University Press is a department of the University of Oxford.
It furthers the University's objective of excellence in research, scholarship,
and education by publishing worldwide. Oxford is a registered trademark of
Oxford University Press in the UK and in certain other countries

Published in India by
Oxford University Press
YMCA Library Building, 1 Jai Singh Road, New Delhi 110001, India

First published 2007
Oxford India Paperbacks 2009
Second impression 2011

ISBN-13: 978-0-19-806026-0
ISBN-10: 0-19-806026-2

Typeset in Adobe Garamond 11/14 by Jojy Philip
Printed in India by Anvi Composers, New Delhi 110 063

For Amit
For abundant love and inspiration always

CONTENTS

PREFACE TO THE PAPERBACK EDITION   ix

FOREWORD BY N.R. NARAYANA MURTHY   xiv

PREFACE   xvi

ACKNOWLEDGEMENTS   xx

ABBREVIATIONS   xxii

INTRODUCTION   xxiv

BACKDROP

1   BEING POLITICALLY CORRECT ABOUT CSR   1

2   LEARNING LEGACY: INDIA'S BUSINESS–SOCIETY
INTERFACE   15

NEW TRENDS

3   SCOURING SOCIAL SENSITIVITIES: AHEAD OF THE LAW   34

4   EYE ON I.T.: PREPARING FOR AND MANAGING CHANGE   54

5   DEVELOPING MARKETS AND MARKETING DEVELOPMENT   81

INFLUENCERS

6   CIVIL SOCIETY ROAR: INDIA'S NGOs AND CSR   94

7   EMBEDDING CSR IN INDIA   120

8   GOVERNMENTS' GROOMING FOR CSR:
GLOBAL AND INDIAN RESPONSE   139

9   LOOKING AHEAD   151

ANNEXURES   167

INDEX   189

PREFACE TO THE PAPERBACK EDITION

Since the hardback edition in 2007, many of the existing corporate social responsibility challenges have deepened, and many new challenges have been added. Business in India has had to respond to extra market and extra legal expectations from it, often in the gaze of a 'noisy' democracy. Business has been asked to be inclusive and not just merit based; to be ahead of the law and not just to run with it; to be consultative rather than just procedural; and to meet global standards and not just local ones. These are also reflections of changed expectations in society.

Other stakeholders who influence business functioning, like the State and the civil society groups, are themselves going through similar transformation. The State, while providing support to business and industrialization, often lags behind the changes expected of it. In such contexts, business, as a partner with the State in industrialization, has had to face backlash as well. Examples from the past have already been described in the book. With deepening economic reforms, newer and more numerous issues are speedily confronting business. A key role of 'public gaze' on such issues is being provided by the media. These factors together are creating new 'risk' factors for business.

Two issues have been at the centrestage of controversy recently. The first arises out of land requirements for industrialization and the second, from managing job redundancies. The lessons here are the same. There is a case for greater awareness, caution, and sensitivity expected from business.

With deepening industrialization, the role of the State in acquiring land for industries under the arcane and colonial Land Acquisitions Act 1894 has come under the scanner. This is to be distinguished from land bought through market purchase. Both, the implementation and the provisions of the mentioned Act have been questioned. The Act, based on the principle of 'eminent domain', allows the State to compulsorily acquire private land for public purpose. Industrial projects which bring public employment and other benefits is included under this purview. With liberalization the use of 'public purpose' provision for private industry is on the increase. Though the State has the prime responsibility for managing this acquisition, business has been drawn into these debates.

In the last two years Indian companies as well as MNCs have been at the receiving end of such protests, at times violent, in several states like Maharashtra, Orissa, and West Bengal. The Singur project in West Bengal is a landmark case with reverberations being felt in the rest of the country and offering lessons perhaps for all future projects.

There is satire in Singur. The pro-industrialization communist government of the state of West Bengal had acquired approximately 1000 acres of land for the corporate giant Tata Motors' pro-people small car project, *Nano*. West Bengal was ironically 'disadvantaged' in having better land distribution, and in being naturally endowed with cultivatable land. Both these factors exacerbated the challenges of acquisition. First, it meant dealing with the presence of a larger number of small cultivating farmers who came into being due to land reform. Second, it was naturally 'disadvantaged' as non cultivable categories of land (less controversial) were available less here than elsewhere. In West Bengal such land constitutes only 1 per cent as compared to the national average of 17.6 per cent.

Despite several provisions to ease the problems associated with 'land acquisition' by the West Bengal government, the emotive and economic and political reasons to protest compulsory acquisition remained. Farmers owning 300 acres of the approximately 1000 acres that were acquired were reluctant to sell. They were given voice and support by the opposition political coalition. Though the Land Acquisition Act leaves much to be desired and an Amendment is on the cards to provide for more caring and transparent provisions and processes, compulsory acquisition will remain a political issue. It is quite clear that legislative frameworks have not matched the social and political democracy and demands have also deepened. Broader questions of how much incentive should be given to industry and what would be the benefits to locals are also raised.

During the construction of the plant at Singur, Tata Motors faced protests on the issue of land acquisition. After two years of work on the construction phase, the company stated that heightened hostility, agitation and intimidation, and assault led it to suspend the start up phase of the plant. In addition to agitation and hostility, Tata Motors cites the 'continuous effect on the reputation and integrity of the Tata Group'[1] as reasons for its suspension and eventual pull out. Tata Motors has been given a new home in the state of Gujarat—but this too has not been without hiccups.

Clearly the battle surrounding Singur, is between different stakeholder perspectives for a conducive but fair climate for industrialization. It has also become clear that market negotiated land deals (though tedious and with problems of their own), as opposed to compulsory acquisition, have delivered larger consolidation of land due to more flexible and satisfactory negotiations, often on a one-to-one basis.

There has been disquiet about land acquisition for some time. A spate of Rehabilitation and Resettlement Policies in 2007, and the Recommendations of the Standing Committee on SEZs 2007 had already paved the way for more 'caring', expanded, and transparent provisions for those affected. The inadequacy of the chilling provisions of the arcane Land Acquisition Act of 1894 (used in Singur), has been exposed and the proposed Amendment Bill (2007) still awaits enactment. Convergence among these would be necessary to cut out loopholes. What is missing is evident from the proposed ammendments to the Act. Transparency and fair pricing provisions and more sensitive rehabilitation plans are embedded here. Rehabilitation plans will have to be made in consultation with affected families. Importantly, acquisitions will need to be discussed in the *gram sabha* and circulated publicly. Moreover, more market responsive direct purchase (both private and public) will constitute 70 per cent of the needed land; acquisitions for companies will be made only for up to 30 per cent of the land required; and further 'intended use of land' will be a factor in determining value for the displaced land.[2]

Land acquisition is clearly an issue because of the 'involuntary' nature of the displacement and the compensations it has offered. However, agriculture is under stress and land has been sold with less controversy through market

---

[1] See Tata Motors' Official Press Releases, 2 September 2008, 'Motors Suspends Work on Nano Plant in Singur', http://www.tatamotors.com/our_world/press_releases.php?ID=385& action=Pull; 3 October 2008, 'Tata Motors to relocate Nano Project from Singur', http:// www.tatamotors.com/our_world/press_releases.php?ID=392&action=Pull.

[2] Note: Civil Society Groups have voiced objections to the Bill in its present form.

processes. The share of agriculture in total employment was 52 per cent in 2004–05. However, the share of agriculture to GDP is only 18.5 per cent (2006–07).[3] The average land holding size and its capitalization is low and farmers often get only seasonal livelihood from agriculture. Only 40 per cent of sown area is irrigated. The majority of the farmers in Singur have accepted land transformation through land acquisition, as have those farmers who have sold the land in even larger projects. The total agricultural land that has changed hands for SEZs (Special Economic Zones) alone is 1,781,000 hectares,[4] many times more than the number of farmers impacted by the transformation.[5]

Business will have to handle land issues with greater awareness and sensitivity in this transformation period where new expectations exist beyond legal frameworks and where governance systems are yet to be effective. This would be more so where land is acquired by the State on behalf of industry. Industry is already beginning to seek clarity. Business chambers have asked for more transparent and flexible terms for land acquisition by the State as also more speedy action on this front.

Another controversy that has emerged before business, in the last few months, is that of negotiating job redundancy. The global financial crises and the sagging airlines industry precipitated this. Jet Airways, in India, undertook 'rationalization' measures that involved retrenchment of 1900 of its staff in October 2008, including unconfirmed and temporary staff. These employees were retrenched with packages but without prior notice or consultation. Though lawyers are divided, there is opinion that such a dismissal did meet legal requirements. Redundancies have been handled for some time but there were three factors that highlighted this controversy. The dismissal, without notice and consultation, was protested as being 'unfair'. Second, protests from a large number of the service staff, as distinct from workers, was a novelty and was highlighted by the media. Third, due to protracted employee protest, support from political parties, and also in the gaze of the visual media, the employees were take back. The message— retrenchment without consultation, in contrast with other kinds of

---

[3] GoI Economic Survey 2007–08, pp. 155, 247.

[4] GoI Ministry of Agriculture http://www.sezindia.gov.in/HTMLS/groundrealities.pdf.

[5] According to the NSSO Survey 2002–03, about 79 per cent of rural households held less than 1 hectare of land. About 32 per cent of this held land less than 0.0002 hectares.

negotiated severance arrangements—was not acceptable. In this case the objectives of cost cutting by the management through this measure, had to be temporarily abondoned and the need for more negotiated settlements reinforced. Kingfisher Airlines had, just months before, embarked upon a downsizing exercise with voluntary separation scheme (VSS) or severance package, putting out of work 300 employees.

Larger redundancies have been managed in the past. In 2001 in a heavily unionized atmosphere and after long protracted negotiations, approximately 100,000 employees of State Bank of India availed the Voluntary Retirement Scheme (VRS). The public sector reform agenda also threw out thousands in short spaces of time in the past decade, across India. Air India had negotiated with 15,000 employees to go on leave without pay for several years. This settlement however came after protracted consultations and negotiations with the associations representing these employees and with political backing as well. The particular case of summary dismissal by Jet Airways however caught public attention. Once again there is good reason to be consultative.

Liberalization brought India 45 million new job opportunities between 2000 and 2005 (GoI Economic Survey 2007–08). The structural shift to the services sector mean that a class of young workers had early choices of unexpectedly lucrative jobs and hard work. Favoured by a huge demand, attrition rates ran high which were estimated upwards of 40 per cent annually in IT and ITES industries. Employers had used all kinds of inducements to stay the attrition. Both employees and company managers are now beginning to face the downturns of capitalism and resulting redundancy. In the absence of labour reforms and social security benefits, flexibilities are being built into existing arrangements through negotiated settlements. These will have to be measured and consultative. There is a message here. The law can be on the side of business, but perceptions of what the law should be or how it is to be implemented have changed, drawing political support as well.

There have been other similar issues that were captured in the earlier preface.

December 2008   MEERA MITRA

FOREWORD

Around the world today, corporations are emerging as the most influential institutions of our time. They dominate investment in both developed and developing countries. In terms of revenues, fifty-one of the largest hundred economies in the world now are corporations, not countries. With the rise of corporate power, businesses today have a significant impact on the economic and social systems of the communities they operate in.

As a result, corporations face increased expectations, to not just achieve their economic goals but also, in the words of professor and writer Philip Kotler, to fulfil the responsibility of doing good. The *good* that a corporation must do is defined by corporate social responsibility (CSR). CSR thus encompasses the ideas of corporate governance, sustainable wealth creation, corporate philanthropy, and advocacy for the goals of the community.

Its Only Business! India's Corporate Social Responsiveness is an informative study on the growth of corporate social responsibility in India. The author, Meera Mitra, investigates the evolution of CSR in India and its relevance to Indian businesses in the context of globalization and a competitive, liberalized market. Mitra discusses the beginnings of CSR in the country—from the growth of 'guilds' aimed at social development in ancient India to Mahatma Gandhi's idea of 'trusteeship' of corporations.

However, following Independence, very few Indian corporations incorporated social responsibility into their business goals. This attitude has begun to change since economic liberalization in 1991. As the role of India's public sector in the economy diminishes, the private sector is increasingly viewed as the key player in driving development in the country. Consequently, as Mitra notes, the Indian public expects businesses to play a leadership role in addressing the country's social and economic challenges.

Indian corporations are beginning to respond to this 'market force of social expectations' through responsible business practices and the contribution of corporate resources to social initiatives and development. Mitra examines the efforts of Indian corporations such as the Tatas, which emphasized CSR since the 1940s, and the initiatives of Maruti, Ashok Leyland, and Infosys—in education, children and women's welfare, and rural and community development. She also discusses the linkages Indian corporations have established with NGOs and the government in their efforts to drive social and economic change.

In addition, as Mitra notes, globalization has brought new challenges to CSR in India with a variety of governance principles and ethical guidelines emerging from different parts of the world—the US, Europe, and East Asia. The author offers a mix of analysis and example as she draws useful distinctions between the various governance codes and regulatory standards that are impacting the CSR movement in India.

The book provides a wealth of insight and information on the evolving nature of corporate social responsibility in the Indian industry. Increasingly, decision makers across Indian companies, today, recognize that following the dictates of a broader, social conscience can help them realize new markets, increased profits, an improved corporate image, and happier employees. At the same time, it enables them to contribute meaningfully to economic and social development in the country.

It's Only Business! is a valuable handbook for managers and business leaders in India who believe that businesses must make profits while embracing broader social goals and affirming a respect for their people, communities, and the broader society they operate in.

September 2006

N.R. NARAYANA MURTHY
Chairman and Chief Mentor
Infosys Technologies Ltd.
Bangalore

PREFACE

Since writing this book, the business–society discourse in India has come centre stage on more than one occasion. Business in India, has had to respond to extra market expectations, often in the gaze of a 'noisy' democracy. In the events of past months, business has been asked to be inclusive and not just merit based, maximal and not just legal, to be ahead of the law, and not just run with it. It seems to have succumbed in a reactive mode. This book has however, focused more on the precautionary and promotive actions by business. But even within this context it is a narrative of different approaches by business to new developments. With globalization there are lessons for transformation in the roles not just for business but for government and civil society as well.

In recent months business has been asked to be inclusive. The possibility of government seeking reservations, in private institutions of higher education and in private sector jobs, for hitherto marginalized groups has re-emerged. The proposed reservations could add up to almost 50 per cent seats in educational institutions as well as for jobs. This is being resisted by business. With such high percentages sought for reservations and dismal ground realities at the lower levels of education and skill development, being both inclusive and competitive at the same time is clearly challenging.

A constitutional amendment paved the way for two proposed legislations impacting the public and the private sector.[1] As a step towards this, the government introduced a bill in August 2006 favouring reservation in government aided institutions of higher learning for the additional groups of Other Backward Castes (OBCs). Even for reservations in government aided institutions this has

---

[1] Reservations in educational institutions of higher learning for the categories of Scheduled Castes (SC), Scheduled Tribes (ST), and Other Backward Castes (OBC), and for job reservations for these groups as well.

led to heated and continuing debate. On the agenda is a plan to legislate—in a staggered manner—such requirements in the private educational institutions and private sector jobs as well. The initial response has been one of industry resistance, and points to the impact this extra market action would have in a competitive and globalized environment—its plea for affirmative action instead did not find political support.

In the face of impending legislation, this has paved the way for other approaches by business as well. Recent submissions by major apex chambers indicate a willingness to engage innovatively. It is clearly recognized that to achieve this inclusiveness of business in higher levels of education, in creation of jobs, as well as for improving the quality of primary, secondary, and technical levels of education, 'government responsibilities needs to be strengthened'. Position papers of Indian industry associations outline their vision as well as their willingness to be engaged in this effort. Together these approaches are *multiscoped*, addressing among other things, changes at the school, technical institutes, and the entrepreneurship level for achieving higher quality education and for linkages with the marketplace. The approach suggests remedial processes and inputs for those who fall through the cracks. The approaches are also *multipronged* in outlining necessary policy changes, the use of fiscal and financial instruments, and operationalizing these through business partnerships. The CII–Assocham position also advocates developing in the interim period, voluntary codes for achieving inclusiveness in industry and monitoring processes to achieve set goals. The overall intent of the Confederation's papers is to create an enabling environment to retain inclusiveness with merit, necessary in a competitive and globalizing world.

The draft approach paper of the Government of India for the XI Plan, for 'faster' and more 'inclusive' growth indicates a strong partnership role for business not just in education but in several other social services sectors as well. These may vary, ranging from purely philanthropic inputs for model-building ventures to incentivized roles of various degrees. It is likely that while the involvement of business in these roles will be extended, both business and government will also be under closer scrutiny. This is an opportunity to develop a broader vision for innovative new roles and deliver systems to bolster the credibility and legitimacy of such initiatives.

Deepening global integration has left in its wake the integration of worldwide social expectations. Business is being asked to work for social advantage not comparative advantage. Business has not always responded well to these ever emerging social imperatives. If there is to be a calibrated process for this, it has not yet found favour in the face of highly emotive persuasions of NGOs, which find place in political processes as well. Often business has also lost out in the communication battle with NGOs and both—the former's image and the business activity—have taken a beating.

The pepsi-coke controversy, regarding permissible limits of pesticides in their soft drinks (outlined in a segment in the book), is still being unraveled. This has reemerged again in 2006. Whatever the technical issues, (there are many and still emerging), the move has been to set higher and more stringent standards for safety. The question as to whether violations have taken place, (in terms of residues in colas not being within the specified limits), is still to be resolved though the perception has all along been (as indicated by the decline in sales of the colas—reportedly to approximately 40 per cent, not to mention political upsurge) heavily weighted against business. Corporate communication has not overcome this, nor has it satisfied customer queries or sufficiently educated the consumers on this issue. There is also the question of 'whom to believe'?

Standards setting mechanisms and processes of government have come into question, as well as the industry's role in colluding with the government on this. Through NGOs, civil society is demanding a space in the processes of decision-making. Industry has acquiesced to multi-stakeholder demands and indicated a willingness to engage for setting new norms as well. India will end up with unprecedented global standards, if end-product norms are indicated for soft drinks.

In the context of globalized business, issues of 'fairness' spearheaded by NGOs is increasingly making inroads into established practices and laws. While this may be viewed as part of an evolutionary process, business as a whole and the concerned industry in particular are often branded for their lapses. In recent months, India has been the public venue for such branding—as in the case of 'toxic' ships moving from the developed to the developing world seeking anchorage.

This case began when the French aircraft carrier *Clemenceau*, allegedly bringing tonnes of hazardous asbestos and other carcinogens, moved in turbulent social and legal waters before it sought entry to India for demolition, at the world's largest ship-breaking yard at Alang, Gujarat. In the eyes of NGOs, the movement of ships for demolition represented the movement of toxic waste from developed to developing shores. This was exacerbated when health and safety conditions of labourers working at shipbreaking yards in India were brought into focus. Greenpeace International and Greenpeace India, IMF (International Maritime Foundation), and the Indian Platform on Ship-breaking (a coalition of non-government organizations in India with union representation as well) highlighted unhealthy work and safety conditions in Alang. The Supreme Court in India and the Court in France were moved for relief. There were several wins for civil society groups. Whether a ship built of material that had carcinogens, moving for demolition constituted the movement of toxic waste and therefore violated international laws were ruled in the affirmative. The conditions of workers in Alang were brought into question. The then French President Jacques Chirac recalled *Clemenceau* home, to port at Brest on moral grounds.

However there were sufficient loopholes and in May–June 2006 yet another ship, now famously known as Blue Lady (also allegedly containing over a thousand tonnes of asbestos), sought permission to enter Indian waters. The Supreme Court of India has allowed beaching rights to Blue Lady on the recommendations of the Technical Committee, for the time being. The question as to how 'safe' existing conditions of work for contract labour in Alang are, will undoubtedly get scrutinized in the months ahead. It is increasingly argued that it is in business' own interest to keep abreast and ensure this.

The globalized world is one of tumultuous change. In the competitive environment, the easiest retreat would be for business to move elsewhere. There is little guarantee though that with a globalized civil society the issues will not move with them as it has in the above case. On the other hand, getting the government to play an impartial, firm, and expeditious role in the face of such changes requires it to transform itself as well. Business certainly has its work cut out.

October 2006 MEERA MITRA
New Delhi

ACKNOWLEDGEMENTS

Corporate social responsibility covers a wide landscape of initiatives, emerging out of the confluence of multiple actors, ideas, and approaches. I have benefited from the perspectives, experiences, and expertise shared with me by many, both inside and outside the business world.

Managers and professionals and CEOs from the corporate world guided me to the approaches and issues in CSR in their respective fields. In the area of information technology and ITES, I am grateful to Sugata Mitra and Anwar Ahmed Khan of NIIT; Vijay K. Gupta and Anand Swaminathan of Wipro; and Kavita Prakash-Mani of Sustainability, UK. For the perspectives from the business chambers, I am particularly grateful to N. Srinivasan, Director General of Confederation of Indian Industry (CII) and to Amit Mitra, Secretary General, Federation of Indian Chambers of Commerce and Industry (FICCI) for raising critical issues in CSR while indicating the vast scope and spread of their approach. I thank the managers of various sectoral programmes of these two organizations as well as those of the Punjab Haryana and Delhi Chambers (PHD) for detailing the range of initiatives and learning—Harry Sethi, Atul shumlu, Dr Hamsa, Teevra Sharma, Ramnik Ahuja, and Narendra Bhatia.

Many international processes are underway to promote CSR related activities in India. I appreciate very much the detailed outlining of the genesis, approach, and challenges before the Global Compact by Uddesh Kohli, former chairman of SCOPE and Senior Advisor and Member, Governing Council, Global Compact Society, India. I am also appreciative of the interest and encouragement of those who read entire drafts of the manuscript. Among those I would like to thank Fred Dubee, M.M. Luther, and Dipankar Gupta.

It is my association with the non-profit world which indirectly led me to this study. Viraf Mehta, CEO, Partners in Change, and before him

Shankar Venkateshwaran, cultivated my interest in this field. Viraf was particularly generous in sharing information on various dimensions of CSR over the last two years. I thank Rashid Kidwai, formerly from the corporate world, now CEO, Grassroots Trading Network, a non-profit company for introducing me to public–corporate–NGO partnerships in development, which this book also draws on.

Chandra Bhushan of Centre for Science and Environment introduced me to CSE's own extensive literature on corporates and their adroit movements. I am grateful to Parna Dasgupta, Confederation of Food Trade Industries, for guiding me through the business perspectives on this. For information and support in many other ways I would also like to thank Krishan Kalra, Arun Chawla, and K.S. Narayanaswamy.

I am grateful to Oxford University Press for their individual and immediate interest in this topic and also for steering inputs for enhancing the book and taking me seamlessly through considerable processes of publication.

It is always difficult to thank family without being inadequate. Amit, Acha, Aditi, Rajiv, and Anubhav had to bear with me during this period. Ever loving, encouraging, supporting, fearlessly critical when called upon to review, and watchful of any remiss in the pace of writing, they left me with no room for excuses.

MEERA MITRA

ABBREVIATIONS

APCM	Assemblée Permanente des Chambres de méteirs
ARED	Association for Rural Economic Development
ASA	Association for Support of Ashalayam
BPOs	Business Process Outsourcing
BT	British Telecom
CEQ	Council of Environmental Quality
CII	Confederation of Indian Industries
CITU	Centre for Indian Trade Unions
CLE	Council for Leather Exports
CSR	Corporate Social Responsibility
DTC	Delhi Transport Corporation
FICCI	Federation of Indian Chambers of Commerce and Industry
FICCI-SEDF	FICCI Socio-Economic Foundation
GLT	Global Leader of Tomorrow
GPO	Grassroots Producers Organization
GTN	Grassroots Trading Network
ICRISAT	International Crops Research Institute for Semi-Arid Tropics
IEAG	India Export Advisory Group for Polio Eradication
IFC	International Finance Corporation
ILO	International Labour Organization
IRFT	International Resources for Fairer Trade
ITES	Information Technology Enabled Services
ITPF	IT Professionals Forum of India

KITES	Katha Information Technology and E-commerce Schools
NAFE	North American Alliance for Fair Economy
NIIT	National Institute of Information Technology
PCB	Pollution Control Board
PETA	People for Ethical Treatment of Animals
PIL	Public Interest Litigation
RCH	Reproductive and Child Health
RUDI	Rural Distribution Network
SDC	Social Development Council
SEWA	Self Employed Women's Association
SME	Small and Medium Enterprises
TBI	Triple Bottom Line

INTRODUCTION

In his book *The New Paradigm of Business*, Michael Ray comments on worldwide transitions underway and the approaches and efforts in corporate social responsibility. He describes these as being akin to 'rebuilding the spaceship while it is still in flight'.[1] The analogy is pregnant with meaning. There is the sense of a hugely different and difficult endeavour, in an unfamiliar, dynamic, fast-moving terrain—hurtling to definite catastrophy, if unattended. Such concerns have been, not least of all, those of business as well. India, described as the second-largest emerging market in the world, also has the world's largest population in abject poverty and thus cradles a major pressure point of such transformation.

In the context of what is happening worldwide, this book is about CSR in India. Chapter 1 on 'Being Politically Correct about CSR' outlines philosophical and political aspects of CSR. There appears to be, as shown in this chapter, a synchronized chorus from political heads across the globe for such an engagement by business. However, this chapter also shows that there are variations, philosophically, regarding the expediency and desirability of such an engagement.

Chapter 2 'Learning Legacy: India's Business–Society Interface' discusses the historical backdrop. In the symphony of the expanding and contracting, and overlapping roles of civil society, politics, and business, CSR is a new injection. However, debates on the role of wealth and business have taken place in the past in India. In the cusp of change, India has a marked legacy in such discourse and practices as well. We are heirs to the tradition set by business in the distant past. Sections of this book show how the ancient guilds in India functioned both in the presence of strong and weak states to

[1] Michael Ray and Alan Rinzler, *The New Paradigm in Business: Emerging Strategies in Leadership and Organisational Change*. G.P. Putnam's Sons: New York, 1993.

engage in social developmental work of various kinds. This went much beyond philanthropy, though there was some of that as well. In more contemporary history, India is also heir to the concept of 'Trusteeship' espoused by Gandhiji. This concept finds new meaning in the context of political economy issues arising out of globalization and is explored here in some depth. Gandhiji's was a call for a paradigm shift away from and almost opposite to the ethos of market societies as perceived today. But Gandhiji was to appeal that this was not necessarily contrarian to or outside the ambit of market-driven economies. The full implications of this thought are explored in this chapter—particularly for India in the context of changes taking place today.

The book principally deals with what is current and new in CSR trends in India. Chapters 3, 4, and 5 on 'Scouring Social Sensitivities: Ahead of Law', 'Eye on I.T.: Preparing for and Managing Change', and 'Developing Markets and Marketing Development' respectively capture these trends. Business has mostly not been apologetic about its business interests in taking up a social development agenda, or developing workplace and other norms beyond the law. Sometimes these have gone so far into the future that one misses the business interests altogether, but we are assured there will be returns.

Chapter 3 'Scouring Social Sensitivities: Ahead of the Law' unravels what has become a fine art by our best-known companies in anticipating social expectations. Business associations have also included the social agenda in strategising on behalf of the firm.

New trends in business have brought new responsibilities as manifested in the IT industry. Chapter 4 'Eye on I.T.: Preparing for and Managing Change' describe this. The industry came with new technology and know-how but the country had an ill-prepared social infrastructure to absorb its bounty. That had to be built fast and built anew. This was done by generating an interest and by investing in building education in general and IT education in particular.

Chapter 5 'Developing Markets and Marketing Development', shows how global and local business take a long-term view to develop CSR and other capacities of small enterprises. For a decade the entrepreneurial but notoriously informal (in terms of various social standards) small-scale sector has contributed between 30 per cent and 36 per cent of our exports. Social expectations from the outside world have underwritten the social aspects of this economic link. It is a continuing challenge to meet these expectations and survive. Another area of such changes is in the rural hinterland where most of India lives. For decades, there has been neglect and deprivation through indifference. Building here means building new institutions—grassroots producer's groups, credit systems, skill, and knowledge enhancement mechanisms—it also means generating new and sustainable employment.

These are the themes of development pursued in the core chapters of this book. Whether this is 'corporate social responsibility', 'corporate social responsiveness', or just 'long-term business strategy' often depends on intents and motives, as much as on the actors who engage in these debates. Here I explore the many models of developmental engagement by corporates, which are emerging, many of which bring immediate business rewards.

Business chambers, associations, and clubs have the advantage of going beyond the individuation syndrome of the firm, of looking beyond the firm for the interests of the firm. Though inputs in the area of social development have been largely ad hoc, there is a slow maturing of approach. These include efforts to sensitize business to issues being raised in civil society, to develop researched information on these issues, and to seek buy-ins for efforts on such issues both from business and governments. It also includes developing models for implementation and in many crises situations, designing, and coordinating efforts in implementation as well. To the giants in this field, Rotary India and the Lions Club of India, must be owed the models of developing a campaign, of leveraging funds, of working in partnership with the government of India to bringing sea change in the social sector on a national scale.

This book is also about other actors who play a role in moulding CSR in India. Globalization has caught in its swirl not just business but other institutions as well. Corporate social responsibility cannot be understood outside the chorus of civil society voices. Chapter 6 on 'Civil Society Roar: India's NGOs and CSR' demonstrates how civil society is increasingly playing a role, globally and in India, in ventilating the concerns arising out of government–corporate behaviour. Cross-border business spans the expectations of different societies and countries. Wherever governments speak less, or are less prepared to address the issues of affected constituencies, civil society can be expected to speak more. Here the tirade ends up not just against government but against what is considered its closest ally, business, as well. The chapter discusses the strength of the civil society networks in India, of the communication strategies that are used, and of the confronting and collaborating approaches civil society engages in to bring about change in corporate behaviour.

Social and environmental disregard by business is increasingly being considered a part of business risk. This has resulted in a move away from ad hoc efforts to more institutionalized approaches to CSR in India. This is the subject of Chapter 7 on 'Embedding CSR in India'. Institutionalizing of CSR in India is also being driven by global forces to a large extent. A plethora of codes, standards, principles, policy prescriptions, and more, are mushrooming in India and worldwide. It has become the new management tool integral to business functioning to endogenize social and environmental risk as part of business strategy. Emerging trends in India are detailed in the chapter.

Chapter 8 on 'Governments Grooming for CSR: Global and Indian Response' shows how governments, particularly those of developed countries of the West, are promoting CSR efforts both internally and worldwide. The economic changes are seen to be sufficiently overwhelming to warrant close inspection and attention to social ramifications elsewhere. The United Kingdom not only has a Minister for Corporate Social Responsibility but an instructive menu of initiatives under its aegis. Other European countries have also assigned high-level attention to this area in different ways described here. The Government of India is taking important steps outside the World Trade Organization to support voluntary efforts at integrating workplace and other practices with global expectations. The chapter looks at the international trends of how government's social policy drives support for CSR and related initiatives.

Amidst the kaleidoscopic shifts in economic reorganizations taking place in nations and globally, there are social shifts to meet these challenges. The concluding chapter, 'Looking Ahead' takes a peek at the new roles that might be emerging, not just for business but also for governments and civil society groups in meeting these challenges. That there are win-win models to these problems is only part of the solution. In the end it will be the shared ethos of humanity that must drive these models, and for that to happen there is much ground to be covered. But for the time being, these new models of development with business and other multi-stakeholder groups acting together are carving a path to be watched and replicated.

CHAPTER 1

BEING POLITICALLY CORRECT ABOUT CSR

The role of globalization in driving voluntary social development initiatives by business has received much less attention than its other transformative aspects. Here it is the direct focus on development issues— necessarily leading from the globalization process and often a precondition to it as well—and not changes that come with cheaper and better products and jobs and skill enhancement that are the issue.

India, surging forward into higher-order economic reforms, is now firmly a part of the inexorable march of globalization. In such a context, corporates have implications, both through the impact they have on the lives of people drawn into such change processes, as well as through the impact on the lives of those excluded from them. In a developing country like India, it is increasingly appreciated, and not least by business, that to become economic players of first-world magnitude, the challenges of a third-world developmental leap have to be addressed. There is also a sense both among business as well as others (particularly civil society and government) that business has to play a leadership role in bringing about this transformation. What this leadership role should be has not yet been settled.

TERMINOLOGY

Corporate social responsibility (CSR), a term being used to describe this role, lends itself to complexity and confusion. In all fairness the term has not evolved from the business world but from outside. There is much to be said for attracting another term for business efforts in this direction. As it stands, the scope of this term can range from following the spirit of the law (i.e. beyond what is strictly law) to following expectations from society. It can cover workplace practices to extra-workplace issues. In a globalized world, CSR can take a geographical leap to cover corporate behaviour in other communities, states, and indeed nations. It can refer to preventive, curative, or promotive action to deal with social issues in the course of business functioning. It will be the intent of this book to show how the market place of ideas and events have already moved forward to carve a place for CSR in India. Business has voluntarily taken upon itself the role of being responsive to its milieu. However, the ideology of a role for business in developmental issues is still hard to digest for a country like India, recently out of the throes of a mixed economic system. This is true both for those in and outside of business. The trends are nevertheless unmistakable and the philosophical arguments against CSR—both from the right and the left really have to fall by the wayside under the circumstances. But it is important to recognize what these arguments are, because they have a nagging way of emerging in all kinds of constituencies and deflecting from the very positive impact that business engagement and partnership in development can have.

IDEOLOGY

Philosophically, there is very little consensus about CSR and 'extra market' engagement by business. It may come as a surprise to business to know that corporate social responsibility is considered as a right-wing conspiracy in some quarters. Critics of CSR from the extreme left have said that the most charitable thing they can say about CSR is that it is an effort to bridge market failures or negative impacts of market success and profits.

However, its implications are interesting. CSR in their view, gives credence and support to the capitalist class and to a system which has also thrown up great inequalities. One section of this view, in the work of David Korton for example, typically holds that the system in its current form is incapable of effective change:[1]

With financial markets demanding maximum short-term gains and corporate raiders standing by to trash any company that isn't externalizing every possible cost, efforts to fix the problem by raising the social consciousness of managers misdefine the problem. There are plenty of socially conscious managers. The problem is a predatory system that makes it difficult for them to survive. This creates a terrible dilemma for managers with a true social vision of a corporation's role in society. They must either compromise their vision or run a great risk of being expelled by the system.

[1] David C. Korten, *When Corporations Rule the World*, Kumarian Press, Inc. and Berrett-Koehler Publishers, Inc.: San Francisco, 1995, pp. 212–13, 232.

Ironically, Korton argues with the same Friedmanian fervour (to be discussed) that such managers and firms 'find themselves developing split personalities'. Social responsibility for Korton is a mere aberration of individual efforts and not destined to survive under capitalism. There are others who fear that corporates will use this as a branding exercise, without any real inputs in CSR. But what they fear more is that it may give legitimacy to corporates and lead to a more acceptable and revamped capitalistic system.

One prominent example of opposition to CSR is that which evolved in the wake of efforts by the United Nations to promote CSR. This has some relevance to India as outlined in later chapters. Following international efforts by the United Nations to get business committed to social development, the Global Compact was fielded at the World Economic Forum in Davos, Switzerland, in January 1999 by Kofi Annan. It was launched in July 2000 as a means of getting corporate involvement in CSR worldwide. It urged business to embrace universal principles in the areas of human rights, labour standards, and the environment as a means to a 'more equitable global marketplace'. This was to be a voluntary effort by corporates.

Almost immediately, the electronic media carried a grave counterpoint of objections from a section of influential international NGOs and personalities calling for an Alliance demanding, a corporate-free UN. They viewed the involvement of corporates in such a partnership with misgivings, as they did the unfettered market systems within whose ambit they operated.[2] The main issues reverted to the debatable issues of a market-based economy and its potential to solve major social problems. The Alliance describes its genesis as growing out of the general consensus for opposition to several international events and programmes seeking closer ties with the corporate world for development efforts. This included opposition to the 1999 campaign by the UNDP for the Global Sustainable Development Facility for a Corporate Partnership Programme, and an NGO consensus effort in Seattle against the WTO Ministerial. This also included counter meetings in Davos in January 2000, and the formalization of the Corporate Free UN Alliance at the September 2000 Millennnium Summit in New York. The purpose of the Alliance and its

[2] Corpwatch website: http://www.corpwatch.org/. Accessed on August 2003.

ideological difference were clearly spelt out in a detailed letter to the UN. The Alliance was to say that major corporate engagement in a market-based economy would not solve problems created by the market.

Many sectors of society do not concur with the Global Compact's vision of advancing popular social values "as part and parcel of the globalization process,' to 'ensure that markets remain open." Many do not agree with the assumption of the Global Compact that globalization in its current form can be made sustainable and equitable, even if accompanied by the implementation of standards for human rights, labor, and the environment.

We recognize that corporate-driven globalization has significant support among governments and business. However, that support is far from universal. Your support for this ideology, as official UN policy, has the effect of delegitimizing the work and aspirations of those sectors that believe that an unregulated market is incompatible with equity and environmental sustainability.

Our second concern is the purely voluntary nature of the Global Compact, and the lack of monitoring and enforcement provisions. We are well aware that many corporations would like nothing better than to wrap themselves in the flag of the United Nations in order to 'bluewash' their public image, while at the same time avoiding signficant changes to their behavior. The question is how to get them to abide by the principles in the Global Compact.

Without monitoring, the public will be no better able to assess the behavior, as opposed to the rhetoric, of corporations. Without independent assessment, the interpretation of whether a company is abiding by the Global Compact's principles or not will be left largely to the company itself.[3]

The UN response clarified that while they were not for 'unfettered markets', they were indeed in favour of 'open markets'. In the context of open markets. The UN favoured voluntarism as a means to bring the required changes did not, in any case, have the mandate to pursue a regulatory approach.[4]

It is not just from the left that there is opposition to CSR. The position taken by Nobel laureate and economist Friedman[5] is an important reference point for discourse on CSR from the right. In fact Indian business leaders, often refer to this position as their mantra for not engaging too much in CSR. It is seen as a position arguing against CSR. This is only partly true.

---

[3] Ibid.

[4] Ibid. (Letter from UN Assistant Secretary General, John Ruggie).

[5] Milton Friedman, 'The Responsibility of Business is to increase Profits', *New York Times Magazine*, 13 Sept 1970. New York Times Company published in Chryssides, *An Introduction to Business Ethics*. Chapman & Hall: London, Glasgow, N.Y., Tokyo, Melbourne, & Chennai, 1993.

We know well Milton Friedman's now famous position that in a free society 'there is one and only one social responsibility of business—to use its resources and engage in activities designed to increase its profits so long as it stays within the rules of the game, which is to say, engages in open and free competition without deception or fraud'. We appreciate less or choose to know less well his further directives in the same article: 'Make as much money as possible,' he wrote, 'while conforming to the basic rules of society, *both* those embodied in law and those embodied in *ethical custom*' [italics mine]. What is this other than a call to, what social anthropologists have long called, economic 'embededness'—or an understanding that business must work within the norms of social expectations?

Friedman's real strictures against CSR lie in another direction. He was more in favour of strategic silence on the issue of CSR by business. In fact, he condemns company branding using CSR in the strongest terms. Friedman saw talk about social responsibility by businessmen as being 'short-sighted', 'schizophrenic', and revelation of a 'suicidal impulse'. 'Whether blameworthy or not, the use of the cloak of social responsibility, and the nonsense spoken in its name by influential and prestigious businessmen, does clearly harm the foundations of a free society.' In Friedman's view such *talk* would transfer costs to consumers and shareholders; would transfer the responsibility of government to corporates; would prompt mandatory requirements; and would invite bureaucratic overseeing and demands on businesses, thus curtailing a free society and by implication capitalism itself. In a country like India, recently out of a command-type economy, this argument is likely to weigh favourably with business. So if corporates are engaging in 'responsible practices' and are also somewhat reticent about it, they inherently reflect a Friedman-like strategic approach and duality in the matter. However, there is real problem of erring on the side of too much reticience and too little attention to this sphere.

Strategic silence by business is unlikely to silence the issues. Since the 1970s when Friedman wrote his controversial article, there have been momentous changes in the institutional and social aspects of economic life, especially in a developing country like India.

To begin with, Friedman's 'ethical custom' has become much more difficult to define today. Global production of business is certainly one component of these changes though not the only one. Global connectedness has meant that local custom and ethics are no longer the only ones to contend with. For instance, multinational corporations have almost doubled since the 1990s from 35,000 to 60,000 and their foreign affiliates have tripled from 170,000 to 500,000.[6] India is strongly integrated into this system. Well before liberalization in the late 1980s, assets and sales of foreign affiliates in India were approximately 23 per cent of the corporate sector in India,[7] not to mention the millions of workers/employees linked to these affiliates both directly and indirectly. The MNC presence and other cross-nation production and commercial processes bring with them social baggage drawn from another social millieu. In these new times, whose custom, law, or ethics to abide by is becoming increasingly blurred.

The issue of silence on CSR is violated by direct concerns from non-business stakeholders as well. Despite disagreement about measuring the size of corporations, it is clear that at least thirty-seven of the top 100 economies of the world are corporations.[8] The fact that the size and financial muscle of business, particularly MNCs, are reputed to be much larger than those of many nation states has added to new concerns. This rearranging of the hierarchy of influence between the state and business is politically and socially discomforting.

Additionally business in general, driven by technological change, is seen to have both creative and destructive components, and the latter, it is felt have not been properly accounted or paid for.[9] Corporates, also seen to be the prime beneficiaries of these changes, suffer from the individuation syndrome, where business exerts itself incredibly for the development of the firm, but rather hesitatingly, for a collective effort to create the social environment for itself to survive and thrive. Many organizations at national and international levels are promoting this introspection and action among corporates. This

[6] Ann Florini, 'Business and Global Governance—The Growing Role of the Corporate Codes of Conduct', *The Brookings Review*, Spring 2003, Vol. 2.1, No. 2, pp. 4–8.

[7] Nagesh Kumar, *Multinational Enterprises and Industrial Organisation, The Case of India.* Sage Publication, New Delhi, 1994.

[8] Martin Wolf, 'Countries Still Rule the World', *Financial Times*, 5 February, in Helmut Anheier, Marlies Glasius and Mary Kaldor (eds), *Global Civil Society*, Oxford University Press, Oxford, 2002, p. 78.

[9] Michael Ray and Alan Rinzler (ed.), *The New Paradigm in Business—Emerging Strategies for Leadership and Organizational Change.* World Business Academy. G.P. Putman and Sons, New York, 1993.

has become an important service in which consultancy organizations and NGOs have combined to integrate and provide their inputs to corporates.

There is another factor driving CSR debates centre stage. This has to do with the interrogation of the state in fulfilling its developmental functions. A substantial body of literature has emerged since the mid-1990s, which says that business now functions as if people do not matter and that the state is increasingly seen as partnering this process. This is squarely attributed to 'globalization'. This view argues that a 'new and potentially undemocratic role is emerging for the state as the enforcer of decisions and/or outcomes which emerge from world markets, transnationals, "private interest governments" and international quanango-like regimes'.[10] Corporates and governments are then seen to be responsible for but non-responsive to the state of things. In this view it is not just that the business of business is business but also that the business of governments is also (only the interest of) business. This, if it were true, would be potentially disastrous.

Understanding these perceptions and possibilities, there is a call from the intellectual right for corporates to go beyond their core but narrow business function and play a more proactive role in the area of social development. This engagement is seen as a part of managing business processes and business risk. Michael Novak, theologian and social scientist from the right compellingly argues in line with his theological/liberal perspective that we are all sinners[11] and that social values must be infused, motivated, regulated, and emerge out of self-interest.

The more corporations become creative agencies in helping things move along, the less the state will have to do. It's in the interest of the corporation to help provide for the poor in its area, because the more we do that privately, one human being to another, the less we are forced to turn to a large bureaucracy to do it, the more likely it will succeed.[12]

The business model of CSR is certainly in vogue. However, it is not without problems and more elevated leadership roles will be expected if many of the core issues are to be addressed.

---

[10] Cerny G. Philip, 'Restructuring the Political Arena—Globalisation and the Paradoxes of the Competitive State 117–138 in Ronald D. Germain (ed.), Globalisation and its Critics—Perspectives from Polictcal Economy, Macmillan Press Ltd., London, 2000.

[11] Marjorie Kelly, 'Michael Novak: The Theologian of Capitalism', in Ray and Rinzler (eds), The New Paradigm, 1993, pp. 190–202.

[12] Kelly, 'Michael Novak', p. 197.

Other emerging world-views see CSR-infused business taking us to new heights of a different kind. Even from the right of the political discourse, pundits are predicting the abolition of private property itself emerging through the medium of corporate social responsibility! Examples of the developed countries have not necessarily shown this trajectory. However, it is of some theoretical interest. This view comes from those involved in the organizational transformation movement, with industry background. Accordingly Maynard and Mehrtens[13] argue that business would have travelled from a focus on financial statements and balance sheets in the first wave, to a grudging second-wave recognition of broader issues like environment and worker satisfaction also impacting the bottom line. The third wave is a 'bridging time' with some sharing of responsibility with wider stakeholders but with continued old methods of financial accounting, but with emerging new ideas for the fourth wave. Social accounting in the fourth wave, 'will become the principle form of accounting'. This will be matched by a demand for accountability and the 'distinction between social activity and corporate activity will fall away'. In their view, 'corporate' will be 'social'. By extension, the whole idea of capitalism with ownership will change. 'Capitalism as we know it having disappeared and been replaced by more positive images of humankind and a more communitarian form of ownership'.[14]

Is there a societal transformation in the offing, in which business will be called to play a more predominant role? Statements from across the political spectrum, and across the globe, offering full support to the market and full support also to extra-market engagement by business seems to suggest that such a transformation is being politically perused.

POLITICS AND MARKETS

Political leadership across the world has for more than a decade participated in these debates The envisioned future is outlined from across ideological and political spectrums around the globe. From the developed world, from the leaders of Britain and Germany, there has been talk of a 'third way'.[15] The

---

[13] Hermant Bryant Maynard, Jr. and Susan E. Mehrtens, 'Redefinitions of Corporate Wealth', in Ray and Rinzler (eds), *The New Paradigm*, 1993, pp. 36–42.

[14] Ibid.

[15] Tony Blair, *The Third Way—New Politics for the New Century*, The Fabian Society, London, 1998.

third way is, in essence, described as one in which 'we support a market economy, not a market society'. It is a way of 'reconciling themes which had been regarded as antagonistic between patriotism and internationalism, between rights and responsibilities, between the promotion of enterprise and the attack on poverty'. More importantly, it is described as being a way of uniting the two great streams of left-of-centre thought—democratic socialism and liberalism.

The United Nations World Summit for Social Development convened in Copenhagen in 1995, organized a series of conferences on this topic. Its report[16] outlines the need for new political cultures and institutions in pursuance of the ends of greater economic growth and development by the global community. In speaking of 'ethical markets', 'humane markets' and 'democratic markets' the report essentially gives the message that markets are social constructs as much as they are the outcomes of individual exchanges, and that both governments and corporates need to imbibe the social aspects more fully. The theme of the subsequent Johannesburg Summit in 2002, with significant corporate participation, also concluded the need to look at and commit to sustainable business, which is one that imbibes the social sensitivities more fully.

In more than one way this debate is seen as taking market forces to new heights, while securing them firmly to the social values and agendas represented in the state. This must be seen as part of a natural process in the evolution of markets in a future world. From the developing world also, echos of this perspective are in evidence. Prime Minister Thaksin Shinawatra of Thailand, while rejecting the view that he was guiding the country to a welfare state through hand-outs, maintained that the government would eventually 'do less and less'[17] once the disparity between groups is reduced. Meanwhile, he termed the interventions as 'social capitalism', which is being viewed as a new social architecture that falls between free markets and government intervention.[18] However, whether this process of support is to be entirely government-based or not is yet to be resolved.

---

[16] Royal Danish Ministry of Foreign Affairs, *Conditions for Social Progress: Humane Markets for Humane Societies*, 1997 Copenhagen Seminar for Social Progress. Royal Danish Ministry of Foreign Affairs, 1998.

[17] Pana Janviroj, 'P.M.'s "social capitalism" needs more debate', in *The Nation*, 8 October 2003.

[18] Ibid.

In India, Prime Minister Manmohan Singh, in an inaugural address after taking office in June 2004 spoke about the mandate that his party had received in the recent elections. He interpreted the mandate as being one which clearly indicated that 'economic growth has to be accompanied with equity and justice'. At the 100th birth centenary celebration of J.R.D. Tata, the Prime Minister spoke on to the issue of partnership with corporates, of corporates walking hand-in-hand with government in taking India on its path of modernization and industrialization. While recognizing the role government must play to create the enabling conditions for entrepreneurship, he urged that corporates consider their obligation.[19]

In discovering opportunities to invest in socially useful projects, in creating new avenues of progress for the under-privileged, in investing in the less developed regions for the benefit of the marginalised sections of our society, corporate social responsibility is not philanthropy. It is not charity. It is an investment in our collective future

In this we are partners. We must walk together on the road to well-being and prosperity.

In addressing business, prime ministers in India have often centre staged issues of corporate responsibility and partnership in development.[20] Former Prime Minister, Atal Bihari Vajpayee, in his address to the 73rd Annual General Body Meeting of the Federation of Indian Chambers of Commerce and Industry (FICCI)[21] commented in this vein.

I have often urged Indian business to discharge its social responsibility in a more visible and effective mannner than has been the case so far. It is an appeal that I make again today. The challenges of India's social sector development are daunting. All of us know, the resources of the Central and State Governments are insufficient to meet these challenges.

Indian businesses should set aside a significant part of their earnings as well as their human resources to improve the conditions of education, healthcare, sanitation and community welfare.

There have been many occasions in the history of independent India when this sentiment has been voiced at the very highest levels. The first seminar

---

[19] PM's address at ASSOCHAM's J.R.D. Tata birth centenary celebration; and Inaugral Address after taking over as PM July 2004.

[20] Sunder Pushpa, *Beyond Business—From Merchant Charity to Corporate Citizenship.—Indian Business Philanthropy through the Ages.* Tata McGraw-Hill Publishing Company Limited, New Delhi, 2000.

[21] Atal Bihari Vajpayee, 'Emerging Contradictions in a Globalizing World—Pitfalls & Opportunities', FICCI, 2000.

on Social Responsibilities of Business in India in 1966 with an august audience consisting of the then Prime Minister Lal Bahadur Shastri, Jayaprakash Narayan (who seems to have initiated the debate), C.D. Deshmukh, and many others met. Their agenda was a relook at the concept of Trusteeship. In these formulations there appears a corresponding drift from a socialist ethos to a charity ethos to one that calls for opportunity solutions which are neither philanthrophy nor charity.

It is not just business in capitalist countries that calls for such leadership. Such voices are also emerging in the developing world, including in communist China. In 1998, in the process of encouraging greater participation by non-state agencies in development, the Ninth National People' Congress in Beijing elected a new administration committed to work towards 'small state, big society'.[22] This is a call for loosening the control of the state on markets and society. Following the policy direction from this, some 20,000 NGOs registered and helped organize, particularly individual farming communities, to receive industry largesse. The household responsibility systems introduced in the late 1970s and the early 1980s freed the individual from the mandatory collectives of the past. In their place grew the new configurations, when farmers began to recognize that the new market economies were 'rewarding economies of scale to the detriment of individual peasants'.[23]

SCOIOLOGY OF ECONOMICS

A great deal of sociological enquiry surrounds questions about connectivities between society and the economy. In this context, CSR is a significant theme. In the sociological view of things, pre-capitalist economic systems bind closely with the social framework. Economic anthropologist Karl Polyani more than anyone else, has talked of the 'embeddedness' of economic structures in the social structures of simple societies.[24] In the terminology of economic

---

[22] Ye Zang, 'All China Federation of Industry and Commerce and the Glorious Cause Programme', in Yamamoto and Ashizawa (eds), *Corporate Ngo/Partnership in Asia Pacific*, Japan Centre for International Exchange, Tokyo, 1999, pp. 67–80.

[23] Ibid.

[24] George Dalton, 'Primitive, Archaic, and Modern Economies: Karl Polayani's Contribution to Economic Anthropology and Comparative Economy', in *Economic Anthropology and Development: Essays in Tribal and Peasant Economics*, Basic Books, USA, p. 11, 1971.

anthropologists, simple societies show perfectly that societies are in essence made up of 'exchanges' and that market exchange is only one of the forms of exchange. The other forms being reciprocity and redistribution. What these studies show is that while markets operate in these simple societies with the same competitive impulse one might see anywhere, the other forms of exchange, namely reciprocity and redistribution, are given priority positioning, almost to the negation and denial of the very substantial active market transactions that take place in these societies.[25]

Capitalism and industrial society are not particularly credited with consciously engaging with the social. However, such systems are not without some inherent morality, unannounced and subterranean. This was the import in the work of famous French sociologist, Emile Durkheim. Writing almost a century ago amidst great criticism of the industrializing societies, Durkheim in his classic expose *Division of Labour in Society*,[26] outlined the inherent morality of the new emerging order of specialization, complexity, and differences. According to him, the new system actually bonds people and societies, though differently from simpler societies. 'Mechanical solidarity' is the organizational outcome of the way simple societies bond through 'likeness' of its parts and segments. Here everyone does more or less the same thing. Codes of behaviour are embedded in the collective consciousness, exercising constraint to conform. Everyone knows and abides by the norms that bind. With increasing economic differentiation in complex societies, the nature of bonding is through what Durkheim calls 'organic solidarity'— the uniting of different but interrelated parts. Here we bond because of the differences and dependence of the various segments on each other.

For Durkheim, this dependence creates a natural legacy of a higher-order morality.[27] Writing almost a century ago, he argued for the need to create new legitimacies to uphold the new differentiation and the new morality which in his view could be satisfied only if 'all men form one society'. With foresight he pointed to the tendencies in European society which 'has some idea of itself'[28] to form a single organization.

---

[25] Ibid., p. 15.

[26] Emile Durkheim, *Division of Labour in Society*, Reprint, The Free Press of Glencoe, Illinois, (1893) 1960.

[27] Ibid., p. 404.

[28] Ibid., pp. 404–5.

The work of his nephew and 'most distinguished pupil' and Sanskrit scholar, Marcell Mauss, further showed the social underpinnings of economic contracts and behaviour. This is highlighted through a comparative study of social contract and gift-giving. Mauss says of traditional exchanges of the past,[29] 'It is not the same as a market where a man takes a thing objectively for a price.' Referring to traditional exchanges he says, 'Contracts, alliances, transmission of goods, bonds created by these transfers—each stage in the process is regulated morally and economically.' Interestingly, and in conclusion of this comparative treatise from different societies, Mauss approvingly points[30] that the ingenious innovation of family funds freely and enthusiastically provided by industrialists for workers with families is an answer to the need for employers to get men attached to them and to realize their responsibilities and the degree of material and moral interest that the responsibilities entail. And again in the example of Great Britain, in the wake of a slow response of the state to support the cost of unemployment insurance, he points to the initiative taken by industry to support this as a step in the right direction.

In competitive and global markets unprotected by monopolistic arrangements, the bonding arrangements referred to earlier are likely to be recognized as implicit for better productivity. The management gurus of India have been at great pains to point out the significance of our values and their relationship to society, which is holistic, integrated, and interdependent. These are identified as the very concepts integral to modern-day management.[31] It is also being pointed out how important it is to address these issues. Sumantra Ghosal, international management specialist, urges that managers,[32]

accord the same priority to the collective task of rebuilding the credibility and legitimacy of their institutions as they do to the individual task of enhancing their company's economic performance.

[29] Marcel Mauss, *The Gift—Forms and Functions of Exchange in Archaic Societies.* Norton Company, New York N.Y. (1925), 1967.

[30] Ibid., pp. 65–7.

[31] B.M. Atreya, 'Teaching of Shastras For Modern Management', Talk Delivered at India International Centre, New Delhi, 11 July 1994.

[32] Sumantra Ghosal, Gita Piralmal, Christopher A. Bartlett, *Managing Radical Change— What Indian Companies Must Do to become World Class*, Penguin Books India, New Delhi, 2000, pp. 330–1.

Far from thinking of their companies as agents for destroying social welfare, most Indian managers believe that their primary role is to create value. Their guilt lies in their unwillingness to confront explicitly the role their companies play in society or to articulate a moral philosophy for their own profession. Through this act of omission, they have left others—economists, politicians, journalists and others—to define the normative order that shapes public perceptions about themselves and their institutions.

The global world that business has created is also a global world of politics and civil society. The voices of these constituencies are increasingly addressing issues of the nature and pace of economic changes and their negative fall-outs. In doing so they highlight the roles and responsibilities of business. It is now in the interest of business to address this as much. Corporates are driven by these new realities to move out of the individuation syndrome of servicing immediate needs of the firm to an effort to support the base in which they survive. Ground realities have overcome the Friedmanian position of silence and restraint on CSR. In India and elsewhere corporates have been intuitively moving in the direction of such an engagement. Whether this is responsibility or response to ground realities—this is a space that needs to be covered and a trend that needs to be supported in innovative ways by various non-business communities as well.

This book is about roles that business in India is playing. It is especially about the new contexts which are driving that process. Fortuitously, it is bringing to the fore social development issues long left to bureaucracy alone. Moreover, it portends a multi-stakeholder engagement by government, business, and NGOs to meet the development needs of the country. In India the movement is already in a fledging stage as later chapters will show.

While globalization is calling for new roles for business and the state, history is witness to roles of responsibility by business in the past, particularly at critical junctures when change was imminent. India is heir to a legacy of ideas and action in this field. This is the natural backdrop to India's current role in CSR and is the subject of the following chapter.

CHAPTER 2

LEARNING LEGACY
INDIA'S BUSINESS–SOCIETY INTERFACE

The concept of business's social responsibility or responsiveness is not new in India. What is happening in the new economic environment of India in terms of business engagement in social development and CSR is the subject of other chapters in this book. But in history we find the backdrop of roles and discourse on business roles in developmental efforts, especially in the context of change.

The concept of Trusteeship, espoused by Gandhiji, in the period of waning influence of colonialism and imperialism, is an important marker in the history for CSR. The full nuances of this concept is addressed here. Another important strand came in the wake of national policy debates of the immediate pre- and post-independence period in India, regarding business's role in development. However, the engagement of business in development also draws from a very distant past. This is evidenced in the work of the ancient guilds over centuries in developmental efforts in the context of states under which they functioned. These different strands of engagement are discussed here.

GUILDS

Guilds and State—Governance Partners

In the early Vedic and later Vedic periods, the work of guilds in wider social development initiatives was evident. A thousand years of history based on both textual and inscriptional data on epigraphs, coins, and seals covering this period is revealed through the work of scholars.[1, 2, 3]

---

[1] Thaplyal, K.K. 1996. *Guilds in Ancient India*, New Age International Ltd: New Delhi.
[2] Mazumdar, R.C. 1969. 'Corporate Life in Ancient India'. K.L. Mukhopadhya 6/1a. Calcutta.

Guilds could draw from a rich tradition and ethos of social giving[4] (see Annexure 2A for interesting renderings on this topic) which echoes modern day concerns of addressing environmental degradation and social exclusions. Additionally they were drawn to play even broader governance roles. The guilds played an important role in governance during periods of state formation, state consolidation, and state dissolution.

The strength and multifarious roles that the guilds assumed in early stages, have led scholars to surmise that these guilds and their offshoots may have even preceded the formation and governance by the state.[5]

In the engaging history of this period, Thaplyal describes[6] an early stage (600 BC and 320 BC) which saw a shifting of loyalty from 'tribal organisations to politico-geographical units' due to overall development. The guilds at this time were so well formed that they had the authority from the king to lay down their own rules and regulations. Moreover the king was enjoined to legislate in their matters only after proper consultation with their representatives. There are references to civil, legislative, judicial and executive powers of the guilds over not just their members but families and classes of persons living within their jurisdiction as well.[7] In this guilds were far from just economic work organizations but shared political and governance roles as well.

Periods of dynastic and state strength as in the Mauryan empire (320 BC–200 BC), or the Gupta period (300 AD–600 AD) actually saw increased strength of the guilds as well. The former period was one of state consolidation and the need for revenue through taxes went with granting relative autonomy and control in civic roles in designated areas of towns.[8] In the Gupta period, especially detailed rules are set for business partnership and there is reference to chiefs of artisans and trader guilds acting as members of the advisory board of the district administration. This has been described

---

[3] Spengler, Joseph 1971. *Indian Economic Thought—A Preface to its History*. Duke University, Durham N.C. Duke University.

[4] Mazumdar, R.C. 1969. Corporate Life in Ancient India. K.L. Mukhopadhya 6/1a. Calcutta, pp. 5–7.

[5] Spengler, Joshep 1971. ibid. pp. 38–40.

[6] Thaplyal,K.K 1996. ibid. 23–36.

[7] Mazumdar,R.C. 1969. ibid. pp. 21–23.

[8] Thapalyal 1996. ibid. pp. 123.

as a 'partnership between city bourgeoisie and the civil servants'.[9] At a period later than 600 AD the state was delegating its own powers, and authorized guilds to collect taxes on its behalf.[10]

On the other hand waning influence of the state coexisted with the continued and further growth of activities in the area of trade,[11] as in the period following great dynasties. The resilience and strength of guilds was somewhat in contrast to the shifting political arrangements. In fact the stability of the guilds is described as being so great that they probably endured the dissolution of formed states as well[12] at various periods. The guilds appeared as a number of sovereign units ... 'comprising of lesser stable units' 'into which larger unstable units decomposed in times of crises'. This political instability at the macro-level led to a natural devolution of decision-making and governance roles to the local level through these guilds.[13]

The new roles emerged in various ways. Quoting from the Yjnavalkyasmritin (100 AD–300 AD), scholars also mention that during this period, besides having judicial authority for its members, the guild also functioned as one of the ordinary courts of law. The decline of the Mauryan empire during this phase 'led to the slackening of state control over administration and economy and the guilds assumed more power and influence'.[14]

The guilds thus got into a meandering path of engagement in social and political processes in the wake of the abilities or disabilities of the state for governance. Moreover there were interesting aspects about this role indicating its embeddness in the moral order of the society. There were systems for formalized commitment to these roles.

Morally Embedded Social Responsibility

The legitimacy for playing such a role by the guilds came from the norms of religious practice prescribed for guilds. The head of the guild and

---

[9] Budh Prakash Aspects of Indian History and Civilization p. 22 quoted in Thapalyal. ibid. 33.

[10] Thapalyal: 1996. ibid. 98–99, 124–125.

[11] Mazumdar, R.C. 1969—31.

[12] Thaplyal, K.K. 1996. ibid. pp. 125.

[13] Spengler, Joseph 1971. ibid. quotes R.C. Mazumdar.

[14] Thaplyal, K.K. 1996. ibid. 29.

executives were to be persons who were acquainted with the Vedas and their duty as proscribed therein and were to have attributes among other things of honesty.[15] Such knowledge and initiation of the Vedas also meant imbibing the values of giving and charity and an understanding of the interdependency between wealth and society. (See Annexure 2A)

The corporate entities including national guilds, city guilds and what is called the enterprise partnership was to have a core objective 'sarva loka hitam' that is well being of the people.[16] There was a religious component as well. Mazumdar points out that social activities undertaken by the guild collectively was also believed to bring merit to each of the guild members as well.[17] These also contributed to gaining confidence, recognition, and social status from the public.[18]

Institutionalization of Developmental Activities of Guilds

Interesting also from our perspective is the formalization of philanthrophic and developmental activities. The strong corporate nature of the guilds, was a remarkable example of joint holding of resources and sharing of profits and other gains. Social and philanthropic activities were also documented in writing as it was supposed to be undertaken as a matter of duty and binding on all its members.

The sources of revenue for the guilds came from member subscriptions, contributions, gifts bestowed by state to individuals in the guild, profits from the execution of orders, fines, confiscated property, and permanent deposits for endowment purposes, whose interest was to pay for charitable works.[19] Endowments in turn came from a wide variety of sources including kings, officials, traders, artisans, and other classes of people. As far as profits of the guilds are concerned there is evidence of a fixed system of contribution as well. A portion of the profits were to be ear-marked for charitable activities.

The post Mauryan phase was also marked by guilds getting into partnerships with larger political units for various public works and acts

[15] Mazumdar R.C.1969. ibid. pp. 49.

[16] Dr. M.B. Athreya 1994. Teachings From Shastras for Modern Management –talk delivered at IIC 11th July 1994.

[17] Mazumdar R.C.1969. ibid. pp. 54.

[18] Thapalyal 1996. ibid. pp. 34.

[19] Thapalyal 1996. ibid. pp. 69–70.

of charity for which they were given permanent endowments of cash and land by the political authorities and sometimes by individuals as well. The purpose of the endowment was often specified—as for tree plantation, or to be used for the benefit of Buddhist monks, or for the sick, for maintenance of religious establishment and so on.[20] Moreover they also functioned as banks, and inscriptions indicate that 'they were an important factor in the municipal government of ancient cities, and were responsible to the corporation of the town for the due discharge of their duties as trustees of public money. They received not merely deposits in cash but endowments of property, as ascertained from inscriptions of the time.[21] During this period the services of the guilds as partners in public works was proclaimed and registered in the town hall, at the record office as was the custom. Thus the role of guilds in such development activities were fairly formalized.

The nature of philanthropy was directed at both its internal members and external society. Internally they helped in training, in providing a congenial atmosphere for the craftsmen and providing sufficient time and opportunity for creativity and originality in the arts in which they were employed.[22] For the wider society evidence from the Brihaspatismriti[23] (300–500 AD) indicates that 'compacts were made by guilds to alleviate distress and for undertaking works of piety and charity. Each guild would determine the way its profits were to be used. Such acts were to be performed as a matter of duty by the guilds and were included in an agreement put into writing, which formed a kind of Memorandum of Articles of the Association that was binding on the members.'

Such acts typically included donation for construction and maintenance of assembly hall, a shed for water, a shrine, a tank, or a garden, help to the poor and destitute in performing sacrifices and sacraments and assistance in times of famine and other calamities. The portion donated from the profits went to the infirm, diseased, blind, mentally disabled orphans, and destitute women and others in need. Historians have suggested that these guilds acted as guardians and in this sense widened

---

[20] Mazumdar R.C. 1969. ibid. 31–39.
[21] Mazumdar R.C.1969. ibid. pp. 30–34; 35.
[22] Thapalyal 1996. ibid. pp. 43.
[23] Thapalyal 1996. ibid. pp. 85; Mazumdar R.C.1969. ibid. pp. 43.

the sphere of Poor Law by including in it the fulfilment of both material, social and spiritual needs.

TRUSTEESHIP: 'INDIA'S GIFT TO THE WORLD'

A significant Indian concept in rethinking the role of business in society, is that of Gandhiji's 'Trusteeship'. While discussing corporate social responsibility in India today, one is likely to encounter the concept of Trusteeship, which Gandhiji described as 'India's Gift to the World.' It is possible to find corporates in India who acknowledge the concept as a guiding force in their CSR work today. Important as these submissions are, Gandhiji's formulation is really very challenging and much broader in its demands. In whatever form we are attempting to capture that spirit, one must pay homage to the vision that the Mahatma had in mind, one whose time is yet to come. However, the issues from which this vision stems are at once familiar and important in today's context.

What were the values and issues driving Gandhiji's concept of Trusteeship? What were the principles of trusteeship? And what is the significance of these principles for us in terms of CSR today? To these queries we turn now.

It is important for all concerned with CSR to recognize that originally Trusteeship, as envisaged by Gandhiji, was most revolutionary in its compass. It was revolutionary in the sense that it was not just a guide to business functioning in society, it was an integral part of a wider world-view of society itself. It was also revolutionary because it rested on a complete reformulation and in a sense negation of the twin aspects of capitalism as we know it—namely, the aspects of private property and competition. It was also revolutionary because, it still envisaged a future society, which could (in Gandhiji's view) emerge within the parameters of a market economy—without violence and on a voluntary basis. Most of all it was challenging because it tried to combine two opposites—despite being anti-market in its approach, it proclaimed itself as not being anti-business.

Gandhiji came to India at a time when the country was in the grip of imperialism—political domination through physical force by a foreign country. To this was added a global economic connectedness at that time as well that threatened to hurtle a fragile self-sustaining economy into mass impoverishment. Gandhiji's aversion to global markets was further justified here. However untenable his solutions may appear, his thinking was instructive in highlighting the great need for thinking economics anew and for bringing the human face centre stage when discussing economic advancement. In the nationalist ethos of India at that time, the question that concerned many was whether the dehumanizing aspects of capitalism would disappear with the British withdrawal. Capitalism's flaws were also being discussed in the West and Gandhiji was familiar with, and engaged in that discourse. It is impossible to understand the concept of trusteeship without this wider political economy backdrop.

RUSKIN: A TRYST WITH TRUST

The single most important influence on Gandhiji with regard to his concept of Trusteeship, was a political economy treatise by John Ruskin. Gandhiji wrote of the 'magic spell of a book' that laid hold of him as he read John Ruskin's *Unto This Last* on a journey from Johannesburg to Durban:

> The train reached there in the evening. I could not get any sleep that night. I determined to change my life in accordance with the ideas of the book—I translated it later into Gujarati, entitling it Sarvodaya.[24]

Ruskin's work had created much controversy when it was first published in Britain in a series of articles in the 1860s. Ruskin, as an influential writer and poet exclusively writing on art and architecture, had for some time been concerned with issues of 'value' in art as a result of the play of market forces. The satirical title of his publication on art, 'A Joy for Ever and Its Price in the Market'[25] captures this preoccupation. His concern widened to include issues of the 'value' of labour and contemporary economics. As in the case of art, he found the valuation of labour based on markets a fundamentally flawed philosophy.

Gandhiji shared Ruskin's philosophical underpinnings for an enlarged entitlement for labour on the one hand, with more limited entitlement for

---

[24] This translation was actually an abstract of important features. M.K. Gandhi, *Ruskin Unto This Last—A Paraphrasse*—which was retranslated into English, (1956) 1999.

[25] Oliver Lodge, 'Introduction' to John Ruskin, *Unto This Last and Other Essays*, J.M. Dent & Sons Ltd; London, 1907, p. vii.

business on the other. Ruskin's work was sufficiently provocative and had to be suppressed, especially since it came from a Tory, who considered himself a Tory to the end.[26] Echoes of his convictions and the tenor of his arguments can be found in the concept of 'Trusteeship' by Gandhiji. All the key issues that concerned Gandhi and led to the formulation of the concept of trusteeship were addressed by Ruskin:

- Ruskin saw self-interest-based economics as bringing 'schism into the Policy of Angles and ruin into the Economy of Heaven'.[27]
- 'For as consumption is the end and aim of production, so life is the end and aim of consumption.'[28]
- An enlarged entitlement for labour on the one hand, with more limited entitlement for business.
- What was morally legitimate for business to claim, according to Ruskin, hovered precariously on survival entitlements only.
- A merchant should, in his call to duty, use his utmost energies not just to produce at the cheapest cost but to distribute at the cheapest price where the merchandize is most needed. In the course of doing this he should be prepared to meet 'fearlessly any form of distress, poverty, or labour, which may, through the maintenance of these points come upon him.'

HINDU PHILOSOPHY AND TRUSTEESHIP

While Gandhi acknowledged Ruskin's influence, he also had indigenous sources of inspiration to mould his concept of 'Trusteeship'. There was much in Hindu philosophy that focused on an amaterial world and non-possession. Vinobha Bhave, the famous reformist and freedom fighter, comments on the religious influences on Gandhi in his formulation of Trusteeship. The concepts of *aparigraha* (non-possession) and *samabhavana* (equalism, sense of equality or oneness with all) are key concepts in the

---

[26] Ibid., p. vii.

[27] John Ruskin, *Unto This Last and Other Essays*, J.M. Dent & Sons Ltd, London (1860) 1907, p. 183.

[28] Ibid., p. 184.

Gita, 'which had taken a strong hold of Gandhiji's mind, and, it seems, that when he began to meditate on how he could apply these attitudes of the mind to practical life, this legal term trustee came to his help and stood him in good stead.'[29]

Gandhi was to say in his autobiography that in studying the Gita the rules of equity in English Law became clearer as did the concept of 'trustee'. In 1891, Gandhiji described the different approaches to law in the East and West: 'Individual property is the rule in the West. Corporate property is the rule in the East'. He talked about this in the context of the joint family system of which he was a part and in which he saw himself as owning nothing.[30] However, the equity in the joint family system was rejected by him, and he was to write in his autobiography how he refused contributions to it (and to his older brother whom he considered as a father). He argued that the narrow view of 'family' should be widened suggesting that his contributions would be to a wider community.

Hindu religious texts are informed with a deep sense of social equity and enjoin giving. The creation of wealth is viewed positively. Prescriptions for enhancing both material and spiritual wealth include its distribution and giving. These religious injunctions found an echo in Mahatma Gandhi's concept of 'trusteeship' which he espoused as the ideological basis on which business should be conducted. His ideas on trusteeship found expression at various periods of his life and are published in scattered contributions to *Harijan* and *Young India*. 'Enjoy wealth by renouncing it', he wrote, for example, in *Harijan*. Earlier (1939) he had maintained, 'I am entitled to wealth which gives an honourable livlihood—the rest belongs to the community and must be used for the community.' And again with respect to the use of non-violence to achieve this goal: 'It has the sanction of philosophy and religion behind it.' In 1941 he describes trusteeship as a gift to the world from India.[31]

---

[29] Vinobha Bhave, 'Introduction in K.G. Mashruwala, *Gandhi and Marx*, Navajivan Trust, Ahmedabad, 1971 [1951], p. 24.

[30] Prabodh Choksi, 'The Gandhian Concept of Trusteeship', in *Social Responsibility of Business—IIC 1966*, Manaktala and Sons Pvt. Ltd, Bombay, 1996, pp. 85, 88.

[31] M.K. Gandhi, *Harijan*, various dates, quoted in J.D. Sethi, *The Gandhian Alterative*, Gandhi Peace Foundation, 1986, pp. 204, 205.

TRUSTEESHIP AND VALUES

Trusteeship Defined

Intellectual debates centring on whether industrialists should be allowed to retain their wealth were common in the India of Gandhi's times and provided the context to deliberate this issue. In the pages of *Young India* and *Harijan*, Gandhiji's own ideas of trusteeship were strewn. Here and in response to many queries implied by this concept, he gave answers but he never collated his ideas in any one place. In 1942, because of the efforts of colleagues, the guidelines for trusteeship were enunciated.

The guidelines drew up six principles, of trusteeship as follows (see Annexure 2B for original draft and comments by Gandhiji):[32]

- Trusteeship provides a means of transforming the present capitalist order of society into an egalitarian one. It gives no quarter to capitalism but gives the present owning class a chance of reforming itself. It is based on the faith that human nature is never beyond redemption.
- It does not recognize any right of private ownership of property except so far as it may be permitted by society for its own welfare.
- It does not exclude legislative regulation of ownership and use of wealth.
- Thus under the state-regulated trusteeship, an individual will not be free to hold or use his wealth for selfish satisfaction or in disregard of the interests of society.
- Just as it is proposed to fix a decent minimum living wage, even so a limit should be fixed for the maximum income that would be allowed to any person in society. The difference between such minimum and maximum incomes should be reasonable and equitable and variable from time to time, so much so that the tendency would be towards obliteration of the difference.
- Under the Gandhian economic order the charter of production will be determined by social necessity and not by personal whim or greed.

This was presented on the occasion of what has been described as the first seminar on Social Responsibilities of Business in India with an august audience of the then Prime Minister Lal Bahadur Shastri, Jayaprakash Narayan (who

---

[32] M.K. Gandhi, *Trusteeship*, Ahmedabad, 1960, pp. 3–49 (A draft prepared by Professor Dantwala and discussed between Kishorilal Madhruwala, Narhari Parikh and Pyare Lal, and approved by Gandhi, *Harijan* 25 October 1952 outlined in J.D. Sethi, *Gandhi Today*, Vikas Publishing House Pvt. Ltd, New Delhi, pp. 153–4.

seems to have initiated the debate), C.D. Deshmukh, and many others. The audience was startled, as Jayaprakash Narayan was to say, by the announcement by one of the participants, Professor M.L. Dantwala, that the draft on the principles of trusteeship had been written by him.

Important was the fact that first version of the draft with Gandhiji's comments written in English and Gujarati along the margins,[33] was made available. Overall, every change made by Gandhi aimed at making the principles less confrontational to business. One change is worth mentioning. The draft contained the following critical Principle

The owner will be duty bound to manage his property for the service of society. As a trustee, he will be entitled only to a statutory commission for his labours. This cannot be exorbitant.

Gandhiji wrote against this principle: 'This is unnecessary. Has been included in clause 2.'[34] Clause 2 had a more expansive scope for inter-pretation of what business could keep and what it needed to give up and was in a sense an escape clause and decreed (as already indicated) that trusteeship does not recognize the right to private ownership of property, except in as much as it may be deemed harmless by society.

However, Gandhiji did give his nod to the six principles after modifications (see Annexure 2B). Whatever explanations he added, did not significantly blunt the expectations from business.

Behind the principles were the key issues of a then globalizing world, which Gandhiji debated. Today we regurgitate these issues in the context of the role, ethics, and responsibilities of business in the new globalization. Gandhiji's views on trusteeship is culled out of his interrelated views on the nature of economics, mechanization, property and entitlements, business morality, and the role of the state.

ECONOMICS OF GOD

To begin with, Gandhi's overall world-view was an economics of humanity taking centre stage. It called for an inclusive society where the marginalized could both partake of and share in the benefits of the economy.

[33] See *Social Responsibility of Business—IIC 1966*, see Annexure 2.2 here for revisions to the original draft.
[34] *Social Responsibility of Business*, pp. 82–4.

Ruskin's view of self-interest-based economics bringing 'schism into the Policy of Angels and ruin into the Economy of Heaven' finds an echo in Gandhi's work.

I offer the economics of God as opposed to the economics of the Devil which is gaining ground in the world to-day. The latter aims at or results in concentrating a million rupees in one man's hands, whereas the former in distributing them among a million or thousands; and in placing the economics of the spinning wheel before you, I am really trying to establish the economics of God. The industrialism of to-day is fast destroying the village in India; it is only by converting every house into a spinning mill and every village into a weaving mill, that we can revivify the village life.[35]

This theme of equity and morality was to infuse his perspectives on mechanization and property. These found crystallization in his concept of trusteeship.

MECHANIZATION WITH A HUMAN FACE

He saw capitalism's twin forces of technology and mechanization as freewheeling and unbridled by any kind of humanity or morality. To return to an element of morality he urged a global and national humanity which even as it empowered some did not disempower others.

To clarify his stand on this issue and in exasperation at being misunderstood as being against machinery, he stated that he considered the body as a most delicate piece of machinery.[36] His objection, was against the craze for labour-saving machines,

Men go on 'saving labour' till thousands are without work and thrown on the open streets to die of starvation. I want to save time and labour not for a fraction of mankind but for all. I want the concentration of wealth, not in the hands of a few but in the hands of all [Italic mine].

PROPERTY AND ENTITLEMENTS

Gandhi's views on 'property' and 'entitlements' were central to the concept of trusteeship. And so unorthodox were these that they have been described

---

[35] M.K. Gandhi, *Young India*, 15 Sept. 1927, quoted in Anand T. Hingorani, *Man verses Machine by M.K. Gandhi*, Bharitya Vidya Bhavan, Bombay, p. 34.

[36] M.K. Gandhi, *Young India*, June 1925, quoted in Hingorani, *Man versus Machine*, pp. 8–9.

as being to the left of communism. Writing on Gandhianism and Socialism, K.G. Mashruwala points out[37] that in the matter of private property, 'Gandhiji has perhaps more radical views than the most extreme Communist. He would like to dispossess every person of all kinds of belongings.' He did not see property as being a productive force as the socialists and communists did. In fact, he associated property closely with exploitation. In Mashruwala's view, if Gandhi tolerated private property it was because he had not yet discovered a non-violent method of abolishing it. Therefore, the injunction to the rich that property should be deemed to be held in trust for the rest of society.

Gandhi, as we have seen, was inclined to the view that the industrialists were to be paid a commission, although he had inserted a more liberal reading of this, which allowed some leeway (see Annexure 2A for original draft with Gandhi's comments). On the question as to what would happen to the successors of trustees Gandhi responded in the *Harijan* that the state would regulate this commission and the children would inherit the stewardship only if they proved their fitness.[38]

Gandhi's message is not so much against private property as for the potential for such ownership for all; not so much against mass production as for production by the masses; not so much against private entrepreneurs as for trusteeship orientation.

MORALITY IN BUSINESS: THE MERCHANT—WHAT IS HIS 'DUE OCCASION' OF DEATH?

The philosophical underpinnings for Gandhi's views on entitlements and business have a close link with Ruskin's formulations. Ruskin opined that it is the object of various professions to render various things—a pastor's to teach, a physician's to heal, and a merchant's (and manufacturer) to provide. It is not their object to seek a fee or stipend. Further, 'It is no more his function to get profit for himself (merchant/manufacturer) of that provision, than it is the clergyman's function to get a stipend'.[39]

Ruskin urged that the objective of the profession (to save lives, to preach, or to heal) must remain even in the face of death—as for a soldier, or a

---

[37] Mashruwala, *Gandhi and Marx*, Navajivan Trust: Ahmedabad, p. 78.

[38] *Harijan*, 31 March 1946, quoted in IIC, *Social Responsibility of Business*, p. 104.

[39] Ruskin, *Unto This Last*, pp. 128–9.

clergyman in the course of his duty, or a physician when attending to a victim of the plague. But, he asks, 'The Merchant—What is *his* "due occasion" of death?'[40] A merchant should, in his call to duty, use his utmost energies to not just produce at the cheapest cost but to distribute the good at the cheapest price where they are needed most. In the course of this he should be prepared to meet 'fearlessly any form of distress, poverty, or labour, which may, through the maintenance of these points come upon him'.

Ruskin's writings were directed at the intelligentsia at large which was debating these issues and as such they were delivered with abrasive sharpness. Gandhiji's translation and paraphrase of Ruskin's work into Gujarati was to show his broad concurrence with its philosophical underpinnings. However, Gandhi was a reformer. He addressed the business class with all the subtlety he could apply to the idea of trusteeship and to this must be attributed its continued attraction for business. The concept, posited a higher leadership by business even vis-à-vis the state and political leadership.

ROLE OF THE STATE AND BUSINESS

The full import of trusteeship must be understood in the context of the kind of development that Gandhi saw the state as providing. He viewed the role of the state with great anxiety. He had been deeply influenced by the Russian and Liberal British tradition on the subject, particularly, Tolstoy (*The Kingdom of God is Within You*) and Ruskin (*Unto This Last*). After his return to India in 1915, and subsequently, he voiced his great discomfort with the role of the state time and again. and his most virulent expression of disapprobation came as late as 1934.[41]

The state represents violence in a concentrated and organized form. The individual has a soul, but as the state is a soulless machine, the state can never be weaned from violence to which it owes its very existence. I look upon the increase of the power of the state with the greatest fear, because although while apparently doing good by minimizing exploitation, it does the greatest harm to mankind by destroying individuality, which lies at the root of all progress... what I disapprove of is an organisation based on force, which the state is....[42]

---

[40] Ibid., pp. 129–30.
[41] J. Bandyopadhyaya, *Social and Political Thought of Gandhi*, Allied Publishers, Bombay, Calcutta, New Delhi, Madras, Bangalore, London, and New York, 1969, p. 105.
[42] Ibid., p. 105.

He alluded often to the absence of the state and the emergence of a self-regulated society, not as the Marxists would have from the conflict between labour and capital, but from the non-violent leadership of the trustees themselves.

In fact, Gandhi also hinted at a wider role for business than just looking after their immediate constituency of workers. On 7 April 1931 Gandhiji addressed the 4th annual session of the Federation of Indian Chambers of Commerce and Industry.

I cannot forget the services rendered by commercial class, but I want you to make Congress your own and we would willingly surrender the reins to you. The work can be done better by you. But if you decide to assume the reins, you can do so only on one condition. You should regard yourselves as trustees and servants of the poor. Your commerce must be regulated for the benefit of the toiling millions.

The idea of trusteeship was a part of his thoughts throughout his life. Following his return to India, it was considered the most 'fanciful' of his notions. Both the right and the left 'considered it as a camouflage in favour of the latter'.[43] The possibility of operationalizing this dream has been viewed critically by many.[44] Gandhi himself was given to self-doubt on the issue,[45] though he never really gave up believing in its ultimate promise.

His extreme views on entitlements in business and its role in creating a new society, expectedly, continue to remain a source of controversy. It must be pointed out that Gandhiji spared no class or section of responsibility in creating this new society. In fact trusteeship was a concept which he applied to many actors, including labour.[46] Wherever there were inequalities of any kind, both for the dominant and subjugated elements in the relationship, transformation was to be through voluntarism or moral appreciation and effort.

[43] J.D. Sethi, *Gandhi Today*, Vikas Publishing House Pvt. Ltd.: New Delhi, Bombay, and Bangalore, p. 138.

[44] See Ibid. chapter on Trusteeship, especially pp. 154–75.

[45] M.K. Gandhi, *Harijan*, 20 Feb. 1937, quoted in Bandyopadhyaya, *Social and Political Thought of Gandhi*, pp. 136, 137.

[46] Prabodh Choksi, 'The Gandhian Concept of Trusteeship', Background paper at the IIC seminar, 1966, pp. 85–110.

INDEPENDENCE YEARS: POLICY DEBATES ON DEVELOPMENT

The role that business played in CSR activities, in the pre- and immediate post-Independence years is comprehensively detailed elsewhere.[47] Here I touch upon some of the significant policy-based trends in that engagement for development.

The eve of Independence in India was a time of great deliberation on the type of system that independent India was to put in place. Socialism, capitalism, varieties of Gandhianism, and near communism were all debated as alternative models. The model adopted would be required to have the gargantuan capability to address the impoverishment of the masses following the imperialistic withdrawal (if it were to happen) and the accelerated rebuilding of the nation. There was a strong anti-business trend, as much as there was uncertainty about taking a path that would lead through the dictatorship of the proletariat as a solution. India chose in favour of a mixed economic model of development.

This was also a time where business engaged extensively in policy debates, both through individual leadership such as that of G.D. Birla, Purshotamdas Thakurdas, J.R.D. Tata, Walchand Hirachand, and John Mathai and collectively through the main business forum of the time—the Federation of Indian Chambers of Commerce and Industry (FICCI). Through these endeavours business came out with its own perspective and plan of action for post-Independence India. This was *A Plan For Economic Development of India*, commonly called the Bombay Plan, published in 1944 and 1945 in two parts. Given the context of the depression years, and the political orientation that was beginning to emerge in India at the time, a socialist model of polity was being proposed by the nationalist political leadership.

Business in India was keenly and acutely aware of the public policy and ideological debate and was to take an active and somewhat unusual stand in this debate. This was partly dictated by the circumstances. G.D. Birla was time and again to strategize and speak out for the true role of business given those circumstances: 'I have not the least doubt in my mind that a purely capitalist organization is the last body to put up an effective fight against Communism.'

---

[47] Pushpa Sunder, *Beyond Business—From Merchant Charity to Corporate Citizenship*, Tata McGraw-Hill, New Delhi, 2000.

Scholars have commented on how the business class in India forwarded its cause in rather unusual ways by seeking to understand root causes of poverty and discontent and addressing it quickly.[48] Though G.D. Birla was its most eloquent proponent, there was considerable support for this viewpoint in the business class. A massive effort at development was considered to be the best situation it could hope for and J.C. Setalvad in 1945 went so far as to suggest that 'collective farming' should also (in addition to cooperative farming) be considered as an option for rural transformation.[49]

In its Bombay Plan business conceded a prominent role to the state in the development process. In turn, the National Planning Committee sponsored by the Indian National Congress had noticeable participation of business in its twenty sub-committees[50] set up for the planning. That kind of inclusion of business has perhaps never since taken place, although there are some indicators of a similar trend emerging today.

An insightful treatment by Aditya Mukherjee of the role of the Indian industrialists acting in their own class interests comments, 'It must be said to the credit of the dominant section of the Indian capitalists that they were capable of looking beyond their short-term class interests, and could visualize and plan an overall development of the economy which was crucial *for its own long-term growth.*'[51] J.R.D. Tata, Walchand Hirachand, A.D. Shroff, and G.D. Birla were all to comment on this aspect. The Bombay Plan looked to effective public–private partnerships to address the development issues of the nation but also conceded an important role to the public sector to bring about the fast changes required by the nation.

In fact, the Bombay Plan and the outputs of the National Planning Committee were strikingly similar except for a few critical provisos. The approach of business at this time has drawn the comment from scholars that 'it is significant that they were perhaps among the first in the world to project as a class a model of welfare capitalism.'[52] The Bombay Plan had

---

[48] Aditya Mukherjee, *Imperialism, Nationalism and the Making of the Indian Capitalist Class 1920–1947*, Sage Publications, New Delhi, California, London, 2002, p. 49, quoted from G.D. Birla to Purshotamdas, 1929, PT papers.

[49] Ibid., p. 46.

[50] Ibid., p. 395.

[51] Ibid., pp. 397, 406.

[52] Ibid., p. 431.

two provisos. The first stated that the socialist economy was acceptable under a nationalist government (not a British one). This was clearly to counteract the effect on local industry of the double impact of socialism and imperialism. Second, there was an attempt to secure space for private industry in the proviso that key industries may be considered for state ownership *only* if industrialists were not forthcoming for the same.

Even while business was an integral part of policy debates, it did not change very much the outcomes of national policies. Gandhi's influence on major business houses of the time cannot be overstated and many leaders had a close association with him. Philanthropy was primarily directed towards the areas of education and health and there were state incentives for this as well. Some of the most enduring educational institutions in India were nurtured and built in the period between 1914 and 1960.[53] The Tatas, Birlas, Bajajs, Lalbhais, Modis, Godrej, Singhanias, Lala Shri Ram and many others were among those who set up premier institutions during this period.

The government granted incentives for business to be drawn into development efforts overall. There were few takers though for efforts in rural areas. This period was also fraught with suspicion and cases of fraud in the working of some trusts were to cast a shadow for a time on the entry of business into developmental efforts. All in all neither at the policy level nor in proposals by business to work in partnership with government yielded any enduring results. Each went its own way.

An exception to non-engagement in rural development came from the Tatas. Forerunner to the famous Tata Steel Rural Development Society, the company had started rural engagement as early as 1949 with developmental efforts among adivasis near Jamshedpur. Very early on in the early 1960s, Hindustan Levers had begun its rural development initiatives. It was much later in the early and mid-1970s that several business houses entered the rural development areas with special tax incentives.[54] Among these were the 1978 Birla Rural Development Association, the Narottam Lalbhai Rural Development Fund (NLRDF) was set up in the 1970s, the Lalbhai Group Rural Development Fund in 1984, the Birla Agricultural Farm and the

---

[53] See Sunder, *Beyond Business*, pp. 179–81 for a comprehensive treatment of the pre- and immediate post-Independence period.

[54] Ibid., pp. 264–7.

Newata Mandal Village Project in 1979, the Escorts Rural Development and Uplift Division in 1971, Excel Industries Vivekananda Research and Training Institute in Kutch for water resources and health in 1976; and the CC Shroff Self Help Centre in 1978.

This was a period when business and government, by and large, went their own way in such efforts. The following chapters show that in the post-liberalization era a whole new type of developmental engagement and ethics have emerged. Global connectivities of all kinds—civil, business, and government—were to signal an altogether different rush of business efforts into CSR-related activity and social development engagements. This period is actively showing a trend towards public–private partnerships—a recall of the distant past under very different circumstances.

CHAPTER 3

SCOURING SOCIAL SENSITIVITIES
AHEAD OF THE LAW

THE GLOBALIZATION CONTEXT

The decade of the 1990s and up to the present has been an era of great change for India. With a newly-liberalized economy, the private sector in India is not only poised to become the leading sector in the country, it is also set firmly on the path of globalization at a dizzying pace. In 1993–4 the total net capital formation between the public and private sector was shared in the proportion of 51.8 per cent and 48.2 per cent, respectively. In the period 2002–3, this position was reversed with 44.6 per cent the share of the public sector and 55.4 per cent that of the private sector. Further the current share of trade in India's GDP is a good indicator of the degree of economic globalizaton. It is as high as 31 per cent of GDP if trade in goods and services is taken together, which is higher than that of USA or Japan.[1] These economic changes are matched by corresponding social rearrangements. Societal perceptions about business and different expectations from business have also changed.

A study conducted under the aegis of Teri-Europe and the New Academy of Business[2] addressed just this issue. It examines perceptions about business across three groups—the general public, company executives, and workers and union leadership—in the cities of New Delhi, Mumbai, Chennai, Kolkata, and Tirupur. At least two conclusions are instructive regarding the expectations and possible role of business in social development.

The first of these conclusions relates to both responsibility and responsiveness of business. Expectedly, the general public overwhelmingly

[1] World Bank, *World Development Indicators 2005*.

[2] Ritu Kumar, David F. Murphy, Viraal Balsari, *Altered Images, the 2001 state of corporate responsibility in India poll*, Publications Unit, TERI India, 2001, pp. 9–13.

held companies wholly responsible for a host of issues related to direct business functioning, including providing the lowest possible prices, environmental protection, fair treatment of employees, reducing human rights abuses, maintaining consistent high standards, avoiding animal testing, and supporting government policies. What is instructive though is that overwhelmingly the general public also held companies fully responsible for other wider developmental issues including increasing economic stability, reducing the gap between rich and poor, and helping solve social problems. The worker groups were not nearly as demanding of the companies fulfilling wider roles- although there were some expectations there as well.

A second interesting conclusion is the legitimacy accorded to business in comparison to that accorded to government. The survey is instructive for that large business was regarded as well (or as badly) as government in terms of working in the interests of society. Expression of trust in business or government for working in the interests of society was more or less similar, with the general public showing a slightly elevated level of trust for business (67 per cent) rather than for government (63 per cent). This leads to the suggestion that a space for social developmental interventions by business is emerging in the eyes of the general public. There is opportunity for new leadership roles for business, for innovative effort both for the management of such initiatives, as well as to reclaim the legitimacy for business to play this role.

Not unexpectedly, corporates are responding to this interest.[3] They are, in a manner of speaking, responding to the market forces of social expectations. One thing common among surveys about CSR in India is that all the surveys show that most corporates are doing something by way of corporate social responsibility. Partners in Change, one of the leading intermediation organizations facilitating corporate social responsibility, conducts an occasional survey on the performance of corporate responsibility. The results of the latest survey[4] indicate that size of the company (from less

---

[3] Comprehensive data-bases of CSR in India are available. See Harsh Shrivastava and Shankar Venkateswaran, *The Business of Social Responsibility*, Books for Change, New Delhi, 2000. An excellent historical account is Pushpa Sunder, *Beyond Business: From Merchant Charity to Corporate Citizenship*, Tata Mcgraw Hill, New Delhi, 2000.

[4] Partners in Change, *Third Report on Corporate Social Responsibility in India*, 2003.

than Rs 40 crore to above Rs 400 crore) has little to do with the overwhelming involvement of over 85 per cent companies in CSR activities. Such CSR is still top driven with 79 per cent of CSR initiated by the owners or CEOs of the companies, but employee-driven initiatives have a small presence as well.

The scope of understanding CSR in India can be overwhelming. Business in India is increasingly addressing different types of issues. Motives are difficult to define. The endogenizing of societal expectations as a business risk has enlarged the canvas of what is strictly business. This has expanded existing engagement in environment, health and safety, worker/employee rights, and community enhancement to encompass every kind of development issue. It also moves the action point from merely curative (righting undesirable impacts already made) to the preventive (being cautious of possible impacts) and promotive aspects of CSR. Additionally, new technology, management of business, and new types of business bring new concerns to the society and business matrix. This expanding and evolving nature of CSR is its key feature.

For late developing countries like India there is another dimension. Such countries actually have compressed time and expanded areas of development to work on in order to meet the global competition. Bridging this developmental space is being done with a new urgency. This is accelerated by increasingly vocal constituencies highlighting the emerging challenges created by business. Companies in India are becoming increasingly adept at being ahead of time in seeing the big picture. Even before these issues came to the forefront, India's favourite companies had already reached there.

AHEAD OF GOVERNMENT RESPONSIBILITY

One of the uncontested leaders in corporate responsibility practices is the Tata Group of Companies. While overall this is well acknowledged, what is less well known is that it has been the benchmark setter for such practices, even before the government had established norms for such practices. Many of the labour laws by government (for government employees and for the nation at large), in fact followed in the wake of those put in place by the Tatas. Some of these milestones reported by the Tatas are shown in the table.[5] As can be seen, some of these measures were thirty to forty years ahead of legislation on these subjects in the country.

Table 3.1: Tata Steel's 'First' in Labour Welfare Measure

Labour Welfare Measures	Introduction in Tata Steel	Enforced by Law	Subsequent Legal Measures
Eight-hour working day	1912	1948	Factories Act
Free medical aid	1915	1948	Employee State Insurance Act
Establishment of welfare department	1917	1948	Factories Act
Schooling facilities for children	1917		
Formation of works committee for handling complaints, service conditions, and grievances	1919	1947	Industrial Disputes Act
Leave with pay	1920	1948	Factories Act
Workers' provident fund scheme	1920	1952	Employees' PF
Workmen's accident compensation scheme	1920	1924	Workman's Compensation Act
Technical Institute for training of apprentices, craftsmen, and engineering graduates	1921	1961	Apprentices Act
Maternity benefit	1928	1946	Bihar Maternity Benefit
Profit-sharing bonus	1934	1965	Bonus Act
Retiring gratuity	1927	1972	Payment of Gratuity
Ex–gratia payments for road accidents while coming to or returning from duty	1979		
Social audit	1980	–	First in India
Pension scheme	1989	–	

Not only were the Tatas, through their social practices, ahead of legislation in the area of labour and other practices in India, they were, on some issues, ahead of such legislation in Western countries as well. The Hitachi Foundation, reporting on Global Corporate Citizenship, has drawn attention

[5] Tata Steel, *Tata Steel—Corporate Sustainability Report 2000–2001*, 2002.

to the extraordinary international landmark set by the Tata Steel Mill. The report points out that when the steel mills were still being built, two of Britain's most prominent social scientists and political activists, Sidney and Beatrice Webb, were brought to Jamshedpur to advise on employment and social policy. The report states, 'By 1912, the company had instituted the policy of an eight-hour working day, long before it was introduced in Europe or the US, and 36 years before it was made mandatory in India.'[6]

No one, least of all business, considers this to have been driven by anything other than business interest. Tata Steel puts these initiatives in perspective:

We do not claim to be more unselfish, more generous or more philanthropic than other people. But we think we started on sound and straightforward business principles, considering the interests of the shareholders and the health and welfare of the employees, the sure foundation of our prosperity.[7]

To the Tatas belongs another milestone in approach. It is often stated that corporate social responsibility is the lowest of all priorities, especially when the economy is weak. A graph of the Tata group's commitment to community development compiled by the Tatas shows the expenditure on CSR against the performance of the company over the years. This shows that the expenditure on CSR was sustained and growing even in a period (1996–2001) when the steel market had taken a downward turn and Tata's margins had been squeezed.

Another type of 'being ahead of the law' is driven by globalization in social and environmental issues and its potential for changing business direction. Increasingly, the message has gone out (market has signalled), particularly in the area of environment, that in the end, minimum or zero depletion of pollutants will be the expected norm, whatever the legal requirements are in India today. We are seeing very diverse trends in response to this. While evidence of non-compliance with existing laws is overwhelming in India, there is also a rush to go environment friendly in many ways.

The growth of a new environment market in India for environment protection includes markets for pollution control equipment and environmental consultancy services. An enquiry into managing pollution has pointed out that,

---

[6] Logan David, Roy Delvin, Regelbrugge Laurie, *Global Corporate Citizenship-Rationale and Strategies*, The Hitachi Foundation, Washington DC, 1997, p. 162.

[7] Ibid., p. 162.

the US department of commerce is said to have estimated the current size of the environment market in India to be \$4 billion, growing at an annual rate of 15 per cent, and the Indo-German Chamber of Commerce estimated the market to be almost double, at \$8 billion. Listing the best prospects for foreign investment in India in 2002, the US department of commerce ranked the sector of pollution control equipment at sixth place (out of 14 investment sectors).[8]

Insofar as it moves society to higher social equilibrium, it must be considered as a socially responsive and at the same time a business move. In fact investment in these areas was made ahead of time. Many companies in India have taken the lead here. The example of Ashok Leyland is only one among many. The company was ahead of environmental legislation[9] in a number of ways, which it describes as being 'ahead of competition'. The company reports that it had incorporated norms limiting vehicular pollution ahead of such legislation in 1987; similarly, more stringent norms for gaseous emissions were in place prior to legislation to this effect in 1992, and subsequently the company found it easy to adopt norms in line with the tightening of permissible levels of gaseous exhaust emissions in 1996.[10] Among the many other initiatives the company has launched is a dedicated mobile emission clinic operating on highways and at entry points in New Delhi. This is meant to check their vehicles for emission levels, recommend remedies and offer tips on maintenance and care. The first CNG-run bus was introduced in India in 1997 by Ashok Leyland in technical collaboration with a foreign company. The technical upgradation for the subsequent introduction of CNG in the Delhi Transport Corporation (DTC) was also supplied by this company, ahead of competition.

Business drives corporate social responsibility in other ways. Corporates are moving in the direction of greater transparency, especially in compliance-driven areas. Despite an acknowledged response bias in CSR surveys (the companies doing most in CSR respond to surveys), these provide instructive lessons. A recent UNDP, British Council, CII, PricewaterhouseCoopers survey of Indian Business[11] shows that enhancing transparency through

---

[8] Aparna Sawhney, 'Managing Pollution', *Economic and Political Weekly*, 4 Jan. 2003.

[9] See Ashok Leyland at http://indianngos.com/1/jnamrolia/

[10] Ibid.

[11] UNDP, British Council, CII and PricewaterhouseCoopers, *Corporate Social Responsibility Survey 2002—India*, 2002.

environmental reporting to investors is gaining ascendancy. Fully 67 per cent of the companies in the survey had undertaken such initiatives. However, it is clearly competition and markets which have driven this process because an overwhelming majority of these companies (85 per cent) were public-listed companies. The trend however has been set for the remaining 15 per cent that were not public-listed companies, who also moved in this direction of disclosure.

Such data should in no way suggest that the public has the benefit of a less polluted environment. Environmental non-compliance is suspected to be much larger than what is reported. On the one hand is an environmental consciousness that seems to be setting a trend of surging ahead of compliance, on the other there is a continuing avoidance of compliance. There is definitely lack of responsibility in non-compliance with legal requirements. Approximately 10 per cent of inspected companies are closed every year for non-compliance.

However, corporate responsibility in meeting compliance requirements is only as good as government responsibility. If government mechanisms and processes are such that they allow some to sneak past compliance requirements, it ends up providing a competitive advantage for some businesses in this respect over others. Worse, we are once again up against perceptions of unfairness, which can drive further non-compliance. The fact that the environment ends up being more polluted than we are legislated to expect, is a loss for everyone and the government has a strong regulatory role to play to ensure that corporate responsibility remains in place.

An environment management analysis by Priyadarshini et al. has pointed out that poor regulation by government can be due to a number of reasons including inefficiency, inadequacy, corruption, and unimaginative approaches on part of the regulatory body, as well as very high compliance costs. In India, the regulatory bodies are understaffed, underqualified, and unable in other ways to play their regulatory role.[12] This study cites that the vacancy ratio against the sanctioned strength of the Pollution Control Board (PCB) varies unsatisfactorily across states, being as high as 65 per cent as in Karnataka. Nor must it be imagined that non-compliance ills plague only the developing world. In the 1990s, a White House Council

[12] Karen Priyadarshini, K. Omprakash Gupta, 'Compliance to Environmental Regulations: The Indian Context', *International Journal of Business and Economics*, vol. 2, no. 1, pp. 12–21.

on Environmental Quality (CEQ) study estimated that compliance with air pollution limits by industries was as low as 35 per cent.[13] Further, studies in the United Kingdom reported a rate of non-compliance with water quality standards of around 48–83 per cent, with the effective rate of compliance being even lower.[14]

In India, the government's lack of ability and/or will to monitor this process also has its ramifications in irresponsible and illegal behaviour. Structural inefficiencies have been suggested by many studies. There are many innovative compliance measures, not based on the command and control approach alone, that have been known to provide better results. More innovative community and civil society initiatives have been much more successful in ensuring compliance, as have been incentive-driven schemes.

THE BUSINESS CHAMBERS AND ASSOCIATIONS*

The business chambers and associations have the task of looking beyond the firm, for the firm. The primary focus of such work for business chambers in India has been on addressing policy issues that directly affect the economics of business. However, increasingly the chambers have taken up the role of addressing wider social concerns as well. All the major apex business chambers in India have some kind of institutional arrangements for social development. These have emerged mostly in the last ten to fifteen years. Under the aegis of the apex chambers, for example, the Social Development Council (SDC) of the CII (Chamber of Indian Industries) and the FICCI Socio-Economic Foundation (FICCI–SEDF) were both set up in 1995. The PHD (Punjab, Haryana, and Delhi) Chambers of Commerce and Industry formalized its social development initiatives even earlier in 1981 with the Rural Development Foundation and the Family Welfare Foundation. The mission of these organizations are described similarly as being the creation of a better environment for social development

---

[13] Ibid., p. 10.

[14] Ibid., p. 10.

* Apart from the CEOs of these chambers who gave me broad perspectives, the CSR professionals from FICCI, CII, and PHD guided to literature sources for their work. I thank Harish Sethi, Atul Shumbu, Hamsa, Ramnik Ahuja, Narender Bhatia, and Teevra Sharma.

and a better image for business as it is an integral part of society. The objectives are to provide institutional arrangement for facilitating corporate social responsibility through creating awareness, multi-stakeholder dialogues on issues, advocacy and design and model building inputs. These efforts have been generated as much out of the internal interests of members and the association, as by the increasing interests of client organizations in the development sector (including government) looking to bringing the resources and managerial abilities of business to development.

As service organizations to industry, these two apex chambers (as examples), have tremendous reach to take this message and the efforts forward. FICCI (Federation of Indian Chambers of Commerce and Industry) has 500 chambers and associations affiliated to it, linking it to 1500 companies and directly and indirectly to over 2,50,000 business units.[15] CII has a direct membership of over 4,900 companies and indirect membership of over 50,000 organizations from various national and regional sectoral associations.[16] Several areas of social development are covered by these two business chambers and many strategies are undertaken to carry the message and initiatives to their members. There is also emerging clarity about their role, particularly as to how to be service providers to business in these areas. It is these trends, rather than a comprehensive list of the programmes that the following pages discuss.

INCENTIVIZING CSR INITIATIVES

Business associations have used the award system as a way of promoting CSR through voluntary processes. Participation for CSR awards is canvassed among member companies, scrutinized by credible jury, and the awards distributed at high-profile meetings. Based on defined criteria, the CSR performance is evaluated. What the awards do, is to create an awareness of issues, their scale, their management, their outcomes, etc. Last year's FICCI awards for CSR set a stringent set of critera that included integrated initiatives, demonstrated sustainability of CSR, the presence of participatory processes in the company for CSR, evidence of institutionalization of processes for CSR together with the company's economic performance.

[15] FICCI 2005, Corporate Office Communications.
[16] CII, 'Business as a Social Partner', n.d.

Equally, the evaluation used multi-stakeholder groups, credible jury, branded consulting groups, transparent criteria, and verification at field level to make this a serious effort at benchmarking performances. Companies use this for brand value as well.

With globalization, there is also effort to meet global standards at marking excellence in these areas. Both the CII and FICCI have international quality forums. In 1994, CII instituted the CII Exim Award for Business Excellence. This was based on the European Foundation for Quality Management model and is among the top awards aspired to by business worldwide. The award focuses on leadership, process, and performance in areas relating to people, customers, and society. It is considered a difficult standard to meet and is awarded only if the criteria are rigorously met. Since its institutionalization nine years ago, only in four years has it been awarded—to Infosys Technologies Limited, Tata Steel, Maruti Udyog Ltd., and Hewlett Packard India Ltd. It is pointed out that Infosys was given the award only in the second year of its applying and Tata Steel in its fourth year of applying. This is viewed in the spirit of improvement and corrective processes. Meeting global social standards in terms of CSR is increasing at every turn (see Chapter 7).

The CII has announced the setting up of a Centre for Corporate Sustainability to meet the global reporting standard of the Triple Bottom Line (TBL), that is people, planet, and profit. This centre has the objectives of (a) advocacy and awareness on environment, society, and people issues, (b) training the corporate world on how to measure TBL, and (c) celebrating, recognizing, and rewarding companies that have achieved best practices.

Despite the high profile of business awards for social development, significant participation of the extensive membership of these apex bodies is yet to emerge.

RESEARCH LEADING TO CSR

The Indian business chambers also work as facilitators of CSR through research. Research in selected fields of development is identified. Often, it is in tune with what are seen to be the most pressing needs in the immediate environment of business and society. Education- and health-related areas have been identified as important not just for national development but for business growth as well. Research leading to 'How–to–do' kind of action has become an integral part of CSR initiatives. For example, under the aegis of the Education and Literacy Committee of the CII, a document was developed for planning and designing school projects.[17] This was stated as an exercise at 'motivating Indian Industry to initiate Social Development Programmes in and around their workplace' in innovative ways. The document highlights the work in school education by member companies through their foundations and also suggests a step-by-step approach for new initiatives. These initiatives have approaches for transforming and expanding the supply of quality education.

This document also focuses on the need for value-added educational inputs to the existing system, rather than the setting up of parallel institutions. Under the category of 'Some Innovative Non-Industry Models to Reflect Upon', the work of the NGOs Eklavya and Pratham are cited. Eklavya primarily integrates new approaches to learning/teaching in existing schools both private and public. Central to its approach is encouraging critical thinking and experimentation, and developing skills for analysis and comprehension as learning methodologies both in science and the social sciences. A number of programmes to achieve this are integrated into the school system in fourteen districts of Madhya Pradesh, covering some 450 schools.

Research can also follow in the wake of critical socio-economic-business issues that surface from time to time. FICCI led research on an issue raised with respect to the football industry.[18] This followed in the wake of a damaging monograph entitled, 'A Sporting Chance' put out by the Christian Aid Society, a UK based NGO, regarding the use of child labour in the supply chain of the football industry in India. This study estimated that the Indian sports industry utilizes child labour to the extent of 10 per cent of the workforce. India has many commitments in principle, both stemming from the Constitution of India and the conditional ratification of international conventions that promote the elimination of child labour. Indian laws, however, do not ban all child labour, and especially not that in

---

[17] CII, *Industry's role in School Education—A Practical Handbook for Planning and Designing School Projects* (undated).

[18] FICCI and ILO IPEC sponsored V.V. Giri National Labour Institute, study, 'Child Labour in the Sports Goods Industry—Jalandhar—A Case Study', 1998.

family-based workshops. The sporting goods industry has a small component of exports (8 per cent). Linked as it was to markets abroad, a closer focus on behalf of the consumers in that market was inevitable. The FICCI study in collaboration with the International Labour Organization (ILO) was done to examine the actual situation with regard to the use of child labour in the sporting goods industry.

The preliminary results of the case study showed that in the registered units surveyed, three of the 144 units did have incidence of child labour. Three children were found to be working in three of the registered units. However, the involvement of children at the home-based level of the industry was widespread. The study particularly focused on the impact of child work on their education and revealed the various dimensions of the problem. The study considered four distinct categories of children in home-based work. These included the 'only working' (OW), the 'working and school going' (WSG), the 'only school going'(OSG), and the 'non-working and non-school going' (NWNSG) children. The maximum number of children fell in the WSG category in the survey.

In the wake of this study, the Indian Sports Goods Manufacturers and Exporters Association has outlined a number of proposals,[19] which, if implemented, would address the problems of each of these categories, and work towards the overarching commitments of the nation, much beyond the purview of law per se (see Annexure 3A). This included among other things, responsibility to ensure sub-contractor compliance on various norms for education and work for children, together with mandatory requirements of not engaging children below a certain age. The Sports Goods Manufacturers and Exporters Association in India also sought collaboration with the World Federation of Sporting Goods Industry, to buy from those Indian companies that are benchmarked in this respect.[20]

The Handicrafts and the Agriculture segment, are new areas of industry focus. These are seen to be areas that have tremendous potential for the economy post-liberalization, yet have some of the most impoverished sections of the country. The potential of developing these segments for overall growth is immense. Both chambers demonstrate a management

[19] Ibid., see Annexure 3A here.
[20] Ibid.

approach to solving both the business and development gap in such segments. The CII and FICCI have researched[21] each of these areas recently. This research indicates a design and role for the private sector in providing inputs for enhancing the productivity (technology, management, marketing, etc.) of these sectors as well as creating mechanisms by which the producers have a better share in the product value.

MODELS AND PILOT PROJECTS FOR BUSINESS

Information and design inputs and model building projects in key social sector areas have been another way for business associations to tap into existing interests of members and scour new areas of CSR. The potential for upscaling the results to wider constituencies is immediately apparent. Health and education are major areas of such engagement. The development of I.E.C. (information, education, and communication material) on HIV/AIDs by the CII is an example of such work, which has become available as training and awareness-generation tools for industry and its stakeholders. CIIs' AIDs at the Workplace Programme is another example of training and awareness services for industry that is conducted by the chamber. The response from members for receiving such training is described as being overwhelming.

Taking the design inputs of IT to the education sector, both public and private, has also been a value-added approach in the area of education by many individual IT companies (see Chapter 4). As a business chamber, the CII has also added this to its own menu, in view of the huge business potential in this field. Shiksha India, a non-profit society was launched by the CII and Global Leaders of Tomorrow (GLT) at the World Economic Forum in 2001. It was aimed at improving the quality of education in Indian schools through IT (see Chapter 4 for IT and CSR). The experience of this model is similar to that undertaken by individual IT companies. The approach is to achieve better integration of value-added quality inputs in education as a whole and IT education specifically through partnerships with schools both private and public.

---

[21] CII, 'Initiative to Improve the Handloom and Handicraft Products of North East', Oct. 2002; FICCI, 'Indian Agriculture Unbound: Making Indian Agriculture Globally Competitive', 2002.

A similar approach is adopted towards programmes in health. FICCI uses the decentralized industry associations to engage in model building projects that aim at better outcomes from existing public health services. The joint venture between FICCI–SEDF and the Rajiv Gandhi Mobile AIDS Counseling Services Project covering Delhi is an ongoing four year project; Reproductive and Child Health (RCH) Projects in collaboration with regional chambers have been implemented in Kanpur, Agra, Moradabad, and Bareilly districts with a focus on improving service delivery for health and creating awareness of RCH issues. The project has achieved successful improvement of indicators relating to coverage of antenatal services, contraceptive rate, and contraceptive social marketing. In a few cases, the chambers also undertake pilot projects, which could provide models. FICCI has itself been a partner with Apollo hospitals, in implementation of community health initiatives in several regions. It seek to provide a greater reach of the community to the public health system and to provide better coverage of family planning and reproductive health programmes. These are in the nature of pilot projects for implementation.

For encouraging model CSR approaches, the CII has developed a code of conduct for its members to adopt. The provisions of the code are oriented mostly to encourage embedding of CSR in member companies (Annexure 3B).

The initiation of such CSR-related activity by chambers is often possible because donors see business as a credible channel for development efforts. Constituencies dealing directly with developmental issues, such as the Government of India, multilateral, bilateral, and other foundation groups have entered into partnership with business associations for such work. The initiatives discussed in the preceding paragraphs have been donor driven to a large extent. For instance the CII initiatives on the AIDS I.E.C. material development were taken in partnership with an international organization. The International Labour Organization, partnered the child labour study of FICCI, while the Population Foundation of India, the German Embassy, and Sifsa supported the reproductive health and community health programme mentioned earlier. To what extent these initiatives have had sustainable impact in terms of further action and/or replication by industry is not yet clear. Assessments of the investment of time, effort, and money and profiling the benefits of such interventions have yet to be undertaken.

RESCUE MODELS

Though implementation of development projects on a larger scale is not, as a rule undertaken, disaster relief and rehabilitation is one exception. Disaster leaves great disruption of social and economic life in its wake. The coordinated response of business is often channelled through the associations and through fund collection. Occasionally implementation efforts are initiated in private–public partnership. Under duress of social distress, many of the routine road blocks to such development-sector public–private partnerships are innovatively and quickly resolved. These can provide learning opportunities for how such partnerships can work and for the resources and skills that different partners can bring to the effort.

India has unfortunately been the site of a number of major natural disasters and health epidemics in the last decade. Throughout the country many chambers and associations have contributed to the national effort to address such disastrs. The speed, scope, and spread of meeting developmental challenges and the management of such efforts have left a learning path.

The Gujarat earthquake in 2001 left 20,000 dead, several thousands injured, and over a million homeless. FICCI entered into a strategic alliance with CARE India to form the FICCI–CARE Gujarat Rehabilitation Project (FCGRP) in collaboration with the Government of Gujarat.[22] The project raised over Rs 57 crore for reconstruction efforts alone. The intervention was a model of a quick-action, multi-stakeholder partnership (affected communities, industry association, NGO, and government) and collaboration, with multi-pronged implementation design. The worst affected blocks of Bhuj, Anjar, Bhachau, and Rapar were identified by the government of Gujarat as needing assistance. The engagement started on day 2 of the disaster and the reconstructions were completed in a record period of one and a half years. The earthquake had led to the destruction of over 70 per cent of construction in the selected villages where the FCGRP was directed to work. The scope, spread, and scale of the reconstruction were tremendous with 4999 houses built in less than two years (Annexure 3C). This included setting up of sanitation facilities, improved access/space

---

[22] Information and project initiated by FICCI–Socio-Economic Development Foundation under chairmanship of P.M. Sinha.

utilization, improved land drainage, waste disposal systems, and regularization of land titles.

The work progressed from relief and reconstruction to rehabilitation and had a mix of short-term and long-term goals (Annexure 3C). The latter were oriented to reconstruction and support for revamping the main sectors of the economy which had been destroyed. In agriculture this included watershed management, water harvesting, efficient irrigation techniques, reconstruction of water sources, animal husbandry, etc. It also addressed off-farm livelihoods related to handicrafts and other support activities. In the latter phase there was the building of institutional arrangements of societies and development committees which could receive information, training, and resources as well as be enduring structures for the future. This intervention paved the way for further developmental investments in this region for the partners (CARE) in this project. The information[23] flow from the project director in 2005 indicates that while the institutions that were created continued to exist a good four years after project inputs and entrepreneurs had developed, democratic community participation had declined. The institution-and community-building aspects needed continued support from government after project completion. The many lessons emerging from this partnership model are to be yet fully absorbed and understood for replication in other circumstances. However, the tragedy brought out a close working in tandem between industry and government, a speedy convergence between government departments, and an active engagement of the local affected communities and the local NGOs to produce the results that it did.

The 2004 tsunami saw the CII engage in disaster relief in Tamil Nadu. Here too the scope, scale, and spread were vast. A full-time team worked there, looking at a three-year engagement. The CII is estimating a Rs 20 crore commitment. The process to meet the set goal was to be a management challenge. One of the competent managers of industry was deputed as project director. In close collaboration with the Government of Tamil Nadu this engagement too is looking at multi-stakeholder processes and a span of attention from relief to rehabilitation, particularly for the fishing community. Bringing together expertise and critical support from corporate houses was

---

[23] I am grateful to Veena Padia, Project Director of Care in Gujarat for follow-up information.

key to the programme. Logistics techniques to collect, sort, and distribute relief, to provision of communication support, and the management of communication in the midst of disaster are examples of what the CII did to address relief. A long-term and upgraded perspective for rehabilitation has brought improved techniques for fishing, boat repair, the use of IT for various activities related to fishing, vocational training in several areas, and more. Similarly the floods in Mumbai saw the setting up of five relief camps in the city by the CII and close collaboration with the police to plan and bring relief in the form of medicine, clothes, and medical services to the victims of this disaster. Engagement in implementation projects by apex chambers in non-disaster situations is occassionally visible. PHD chambers have two decades of work in this area. Eight hundred acres of wasteland development in three states and 50 watershed development projects in three states has coverage benefits for 8.5 lakh and 50,000 populations, respectively.[24]

Unlike the chambers, there are other institutions linked with business whose social development work is their very raison de etre. These are the famed international Lions and Rotary Clubs with their branches in India. Both were started by individuals in professions in the early 1900s[25] who wanted to bring community orientation to extra-business activity in the West. Rotary came to Asia in 1920 and one of its first chapters was set-up in Calcutta.[26] The expanse and reach of their work in developmental areas far exceeds what any one business can do.

Any discussion of business initiatives in India for development work would be incomplete without mention of the work of these two organizations. To mark the entry of this organization into the second century of service, Rotary in 2001–2 outlined seven major goals for itself.[27] These goals were said to have been developed after careful consideration of data

---

[24] Teevra Sharma, PHD Rural Development Foundation and Family Welfare Foundation.

[25] http://www.rotary.org/aboutrotary/history/index.html. The Rotary Club, was formed on 23 February 1905 in Chicago, Illinois, USA by Paul P. Harris, an attorney who wished to replicate the same friendly spirit in professions and business that he had felt in the small towns of his youth. The name 'Rotary' derived from the early practice of rotating meetings among members' offices.

[26] http://www.ri3240.com/RI/roindia.htm.

[27] http://www.rotary.org/aboutrotary/strategic.html.

collected at various levels of the organization and represented the important issues and challenges that Rotary faces in the coming decade. Among these goals was the goal to eradicate polio worldwide. That objective is of critical importance for curtailing the disease in India. With confirmed new cases totalling 15,561, India represents 85 percent of new polio cases worldwide. The northern state of Uttar Pradesh accounted for 66 per cent of cases in the world. It was the commitment of Rotarians worldwide and in India to deliver a polio-free world in 2005.

What is again noticeable here is the upscaled effort (aiming at elimination of the disease worldwide within a time frame), promoting ownership by the concerned government entities at national and state levels in India; managing multi-pronged partnerships (this has been a joint initiative between the WHO, Rotary International and the Centre for Disease Control and Prevention CDC in collaboration with other funding bodies and governments), the mobilizing of a gigantic volunteer force (over 1 million Rotarians worldwide have been inducted into this effort); scientific surveillance and monitoring process; and bringing and raising considerable resources for the endeavour. The Rotarian contribution was more than US$ 500 million, with an additional US$119 million raised by Rotary as resources in 2003. In addition, Rotary's Polio Eradication Advocacy Task Force has played a major role in decisions by donor governments to contribute over US$ 1.5 billion to the effort. Thus the funds from direct and indirect efforts by Rotary are reported to be more than half the money needed for the entire global polio eradication programme.

The results of this effort for India are reported at the IEAG (India Expert Advisory Group for Polio Eradication) New Delhi, 3–4 May 2005. The IEAG is a high-powered group including senior medical and other professionals, government representatives from various ministries, and representative partner organizations. Their conclusion after review of the epidemological and programmatic data was that 'India has made its most important progress to date during 2004 and early 2005'. This conclusion was based on the findings that the polio cases were now focal (localized) at very low levels in western UP and Bihar, and the programme had achieved almost complete elimination of type 3 polio. Its achievement was also that it managed a very effective vaccination of the HRA (high-risk area) with less than 5.6 per cent 'missed children'. Despite the marked and significant decline in the incidence of fresh cases over the last ten years in India certification that the desease has been eliminated require other conditions to be met. There would have to be a sustained surveillance report to the effect for a continuous period of three years, beginning at the end of 2005.

The commitment to a large-scale impact through single causes is also the hallmark of the other international business organizations with chapters in India. The International Association of Lions Club began as the dream of a Chicago insurance man Melvin Jones, who endeavoured in 1917 to use the concept of a business club to expand the horizons of business from purely business concerns to the betterment of local communities and the world at large.[28]

Lions India makes an annual yearly contribution to Lions International through its membership.[29] Many of the developmental issues taken up internationally are of particular significance for India, in the areas of health and literacy. 'Sight first' has been the foremost of Lions activities in India (15,000 cataract operations are done every year through this programme in Delhi alone). This has been expanded to addressing measles in a joint programme with UNICEF. Also on the cards is a programme for bringing adolescent youth closer to teachers and parents.

The potential to upscale the outcomes is there. For example, there is active engagement with government to eradicate illiteracy through a huge volunteer force (5000 in India) with 1.75 lakh members spread in forty-seven districts. Lions India's adoption of 'literacy' as a national programme for five years, has tied in with Government of India's priorities in this area. Its objective is reported to be to multiply government efforts in this field. For disaster relief and the 2004 Tsunami in India, Lions contributed Rs 200 crore for the entire region.

Industry associations are uniquely placed bodies that look beyond the firm for the firm. Overall development of the country is now seen as being in the long-term interest of business. Partnership with government to achieve upscaled results and to provide models for development management

---

[28] http://www.lionnet.com/history_of_lions.html

[29] I am grateful to Mr Jagdish Agrawal, District Governor Lions, for most of the information relating to Lions activities in India in this segment. Lions has a membership of approximately 1.6 lakh, each contributing $40 annually.

portends more things to come. Meanwhile, a new trajectory of effort is emerging also from business. This is tied to the new economy and linked to individual firms that are bringing a stream of change somewhat more imperative and immediate to business functioning. Chapter 4 addresses the issue of CSR in the context of new economy imperatives in the IT and outsourcing sectors.

EYE ON I.T.
PREPARING FOR AND MANAGING CHANGE

India is poised to take off in what are called the new economy areas. Information technology is a key aspect of that new economy. Through its reach, information technology holds out the promise of touching almost every aspect of human engagement. Anything so all-encompassing calls for not just infrastructure but building capacities, skills, and orientations. Access to these capabilities holds out the promise of adding great value for individuals, business organizations, and the nation as a whole; exclusion can spell disaster through a politically volatile digital divide. Recognizing this, this industry segment appears very tuned to the enlargement of social responsiveness initiatives.

CREATING THE EDUCATION BASE

In India, IT has close to doubled between 1999 and 2002 from a Rs 362 billion to a Rs 642 billion industry.[1] Further this industry has been tracking exceptional growth, contributing an estimated 2.8 per cent share of GDP in 2002 and aiming for a potential 2.2 million jobs in IT by 2008. This industry grew in India in the phase of liberalization, and was relatively free of governmental controls. Essentially, it is an industry that was less constrained by traditional physical infrastructure (such as ports and roads, etc. which other industries felt in short supply). On the other hand, it does not have in place an adequate social infrastructure for its future growth—namely, an educated base to wing the IT transformation through all sections of the population.

In a highly competitive environment, a key requirement of this industry is to have a knowledge-and IT-centred employee base to serve and develop

[1] NASSCOM, India Embassy Report, 2003.

it, and a knowledge-centred consumer base to reap the benefits of this sector. This industry has very good business reasons in India to look at the educational profile of the country in a serious way, and to encourage models to address this developmental issue. This need also derives its impetus from forces reaching into the future and from forces outside of India as well. It is fully expected that the global IT employment boom in 2020 will not be matched by the available 25–35-year olds skilled in this field in the developed world, resulting in an added reason to develop this talent.

School education is primarily a government engagement in India, but with dismal results. As per the census of 2001, as much as 34.68 per cent of the population is excluded from literacy. As much as 42.6 per cent of those in the 11–14 age group and 75.4 per cent in the 14–17 age group are excluded from formal enrolment.[2]

The top information technology companies are in one way or the other involved in supporting and partnering the government in the primary education segment and in initiating IT education as well. This has given rise to a new focus on the approach to education, both in terms of spread as well as quality, content, delivery, and evaluation. It has also provided experience of public–private partnership, models for better governance in this and other areas, and raising new issues in CSR engagement as well. Three examples of IT companies—Wipro, Infosys, and NIIT—having undertaken engagement in this area are outlined below. Many other companies in this segment are doing likewise. Satyam Computer Services Ltd. for instance not only has several innovative wide-ranging CSR engagements, but has also been collaborating with its own potential global competitors in enhancing school education in India.

WIPRO

Wipro Technologies is one of the leading IT companies in India. Wipro's engagement in social development work is prompted by a cultivated consciousness of its stated mission: 'Wipro believes every entity has a responsibility to improve the system it inhabits. Wipro is a key member of the Indian society and is favourably positioned to create positive impact.'[3]

[2] IAMR, *Manpower Profile on India Yearbook*, 2000.

[3] I am grateful to Vijay K. Gupta, Vice President Brand, Corporate Communication & Corporate Planning at Wipro and Anand Swaminathan for an interview on Wipro's approach,

The focus of the company is on education. 'Education' it states, 'is the fundamental enabler of economic development and social change. Hence, Wipro has decided to focus single-mindedly on "education" as the key issue. Wipro's engagement in education and social development comes through at least three different mechanisms.

- Applying Thought in Schools
- Wipro Cares
- Azim Premji Foundation

The Foundation, though not directly a part of Wipro, was set up through the personal contribution of Azim Premji, Chairman of Wipro Corporation. Due to the extensive nature of the Foundation's work, initiatives are under way to bring some convergence between this organization and the two other mechanisms through which Wipro's work is done in the area of social development.

Applying Thought in Schools

Mission

Applying Thought in Schools is institutionalized under Brand, Corporate Communication, and Corporate Planning, headed by an executive of the stature of the Vice-President of the company. Wipro's engagement here is with primary education. A key feature of the programme that began in January 2001 is that it is not necessarily IT-linked in its present form. 'Wipro would like to influence a movement towards quality in education.' Interestingly positioned under Brand, Corporate Communication, and Corporate Planning, Wipro sees this as an intervention in the area of community development.

Scope

Through this initiative, Wipro targets the quantitative and qualitative performance of primary school education in not just several private schools, but also a variety of educational institutions of the state/government/NDMC. The current coverage is primarily, though not exclusively, through private

---

as well as Wipro Applying Thought 2003. Presentation by Vijay K. Gupta 'An Overview', p. 1. The rest of this segment is largely based on these information sources.

schools. However, the scope of the initiatives is wider and includes working towards a 'paradigm shift in the philosophy of education', itself. The approach is also holistic with its roles being perceived as networking, advocating, and intervening to achieve new models of education. In the last of these, a key part is the R&D initiatives of what education should be about.

Approach

The objective of value-added educational inputs is further defined as contributing to changing the existing school system in the following ways:[4]

From	To
Examination Centric	*Development Centric*
Content of Delivery	*Learning Facilitation*
Compartmentalized Subjects	*Interrelated Diciplines*
Teachers who Teach	*Teachers who Learn*
Improving Memory	*Developing Life Skills*
Grading to Judge	*Assessing to Improve*
Boring	*Interesting*
Straightjacket Students	*Unleashing the potential in every Child*

Mechanisms

In order to achieve this, Wipro's Applying Thought works through a number of initiatives, for example,

> *Teacher Empowerment Program*
> *Education Leadership Program*
> *Parents Empowerment Program*
> *Eco-system of Partners*
> *Boards of Education*
> *Teacher Training Colleges*
> Coverage

Wipro's reach through these programmes extends to ten cities (Ahmedabad, Baroda, Bangalore, Chandigarh, Chennai, Cochin, Delhi, Jaipur, Hyderabad, and Mumbai) with plans to extend to five more cities (Pune, Kolkata, Dehradun, Bhubaneshwar, and Cuttack). The figures in terms of

[4] Vijay K. Gupta 2003, ibid.

coverage are constantly revised upwards. In 2003, Applying Thought in Schools covered 2006 teachers (3–7 standard) and 150 principals across 94 schools in 13 cities.[5]

Networks

Wipro works with a large number of NGOs from diverse fields to meet its objectives. Wipro contributes up to two-thirds of the budget for such training, while the schools contribute in cash/kind the remaining one-third. Evaluations of these interventions are done by partnering NGOs. The overall response to a client-centred (students/parents/teachers/school systems) approach is reported to be overwhelming as shown in the assessment by participants in such programmes. However, this is clearly only a beginning, albeit a very important one, and the company still needs to show other indicators of success. Changes in enrolment and drop-out rates, student performance, and other indicators of growth are yet to be evaluated.

Azim Premji Foundation

The Azim Premji Foundation has been set up and maintained through the personal contribution of Azim Premji. However, linkages are in the process of being developed with Wipro's other initiatives in social development. This is being done so that there can be a beneficial convergence of learning in these organizations. The Foundation has the mission to 'transform the lives of millions of children in India by catalysing universalisation of elementary education'. The experiments have been an exercise not just in value-added education but also in management of a viable model and of taking the model to different regions, holding out the promise of transforming education altogether.

Partnering with Government

One of the key aspects of the Foundation's work is that it operates in partnership with government and is focused on schools in rural areas. This has enabled coverage of considerable proportions and in early 2003, the coverage was as follows:[6]

---

[5] Ibid.
[6] Ibid.

- 3700 villages and an equal number of schools in seventeen blocks in the state of Karnataka.
- 500 villages and an equal number of schools in ten mandals in the state of AP.
- 300 municipal schools in three cities in Gujarat.

During April 2002–June 2003, the Foundation would have trained approximately 1,00,000 educational functionaries.

The Foundation's work began with the setting up of Community Learning Centres (CLCs) at the behest of the Karnataka state government in thirty-four schools where a room was provided for this facility. Computers and basic software content in local languages were provided in these schools.

This exercise is important in that it spells the beginning of new types of engagement in social development. There are two major aspects to the 'newness' in this engagement. The first is that the government invites a partnership with the corporate sector in fulfilling its own (government's) social-sector obligations. This means that the government opens itself to receiving design, organizational, and management inputs and non-monetary and monetary contributions to the IT education sector. The scope of interventions through such value-added inputs becomes more focused to national requirements than what the company could do if it were to operate on its own.

Sustainability

The second part of the 'newness' comes from the sustainability aspects that are built into the development of the programme. This provides business opportunity to recover its costs of experiment in this area, as well as to develop a local pay-for-services model in the community, while providing cost-free services as well. These include:[7]

1. The CLC (Community Learning Centre). The facilities at the CLC are available free of cost during school hours for children of that school, and on a pay-and-use basis for the general public before and after school hours and on holidays.

[7] C.V. Madhukar (Head of Technology Initiatives with Azim Premji Foundation), Digital Divide: Concern for Equity and Social Justice.http://www.azimpremjifoundation.org/downloads/CVMarticle-NIEPASeminar.pdf

2. CLCs are run by local youth called the Young India Fellows (YIFs). These YIFs receive a fellowship of Rs 1500 per month for a period of twelve months from the Azim Premji Foundation and thereafter they are responsible for generating enough revenues to ensure the upkeep of the CLC.

This experiment is yet to be wholly evaluated. However, there are indicators of early successes in the government invitation to set up another fifty-five CLCs in eleven identified *taluks* in the state—covering some of the poorest regions. The third aspect of the newness is the stake that local communities have as per the design of the project. The C.V. Madhukar case studies show that ownership at ground level is bringing encouraging results, which are documented.[8]

Engaging with clients

Anoor is a small village with a population of about 1000 people in Sidlaghatta taluk of Kolar district (Karnataka) which is considered a socially and economically backward district. Sidlaghatta is well known for its sericulture industry. Farmers grow the mulberry crop while the silk producers rear the cocoons and produce silk yarn in the process. Anoor government school is one of the five schools in Sidlaghatta where Azim Premji Foundation put up computers in April 2001. There are nearly 180 children in Std. 1 to 7 at this school.

There are 4 computers in Anoor school, where children take turns to use these computers about 2–3 class periods a week. The Young India Fellow in-charge of managing the Anoor schools is 21 year old Radha who has completed her BA and then taken up some computer certification courses. For a year, up to March 2002, Radha received a Fellowship every month of Rs. 1500 to manage the CLC. Since then she has had to depend on the community to generate revenues as well as seek community contributions to support the activities of the CLC including a monthly 'salary' to her of Rs. 2000—up from a Fellowship of Rs. 1500 last year!

Radha and the school head teacher were informed by Azim Premji Foundation at the very beginning of the programme that at the end of the first year in April 2002, the onus of meeting all the operational costs will lie with the school. If the school is unable to sustain itself financially, then the computers would move to one of the nearby government schools that had shown interest in getting the facility in their school and had offered to sustain it financially.

Radha tried hard to generate revenues and had only marginal success. The village is small and there are very few people who are keen to receive computer training after school hours, especially in the absence of credible certification that can help get jobs. Some of the other initiatives

[8] Ibid.

taken up by Radha did not result in enough revenues either. So a meeting of the parents and the community was called, and a decision was taken to get money to the school in the form of donations, from parents and other well-to-do members of the village. The necessary money was raised and the community also gave its conditional support. Radha also received a 'rule-book' developed by the community with the following main points:

1. *Now that we are paying for the facility, we would want to ensure that Radha does not take more than one day off in a month*
2. *If there is a power cut during school hours, Radha will stay back for an extra hour after school to ensure that children get to use the PCs adequately*
3. *The educational software content CDs that were given last year have now been used by the children repeatedly. We want a fresh set of CDs teaching more academic content to be given at the earliest.*

A transformation in the making from non-involvement of the community in school affairs, to close involvement in the running of the CLC and broader issues of governance through community participation is in evidence here.

Participatory education finds a place at the Azim Premji Foundation in another way. This is the Learning Guarantee Programme[9] of the Azim Premji Foundation. There are a number of interesting aspects to this programme, one of which is its scope. It was piloted in 2002 in north-east Karnataka which contributes 50 per cent of drop-outs in the state. It is one of achievements of this three-year programme that out of the 9270 government primary and higher primary schools in the region, 1888 schools have participated in it. The main thrust of the project is to encourage school performance through recognition and award, with inputs from many stakeholder groups including the community as well as the government. (see Annexure 4A)

Apart from the extensive scope of the programme, another aspect is that there is no compromise on conditions of excellence for school performance. However, it allows for various levels of achievement which can keep lower performing schools in the race as well in important areas of school management like enrolment, attendance, and competency.

In the case of enrolment, for instance, the schools would have to achieve '100 per cent enrolment of all children in the habitation in the 6–11 age group, as per the child census survey of 2002'.[10] Equally, learning

[9] Anjali Prayag, 'Premji's Passion', *Praxis*, December 2004, pp. 18–23.
[10] Ibid., p. 21.

competency critieria that have to be met by the school require schools to show that 90 per cent of required competencies have been acquired by most students. The school would be deemed to be of A, B, or C category on the basis of the percentage of students who have achieved this 90 per cent competency. Schools that are able to ensure coverage of 60–80 per cent of students with this high level of competency are eligible for being incentivized through cash and other awards.

The approach to the whole programme is participatory (with a role for parents, children, and school staff) and incentivized with a monetary award to both the schools (Rs 20,000) that meet the criteria of evaluation, and to students as well. This allows the winning schools to invest the award money for further improvements. Most of all what appears significant in all this, is the management and communication strategy. This has whipped up the imagination and enthusiasm of all stakeholders, parents, teachers, school staff, the government, and the corporates to carry this forward.

The interest shown by other state governments—Madhya Pradesh, Orissa, Gujarat and Uttaranchal—to seek the experiment in their state, the extension of the programme in other areas of Karnataka, and the voluntary application of over 50 per cent schools in a given block to be part of the programme are all indicators of its success.

Wipro Cares

Wipro Cares was set up in 2003 to create an avenue for tapping existing and new efforts of individual Wirproites volunteering for social development initiatives. The volunteering efforts are both in terms of cash offerings as well as through inputs in other ways. There is a fund base of financial contributions made by Wiproites matched by contribution from Wipro Corporation.

Wipro Cares has much broader scope than the other two Wipro organizations already discussed and it is flexible to several requirements. The earthquake in Gujarat and the rebuilding efforts drew a total contribution of Rs 2 crore. Wipro Cares is managed by one full-time employee and has approximately 200 volunteers. Wipro offices with 500 or more employees were encouraged to open a chapter, and it is through this mechanism that the volunteer force is identified and has grown. For a total workforce of approximately 30,000, this is a small but significant beginning.

Child development, senior citizens, and environment are other areas of voluntary effort at Wipro Cares. These interventions are employee driven in that the employees identified these areas as ones that Wipro could devote attention to. This was done through a survey. Recently, there have been strategies to enter the field of child education as well—so that the learning and experience from Applying Thought in Schools and the Ajim Premji Foundation can be fruitfully used.

Together with placing emphasis on primary education, Wipro maintains that primary health care is fundamental to all round development. While Applying Thought in Schools and Azim Premji Foundation are concentrating on primary education, Wipro Care is poised to make value-added improvements in the existing health care system. The approach is to target improvement of the Primary Health Care system of the government and work to resolve critical issues on a sustainable basis. In this, partnerships resources from government and private organizations will be sought. In three cities—Bangalore, Pune, and Hyderabad—model projects for health care delivery, sanitation, and hygiene are under way in slum communities. Over 100 Wiproites are involved in these efforts.

NIIT

NIIT Ltd. is a leader in IT educational services and IT-enabled training. It is best known for its software services. It has openings in thirty countries and is on an expansion course. Like other companies in this sector, NIIT's social development initiatives in education comes through diversified mechanisms within the company. While India, with its population of approximately 1 billion, poses an enviably wide landscape for an IT company, the largely illiterate populace, both in the adult and child category, is a special challenge for the current and future presence of an industry catering mostly to an 'educated' constituency.

To meet these needs, NIIT's strategy can be seen in at least two different directions. On the one hand there are initiatives to examine the possibility of IT being more inclusive for a less educated population. On the other hand there are, as in the case of other IT companies, partnerships to bring IT integration into the school system as a whole. These are represented in the two main programmes: Hole in the Wall (minimally invasive education); and K-12 (Kindergarten to class 12).

Hole-in-the Wall: Creating Outreach

To understand the acceptability of computer kiosks, especially in the rural areas, business interest at NIIT led to a number of R&D initiatives in this field in 1999.[11] 'Hole in the Wall' is one of these. It is so called because it delivers computer education in rural areas or slums through strategically placed computers mounted on walls in the vicinity or within the compounds of schools and other public buildings. This initiative embraced the view that technology could be accessed by all classes of people, even in the remote areas, and particularly by young children with little or no education. The challenge remained, as stated by NIIT Chairman Mr Pawar, that 'the rapidly spreading use of the Internet in India is restricted to affluent urban areas, thereby creating a knowledge gap in society.... This project will broaden access to the Internet and provide education to children of all social classes.'[12]

For a country with a huge illiterate and poor population, this was an experiment many watched. The media hailed the experiment as having the potential to bridge the digital divide that had been predicted in the wake of the IT revolution. The early successes of the experiment attracted the International Finance Corporation (IFC) to invest US$1.6 million in 2001 to develop internet-based education for children living in India's urban slums and rural areas.[13]

Aspirations ran high and Mr Bernard Pasquier, the IFC's Director for South Asia called information technology 'an incredible instrument of change in India', and referred to the NIIT experiment as marking the way to help 'eradicate illiteracy in India'.[14]

Dr Sugata Mitra, Chief Scientist, Research and Cognitive Systems at NIIT and in charge of the Hole in the Wall programme explained that it substantiated the hypothesis that computer literacy, was possible with minimally invasive education. Computer kiosks were placed in slum and village environments, specifically designed to attract children in the 8–13-

[11] I am grateful to Dr Sugata Mitra, Chief Scientist, Centre for Research in Cognitive Systems, NIIT for insights and information presented in this section. Monday, 22 March, 2004.

[12] Bridging the Knowledge Gap, 2001.

http://web.worldbank.org/WBSITE/EXTERNAL/NEWS/0%2C%2CcontentMDK:200 19704~menuPK:34460~pagePK:64003015~piPK:64003012~theSitePK:4607%2C00.html

[13] Ibid.

[14] Ibid.

year age group. Close to eighty-eight computers have been placed near or outside schools, both in India and outside as a part of this programme, which was undertaken in partnership with government bodies.

A significant aspect of this programme was that it was closely watched and had monitored results. It showed that with no guidance children, even illiterate children, could master many functions of a computer and of a given software programme. With minimal guidance children could rise to another level of mastery. The close evaluation of the programme showed that this technology was quite unlike other technologies. The hypothesis that computer education was possible with minimal intervention of technology was not rejected, and it showed that minimal invasive education was not only possible but that it held across location, gender, ethnicity, and many other socio-economic factors and in the lowest socio-economic fractiles as well. Here was the case of a corporate taking on the initial investment and R&D initiatives for social development with the full expectation that it would have ramifications for its own business as well.

Following the end of a three-year contract with the Delhi government to take the experiment to Madangir slum, the Delhi government made an independent survey of the results. It showed that between 42 per cent to 58 per cent of all children in this socio-economic group used the machines. The placing of a single computer in the playground environment is estimated to attract use by as many as 500 children, as compared to about forty children in a lab or classroom environment. The Hole in the Wall application of computer learning is best suited for those who do not have access to formal educational services.

These results were so overwhelming that the survey was repeated three times, with no appreciable difference in the results. The Delhi government has agreed to renew this experiment. They have estimated the cost of such interventions to be approximately Rs 2 per child per day.

In a very short time, by 2003, NIIT was able to report expansion of the experiment[15] to other locations in Delhi, several states in India including Madhya Pradesh, Uttar Pradesh, and Maharashtra, and other countries such as Alexandria and Cambodia. Most of these projects were funded collaboratively by NIIT, with government support.

[15] Ibid.

NIIT now looks at three models for the distribution of this technology.

- It is prepared to give design inputs free, with the physical construction being done by the client.
- NIIT will do the physical construction for a cost.
- NIIT will build, operate, and transfer all aspects of this technology and software, at an approximate cost of Rs 3–5 lakh for three computers, servicing some 1000 students.

Already there are client enquiries and delivery to Cambodia of the build, operate, and transfer model. In Alexandria, the hardware model is being disbursed. In the next phase, NIIT is to deliver structured educational material as well. The early experiments have also drawn the interest of other companies and of multilateral organizations planning to replicate this model.

K-12

K-12 became NIIT's exclusive solution for the Indian schools domain. Not only did NIIT enter into partnerships with leading state governments such as Karnataka, Andhra Pradesh, and Tamil Nadu to provide computer education to government schools in these states, it also launched a major IT training drive within the private schools.

K-12 is NIIT's kindergarten to class 12 programme, which focuses on classes 6–10 in government and private schools as well as teacher training through LEAD (learning, experience, adventure, and discussion).

Business and social interests are well matched here as stated by the Zonal Head, of this programme.[16] NIIT had strategized to get involved in the school education programme because it would have an entry to grow with this segment through its life-cycle. It represented a huge potential market, one which would increase the potential of students and society as a whole.

The initiative in India was preceded by a contract based engagement in a Malayasian school project where NIIT was the content partner. The Indian market for this kind of initiative was assessed to be considerable:

Government schools	7,43,568
Private schools	2,62,226
Star schools	900 +100

---

[16] Interview with Anwar Ahmed Khan, Zonal Head North, NIIT, 2004.

NIIT's K-12 intervention in Karnataka started around 2001. The inputs included various kinds of software related to the requirements of school education as well as school administration. The evaluation of the programme after three years reported the following results:

- there has been a marked enrolment increase in the 6–10 classes in three years in the schools where the intervention was conducted.
- Also within a given *taluk*, there was migration from private schools that did not have such computer-related programmes to government schools that did.

NIIT addresses all types of school needs. This includes needs of government schools to private schools and star schools. There is progressive inclusion of foundation and IT courses, IT-enabled services, virtual school and technical applications for the different types of schools.

The approach to provide such services is through the BOOT, that is build, operate, own, and transfer model and various combinations of it—with differing inputs from the school system. In the case of private schools there is a service charge for the students and NIIT's investment is recovered in a short period of time. There is another model being followed for government schools. In the latter case, the amount due for services by NIIT is leased over the period of the contract.

Partnering with government, while offering the opportunity of a huge market, is not without its challenges. Support from leadership at the highest level in government gave the impetus for quick results. There were partnership culture challenges, like timely payments and security to the service provider. Additionally, there were infrastructural challenges like power and telephone lines.

The office of the Northern Zone reports the kinds of positive externalities that these partnerships brought. In Karnataka, fifty out of the 700 school projects were in areas where there was no electricity. NIIT had a contract to put the software systems in place in forty-five days and power infrastructure was reported to be provided in that time as well in many of these instances due to the active interest and collaboration of the government.

NIIT reports over 2000 schools in the government as well the private sector opting for K-12. The integration of free computer education by NIIT in government schools through the Sarv Shiksha Abhiyan has traversed an impressive path. In 2005, Himachal Pradesh partnered with NIIT for this integration. Outside the country there have been similar initiatives by NIIT. From the development perspective, these engagements deliver much more. They are closely tied with the creation of infrastructure, systems integration, facilities management, education delivery, and teacher training, thus delivering both computer-education and computer-aided education. This initiative has also gone beyond India. In Malaysia, it is being implemented in the Multimedia Super Corridor Smart Schools projects to create education content for the country.

The kind of overall impact and coverage that NIIT's early initiatives have achieved have been in the extensive reach of their programmes for both rural and urban government schools providing coverage for lakhs of students, across several districts and several hundred schools.[17] It also covers the design of local language courseware and textbooks, which in some states have been adopted as part of the state syllabus, as in Tamil Nadu, Karnataka, and Andhra Pradesh.

These investments in the social sector of education—where business and social interests can be expected to converge in the future—are not the only ones by NIIT. There are other areas where returns are likely to be long term and more directly fit the description of being 'social'. These include:

- Converging with the government's Sarv Shiksa Abhiyan. NIIT integrated with the Himachal state programme in 2005, with 210 government schools being provided computer literacy free of cost in the first phase. Among other things, NIIT holds a contract valid up to 2007 for this engagment which is extendable to 2010. The services provided will include faculty for computer education, teacher training annually, coverage for class 6–8 students, and the provision of courseware in Hindi.
- A Computer Assisted Teaching and Rehabilitation project for the disabled has been undertaken by NIIT in collaboration with The Spastic Society of Tamil Nadu and the Rajiv Gandhi Foundation.[18]
- Bhavishya Jyoti Scholarships which were introduced over thirteen years ago and have touched over 1,00,000 Indian students. The scholarships

---

[17] http://www.niit.com/Education/programs/niit_school/school_govt.asp#1

[18] http://www.niit.com/niit/corporate/aboutniit/society.asp

including fee waivers ranging from 15–100 per cent are targeted for meritorious yet financially challenged students in other models provided by NIIT.

INFOSYS

Infosys Technologies Ltd is one of the leaders in the field of information technology and systems. Among IT companies, its Chairman, Narayana Murthy, has been the foremost to champion the role of the 'good corporation'. Narayana Murthy's favourite theme was reiterated at an international meeting, 'We should look for the public good, and private good will automatically come.'[19] Seamlessly integrating the issues of corporate governance with corporate responsibility, he talks of the expanded definition of corporate governance to mean maximizing of shareholder value on a *sustainable basis* while ensuring fairness to all stakeholders. In this terminological swirl is carried the need to be the good corporate to employees, vendors, suppliers, consumers, and of course, shareholders, even where it appears to be at the immediate cost of the company. Many of the issues of corporate governance are addressed with the same world-view which gave employees a strong stakeholder position at Infosys Technologies. This is the company that strengthened the employee stakeholder process through opportunities for ESOP options for company ownership, and which is reported to have Indian rupee and dollar millionaires among its employees as a result. In the following section, education and other social sector engagement of this company are discussed.

The Infosys Foundation

The Infosys Foundation set up in March 1996, is the mechanism through which Infosys's social support initiatives are formalized. It was set up by Narayana Murthy and his wife Sudha Murthy, who is Chairperson and a Trustee of the Foundation. The company has a transparent system for its commitment to development and its foundation receives 1.5 per cent of the company's after-tax profits.[20]

---

[19] Narayana N.R. Murthy, 'Corporate Governance—A Luxury or a Must' in *India-ASEAN Partnership in An Era of Globalisation*, 2002, p. 254
[20] See Centre for Social Markets, *A Resource Guide*, 2004.

In line with its stakeholder driven approach, the allocation of funds at the Infosys Foundation is also based on participatory processes. The geographical area of expenditure of the Foundation is rationalized according to the ratio of its employees in the four states, where it has offices. Accordingly, the state of Karnataka gets 70 per cent of the funds, Maharashtra 15 per cent, Orissa 5 per cent, and Tamil Nadu 10 per cent. Additionally, there are sectoral allocations with a variety of committments. There is a 30 per cent allocation to old people, the destitute, and the handicapped; 15 per cent to rural development; 30 per cent to education of talented but poor children, 15 per cent for cultural activities, and 10 per cent for healthcare in villages and cities.[21]

At Infosys Foundation, there is little that can be construed as the 'business model' of development in any immediate sense. There is a strong focus on the underprivileged. The work of the Foundation is spread over health care, rural upliftment, social rehabilitation, learning and education, and the arts. Health and education have a significant focus. The approach appears to concentrate mainly, though not exclusively, on strategic support for the development of infrastructure at credible institutions already catering to the poor, the destitute, and the marginalized. The support is for expanding, remodelling, or upgrading existing initiatives, resulting in the possibility of improving the quality and scale of coverage.

In health, for instance, it is in the form of support for expansion, wherever needed, of existing hospitals catering to disadvantaged groups. For the Swami Shivananda Centinary Charitable Hospital in Tamil Nadu there were additional blocks constructed. The Kidwai Cancer Institute, Bangalore got a Dharamshala. For the Capitol Hospital in Bhubaneswar, which caters to poor patients, a paediatric hospital was added. Wards were built for the Swami Shivananda Memorial Charitable Hospital in Pattumadia, Tamil Nadu; a hospital for tribals at H.D. Kote, Mysore; and improvement made to a rehabilitation centre for mentally-retarded women in Chennai. There are also independent philanthrophy efforts in providing medical aid and support for the impoverished, the destitute, the aged, and orphans.

---

[21] The Centre for Communication and Development Studies information servicehttp://www.infochangeindia.org/CorporatesrIstory.jsp?recordno=322&section_idv=11.

There seems to be a similar approach in the area of education. Under the 'Library for Every Rural School Project, the Foundation has set up 10,150 libraries in rural government schools. In another effort at a different level of education, the latest books in hi-tech streams like medicine and engineering are made available through libraries in Hubli and Bangalore that can be accessed by underprivileged students. There is a deposit of Rs 800 which permits them use of this facility throughout their education.

As in the case of health, there is support to existing educational organizations catering to disadvantaged groups. The Foundation has supported the construction of girls' hostels, for blind students helped in the reconstruction of fourteen government schools in slum areas and the renovation of several other Kapikad Zilla Panchayat schools in Mangalore, Karnataka. The construction of a science centre at a rural school in Kolar district of Karnataka is an example of reaching services to an educational hub. It is described as a 'one of a kind centre in the entire district—which caters not only to the school where it is constructed but to children of neighbouring schools as well.'

Expanding the reach of computer education in rural areas is only part of an overall framework of philanthrophy and this is done through donations for computer centres, for the development of literature in regional languages, for easy computer education, and so on. In 1999, there was a government provision that 'used PCs' imported by export-oriented software organizations can be donated free of duty to educational institutions (earlier such efforts were not allowed). In the wake of this provision, Infosys initiated a pro-gramme with Microsoft to provide computers to schools which could not afford such investments. From the first consignment, forty-three schools in Bangalore and Mangalore benefited. After the launch both Infosys and Microsoft described it as a programme they wished to expand and continue to support.

One other important sector of support by the Foundation is in the area of the arts. The Foundation support for the arts focuses on artists in rural areas. This is done through multiple strategies of direct support on a 'need basis', promoting dying arts, giving recognition to artists, supporting exhibitions, and providing other marketing support as well.

The full menu of CSR efforts of Infosys in the major categories of its work—healthcare, rural upliftment, social rehabilitation, learning and education and the arts—is extensive. However, there is a clear focus on reaching the impoverished sections in all of the five major areas of the Foundation's work. Support for mainstreaming through general education and through IT education is a significant part of this work.

IT Association Partnership with Government

The most ambitious launch of partnership between corporates and government for such work is still unfolding at IT-industry association levels. This is the Mission 2007: Every Village a Knowledge Centre. Programme. The IT industry association is closely linked to the project through its Foundation. The key partners are NASSCOM Foundation, Microsoft Corporation India, and the International Crops Research Institute for the Semi-Arid Tropics (ICRISAT) This is also an alliance of 180 partners from government, civil society, and industry set up in 2004. This national alliance is led Professor M.S. Swaminathan. It has the aim of linking 6,00,000 villages through such knowledge centres. These rural knowledge centres will be a vehicle for delivery of IT skills and services at individual and societal levels. In the latter category, they will also provide a platform for engagement with initiatives such as micro credit, disaster management, and security. The Union Finance Minister has indicated support to Mission 2007. The first Rural Knowledge Centre under the aegis of this project was set up in Ocrober 2005.

These profiles of IT companies' engagement in the social sectors and particularly in IT education are instructive in many ways. They provide models in government—private partnerships for a range of education-related efforts including school administration, teacher training, software content for syllabus. It also profiles the kinds of roles that government has been playing to bring these changes.

MANAGING CHANGE: NEW ECONOMY JOBS AND ETHICS

The digital divide is one of the key issues within India to which corporate social responsiveness is directed as described in the previous section. Quite a different dimension of CSR has emerged in the information technology enabled services (ITES) and business process outsourcing (BPOs).

According to the NASSCOM survey of 1999–2000 there had been a reversal in the mode of IT services offered by India. In the early 1990s, it was basically an on-site service industry with offshore services accounting for only 5 per cent of services; in 1999–2000, the offshore business had increased to 40 per cent correspondingly reducing the percentage of on-site services. The US-based technology research house Gartner has predicted that India will represent two-thirds of the international 'offshore market'—jobs done outside a client's region—within three or four years.[22] Like many other industries, the global markets have created new social scenarios to contend with.

BPO is very much a part of the globalization process and the market's search for cheaper options, in this case that of service provision from developing countries. Companies coming to India in this segment are having to contend with social issues that have been unleashed as a result. Loss of jobs in the developed world and new environment of work in the developing world 'host country', have led companies to reach both forward and backward to address corporate responsibility issues in home and host countries.

The efforts involved in the British Telecom (BT) engagement in India provide a typical example in understanding CSR in BPO issues.[23]

CSR In the Home Country

The 'Sentiment' Of Lost Jobs

In the private-sector-led economies of the developed world, employees and workers are not unfamiliar with hire and fire situations. However, there is something about the loss of jobs represented in the BPO segment that appears to have drawn a strong response. This has a lot to do with sentiments about the circumstances in which jobs are lost. India is currently in the happy position of gaining jobs. But in the global context, as cheaper options become available, these issues would come home to this country as well.

In the context of outsourcing from the UK, it has been pointed out that there are several types of outsourcing with different 'social acceptability' aspects attached to them in the home country. At least four different kinds of patterns have been identified with respect to outsourcing from the UK.[24]

[22] Agence France-Presse, New Delhi, 9 December http://www.hindustantimes.com/news/181_488912,0003.htm

[23] I am grateful to Kavita Prakash-Mani, Senior Advisor Sustainability for appraising me of the issues regarding BPO in India. See Judy Kuszewski, Kavita Prakash-Mani, and Seb B. Beloe, *Good Migrations? BT, Corporate Social Responsibility and the Geography of Jobs*, 2004.

[24] See George Monbiot, 'The Flight to India', *The Guardian*, 21 October 2003.

Outsourcing within country to a different company represents the first kind. The other three types of outsourcing fall within the broad category of offshoring of services, where services and functions are taken to another country. Within its ambit can be found several different kinds of arrangements. A first type in this category is outsourcing abroad to another servicing company. A second type of outsourcing abroad is represented by an in–house activity transported to another country but conducted under the aegis of the company itself. Remote Sourcing represents a third type of outsourcing abroad. In this case services are given to another supplier company offshore, but the host country company retains ownership and sometimes managerial and other roles as well.

Different sentiments are attached to the lost jobs in each of these cases. Where company ownership persists across borders, as in the last two categories mentioned, it is experienced as most onerous to labour in the developed country. Loss of jobs due to these developments is not because of the failure to compete with cheaper imports, but because (of the additional factor) of the company's own strategic decision to fire workers in the home country to hire workers in a developing country like India instead. These represent most transparently what the search for profits does to jobs. In the same context, different sentiments may attach to whether the services and functions offshored were new or existing ones, adding further categories to the sentiments issue.

Offshoring decisions by companies to India have been watched closely by unions in the developed countries by a wide coalition of organizations. British Telecom workers in Glasgow staged strikes to protest the company's decision to open call centres in Delhi and Bangalore. Elsewhere, the NAFE (North American Alliance for Fair Economy), an alliance of sixty organizations of non-standard forms of employment in North America, voiced its concern. Its spokesperson, Tim Costello, maintains that 'this signals a new phase in globalisation, where knowledge-based jobs are moving because corporations want the lowest paid labour'.[25]

Industry, in some quarters, has come to realize that some of these issues have to be addressed. The year 2002–3 saw BT reorganize its existing call centres and investment in the UK and expand into India. In India, this meant that Delhi and Bangalore would have new capacity with 2200

[25] News and Features Infochange http://www.oneworld.net/external/?url=http%3A%2F%2Finfochangeindia.org%2Finfochange_wsfBG.jsp

persons employed who would be handling marketing, administration, and sales functions. This would of course replace the same number of jobs in the UK.

In the wake of controversies surrounding outsourcing from the UK to India, BT commissioned a report by Sustainability, the well-known UK consulting company. This was a conscious step on part of the company to understand what the possible CSR issues might be in this segment and what BT had done in its mission of corporate social responsibility and what it could further do.[26]

The study included broad-based objectives of understanding CSR in the context of BPOs, for BT itself and for others interested in this issue. It sought to understand the specific impacts of BTs offshoring decisions and the processes followed both in the UK and in India in terms of the social issues. The study was also to offer recommendations for enhancing CSR actions in this segment.

A number of issues were identified. As a result BT worked with home country government in managing the transition for those who lost jobs in the home country. It set new norms for outsourcing and as part of that process 'involuntary redundancy' was eliminated. Through partnership for skill development and placement all (except four of the 2000 employees) found new positions in BT. The four are stated to have left the company through voluntary redundancy and normal attrition.

On the issue of consultation with stakeholders with respect to restructuring, the outcomes were mixed. There were processes put in place for protecting the interests of workers through consultation with the main managerial unions. The engagement with call centre representatives was not fully secured and was seen to be an area where there could be improvement.[27]

CSR ISSUES IN THE BPO SEGMENT IN HOST COUNTRY INDIA

Ensuring Supplier Standards

India as a country of destination for BT outsourcing was not without CSR issues. Some of these were triggered by home country sentiments of global supply chains and sourcing norms for operations abroad. Others were

[26] Kavita Prakash-Mani, ibid.
[27] Ibid.

specific to the new organization relating to a completely new environment of work in the segment of call centres.

BT already had in place a document entitled, 'Sourcing with Human Dignity'[28] which addressed some of the CSR concerns with cross-border production and sourcing. Call centre supplies fall within the ambit of these sourcing codes. The document recognizes the global impact of its operations and asserts a conviction that it is by enhancing economies and acting with social responsibility that BT can ensure sustainable presence 'now and for generations to come'.

In this document BT claims to be guided by a series of principles and standards to be maintained in its supply chain, as per guidelines primarily of the United Nations Universal Declaration of Human Rights and the International Labour Organization Convention.

The approach here is very much like that of other companies in the global supply chain, that is to be flexible and developmental in bringing about changes. This follows the trajectory of working collaboratively and guiding processes to achieve standards with suppliers rather than actually meeting these standards.

In India, this approach translates into a setting of guidelines on issues like joint problem solving, setting performance standards jointly for suppliers, local recruitment for employment, setting wages as per local standards, and including non-wage benefits, health facilities and a com-mitment to equal employment.

Job Security and Working Conditions

However, the segment has thrown up many other issues as well. An international network of labour unions who are urging for better standards of workplace practices have articulated these issues. One of the main concerns revolves around the uncertainty of jobs in this sector. Labour union leaders in Britain warn Indian workers that they are as vulnerable as themselves were to the forces of globalization.[29] Indian trade unions echo these sentiments. The Centre for Indian Trade Unions (CITU) General

[28] BT, 'Sourcing with Human Dignity' http://www.selling2bt.com/working/humandignity/gs18.asp

[29] http://www.oneworld.net/external/?url=http%3A%2F%2Finfochangeindia.org%2Finfochange_wsfBG.jsp

Secretary, M.K. Pandhey, points out that 'the jobs are coming because the daily wages in India are equal to the hourly wages in the UK and US. But over the long term, this will not be good as these [jobs] could easily move elsewhere'. The question of CSR issues emerging for lost jobs may well emerge in a host country like India as well.

Despite the furore over lost jobs in the UK, according to a DTI report[30] there is another trend. It is 'onshoring' in computer information services in the UK. The government report points out that 'onshoring' in the UK actually exceeds 'offshoring'. In fact, India's own HCL Technologies Ltd, has acquired a 90 per cent stake in BT's Northern Ireland operation. Even as BT offshores to India, HCL finds it the best option to continue its operation with 1000 employees in Belfast. This would also tie in well with BTs and the UK government's approach and policy of limiting redundancy. It also portends the movement of jobs away from India and the concern for lost jobs here as well.

However, as of now attrition levels in this industry in India are variously estimated and run upwards of 45 per cent, where approximately 40 per cent are expected to switch for money. But there is a massive pool to be drawn from and there could be variance in the ways in which this is addressed. Companies like BT are reported to seek retention through other benefits like partially-funding university and college education. This, together with other employee-friendly approaches, has meant that BT's attrition rate in call centres at Delhi is reported to be amazingly low, far below the industry average and is said to be around 1 per cent. This is attributed to pay and employee development and satisfaction.

Union Representation

One of the most contentious issues that has emerged in India in 2005 is that of unionization of BPO employees. The IT segment in general and the BPO employee in particular are seen as part of the new face of India and its success and not without reason. Corporates point out that this is a segment which has higher than average entry-level salaries (average salaries are reported to be sometimes twice as high as entry-level positions in other upper professional areas). It is also a segment which sees faster career growth.

[30] Department of Trade and Industry, 'Making Globalisation a Force for Good' Crown Copyright; Norwich, 2004.

From the employee's point of view this is a segment which has the advantage of being in demand-driven work environments having one of the highest attrition rates (for better opportunities) in any sector. It is also one where training and skills can be easily imbibed. For India as a nation, the growth and employment potential of this segment of work is well recognized.

Being relatively new, this sector also represents untested ground, especially in terms of the nature, environment, and organization of work as well as the nature of employees in this segment. Many of the issues represented here were brought centre stage by a controversial study which described the BPO worker as a 'cyber coolie'. The fact that the study was done by an autonomous body[31] under the Ministry of Labour in India in 2004 led to more articles probing these issues. Not unexpectedly, unions found this to be a basis to enquire into the unionization (or lack of it) in this segment.

It is important to recognize that these are two different though related issues. It is quite clear that the health and safety standards for this kind of work needs to be reviewed and addressed continually in the context of new learning. Equally it is clear that this segment has not really indicated a proclivity for unionization for all the reasons cited earlier. Companies like BT report grievance committees and helplines and problem-solving approaches and conducive facilities for work. A recent survey of BPO workers[32] reported that two-thirds of the respondents voted against unions in BPOs. Companies' view of unions was expectedly that unions were not necessary in the industry which was very employee oriented. It is important to point out that industry had the law on its side as well. There was the supporting role of states in creating a special definition for this new category of employment which clearly put its employees outside the definition of 'workmen' and thereby outside the pale of the ensuing rights including that of unionization.

Interestingly falling within the purview of states,[33] different states have acted differently in order to make enabling provisions for this much-needed

---

[31] B.P. Ramesh, 'Labour in Business Process Outsourcing: A Case Study of Call Centre Agents', NLI Research Studies Series No. 51, V.V. Giri National Labour Institute, Noida, 2004.

[32] India Times News Network, Reports on the economic times survey of BPO employees, 25 October 2005.

[33] West Bengal ITES Policy 2003 and Kerala ITES Policy 2001.

industry. These variations contribute to a grey area of social sensitivities, which threaten to erupt every now and then. Generally the trend has been to categorize call centres as falling under the Shops and Establishment Act. Under its provisions, workmen are characterized as those who are neither managerial nor supervisory staff, but call centre employees are considered to be neither of these, and are not workers either. Some states have also determined a salary ceiling for defining workmen. With the very favourable salary terms of call centre employees, most of them would not qualify as workmen. West Bengal and Kerala have been in the lead in attracting investment and flexibility of legislation in dealing with employees in this segment. In fact, both of these states have also additionally declared this industry sector as falling under 'public utilities', thus further restricting the scope for strikes.

Corporate social responsiveness issues really operate in the gap between law and expectations and lean towards understanding sensitivities and ensuring voluntary compliance. With the diversity of conditions in this industry, the issue of unionization is far from settled in this industry. What appears to be happening is a whole new hybrid mechanism for mature worker representation.[34] The IT Professionals Forum of India (ITPF), as the name suggests, is a part of that hybrid process. It includes in its agenda the protection of BPO workers, and is also linked to the international network of unions.[35]

Overtime/Night Shift

Another issue emerging from categorization as non-workers is the implications for overtime work. Professional staff does not normally qualify for overtime benefits. The calculation of this for the BPO employee, however is more imperative and is known to be accorded in some operations. Health and stress and security factors relating to this kind of work—involving light schedules and graveyard shifts—are beginning to be debated and still have to be fully addressed. The law has also been responsive to these issues creating legislation to ensure that corporates provide support and security for women in the night shift and ensure safe travel arrangements as well.

[34] Ripunjoy Kumar Sharma, 'Industry Jittery on BPO Union Issue', Times Network, 25 October 2005.

[35] Gangadeep Kaur, 'Will We Hear the BPO Guy Say Inquilab?', *Economic Times*, 3 November 2005.

False Accents, Names, and Locations:
The 'Deception' Issue

Apart from job-security-related issues, there has been enquiry into what is said to be the 'deception' issue which is another grey area. This relates to the false accents and names which are said to be misleading to the consumer and suggestive of loss of dignity to the employee. Here again there are variations. Companies like BT have policies against name changing, training only for a 'neutralized' accent and allowing disclosure of location from India when asked. The practice of accent change continues, but the assessment is that companies are seeking to enhance listening skills, clarity of diction, and speaking slowly as ways to promote comprehensibility.

Community Development Support

Like many Indian companies in this segment, BT supports community development through bringing information technology, to a wider constituency. Katha, a local NGO, has been the vehicle for BT for taking IT training to underprivileged children in a slum in Delhi. Katha is the recipient of £50,000 at inception for a three-year programme (with a further commitment in 2003 for another £50,000 for this programme). Katha Information Technology and E-Commerce Schools (KITES) are oriented to bringing education and skill development to local children and adults to 'enable them to take part in the IT revolution. Many of the supplier companies to BT like Infosys, HCL, and Mahindra and Mahindra have their own community development initiatives independently. BT's support still has to find ways to ensure that these efforts are sustainable as well.

CHAPTER 5

DEVELOPING MARKETS AND
MARKETING DEVELOPMENT

Another aspect of change comes in the form of efforts to support the 'completing of markets'. This refers to filling the gaps that are necessary for mainstreaming small, medium, and marginal enterprises into wider processes. The trend for corporates to facilitate these processes in India is evident in a number of instances. Such facilitation could emerge from recognizing the long-term significance of such inputs for business and society. Equally this could emerge from more immediate business interests as well. It typically considers aspects relating to the environment of work, the management and organization of work, and the quality and scale of existing work.

Two trends are discussed here. The first relates to bringing international workplace and related norms to the small and medium sector in India. The second trend is the facilitation of grassroots producer organizations for better linkages, creating employment and better returns particularly, in the rural areas.

EMBEDDING SOCIAL NORMS

India is one of those countries which is increasingly feeding cross-national production via the manufactures of a huge constituency of small and medium enterprises. Since the early 1990s, approximately a third of India's exports (between 31 and 36 per cent of total exports) have come from the small-scale sector.[1] The sector as a whole employs over 17 million persons. The food and apparel industries are among the major exports groups in this sector. The small-scale sector is known as much for its skill and entre-preneurial abilities as it is for informal workplace and other practices. It is

[1] Annual Report of the Ministry of Small Scale Industries (SSI) and ARI, 2000.

also a segment hovering on instability with sixteen times as many sick units as there are stable ones.[2] This indicates the potential and challenges before this segment.

While free trade negotiations are battling the issues of 'social clauses' and 'protectionism' on a formal and national scale, transnational corporations and international business find it imperative and possible to start addressing these issues with their contracting units of small as well as medium enterprises, outside of negotiations at a national level and on a one-to-one basis. What is politically difficult to achieve is becoming a matter of routine business engagement with individual partners. This typically, but not exclusively, entails seeking to bring compliance and norms on labour issues in the vendor and supply chains among developing country partners. It also includes bringing technological changes and addressing community-wide impacts for improvement of environmental and other issues related to the product. Funding for such changes is for the time being generated in part by the client groups either among themselves or from outside. Producer groups are also expected to contribute in some way.

Indicating the diversity and trends in this engagement are several examples from India, from where a whole range of products are sourced and a variety of CSR models, actors, and CSR engagements are to be found.

BUSINESS TO SMALL-SCALE SECTOR

The case of B&Q plc is typical of how the extending arm of CSR from business in the developed world reaches the small-scale sectors in India.[3] B&Q plc is a British company that is a leader in the home improvement segment and is also considered a leader in CSR. B&Q is connected through its sourcing to a range of products, which also means that it is connected to a range of CSR issues. As early as 1990, B&Q started to assess the environmental and social impact of its suppliers across the globe. Its first focus was on India from where it sourced many products, which were typically made in the small-scale and informal sectors, linked to non-

---

[2] Ibid.

[3] EU–India CSR, European Institute of Asian Studies, Belgium, 'Corporate Social Responsibility in Europe and India: A Comparative Analysis', in FICCI *2001 India-European Union Conference on Corporate Social Responsibility: The Cross-Cultural Perspective*, New Delhi, 2001, p. 23.

standard environments of work and production. Among the focus areas taken up for such scrutiny were the brassware manufacture and weaving segments. In these and other cases the issue has been of informal work, leading to health and environmental issues, poor wages, and poor access to finances. In the case of B&Q, this led to intervention for safer casting for brassware and the setting up of a health clinic for 800 weaving families. B&Q also became the pioneer in stocking Rugmark rugs made without using child labour.

B&Q is also linked to sourcing of other products from other informal sector units as in the case of coir matting from Kerala. The supply chain is now looked at closely for issues revolving around improving wages as well as starting a savings scheme for women involved in the production of coir matting. Additionally, to satisfy the expectations of the wider constituency in the host country B&Q has introduced a water treatment process to reduce lagoon pollution, an integral part of coir processing. Such efforts are reported to be extended to all its thirteen suppliers and fifteen factories in India as well as the other countries of its operation. Reporting on the results of this work to serve as a model for others has also been initiated. These initiatives sometimes converge and, as in the case of sourcing tea, B&Q has in addition to detailed product and quality specifications also introduced social codes with its Indian tea suppliers.

ASSOCIATIONS TO SMEs

Apart from B&Q-type single business initiatives, consortium of partnership inititatives are also in evidence. There are, for instance, business linkages between associations of small and medium enterprises (SMEs) across countries with goals of achieving similar outcomes. A case in point is the French and Indian SMEs working in tandem for taking the social and environmental issues relating to their business. The French SME association, Assemblee' Permanente des Chambres De Metiers (APCM), working under the aegis of the EU–India Network for Corporate Social Responsibility, has a series of partnerships with Indian SMEs in the crafts sector.[4] These include proposals for artists in the Indian SMEs to be recipients of technical

---

[4] Assemblee Permanente des Chambres De Metiers, 'Partnerships between the French and Indian Craft Centre', 2001, pp. 39–46.

development and know-how (training for quality of products, delivery on schedules, etc.). It also includes facilitation to meet specified social standards and norms relevant for the industry in question, as well as to the wider community.

In fact, there appears to be a market developing for initiating 'socially acceptable producer groups'. NGOs are developing new kinds of entrepreneurship for this either on request by business or even as initiators of developing a constituency in anticipation of future demand for such producer groups as well. These provide models for drawing into the global economic scene many who may otherwise have been left out. The Association for Rural Economic Development (ARED) in partnership with the Foundation of Pierre Abbot set up initiatives in south India in 1997, which is run on three sites all located in the state of Karnataka and targeted at 25,000 underprivileged groups of untouchable women and Tibetan refugees. It is looking for financial or commercial collaboration with Indian companies contributing to this goal. The focus of the former project is vocational training and apprenticeship and education, and selling and exporting skills of the refugees.

Similarly, the Association for support of Ashalayam (ASA) located in Paris supports Ashalaya, which provides vocational training to street children. These children work and learn new skills but the sales of the craft produced by a child go directly to his or her personal banking account.

COOPERATIVES AND NGOS TO SMEs

Beyond SMEs, cooperatives have also been drawn into this scenario. The Diamond Workers Co-operative Society in Surat, which was a part of the parent body of the South Gujarat Diamond Workers Co-operative (SGDWA) was contacted by Fair Trade e.V., Germany, a non-profit organization, with a proposal. The proposal was for polishing and cutting rough diamonds provided to them. This would link the diamond workers' society with the buyer and supplier of raw diamonds, a women's cooperative of diamond mine workers based at Lesotho. The buyer and the Surat Diamond Workers Industrial Co-operative Society Ltd. agreed to work together on the principles of fair trade. It is believed that following the principles will enable the Society to manage the fair trade project effectively in the long term.

A large number of intermediary organizations, often serving particular importing country business, have begun to provide services to meet these requirements. The International Resources for Fairer Trade (IRFT) is one such organization with an Indian counterpart body. Its recent projects in this area have spanned SMEs of export importance to India, having among its clients both corporate importers from India as well as significant exporters. The IRFT has, for instance, been contracted to address CSR issues in Basmati trade by Sainsbury, a key player in the Basmati trade between India and the UK. Aproximately 15 per cent of the Basmati rice sold in the UK is through Sainsbury. Similarly, the IRFT is also party to CSR interventions in the brassware industry in Aligarh. This industry reportedly provides direct/indirect employment to over 1.5 lakh people and has a 50 per cent share of all industries in the region. The industry is over a hundred years old, with a majority of enterprises belonging to the small-scale sector.

The IRFT's intervention in this sector and other sectors on behalf of the company includes researching potential CSR issues in the production processes for different products, and intermediating with local NGOs for implementation.[5] The interventions in brassware, weaving, and Basmati rice procurement have all been different. For instance, the areas surrounding the rice mills in Kaithal, Karnal, and Kurukshetra in Haryana were found to have alarming rates of tuberculosis. Awareness, detection, and treatment in areas where the sourcing is done is a key aspect of CSR interventions here. Efforts are also directed through linkages with the local Primary Health Centres and hospitals.

The IRFT is one of the organizations serving more than one client customer in setting up processes for achieving the environmental and social norms in any given industry. Such norms have begun to emerge in India in all kinds of ways. The examples discussed are typical of win–win scenarios of CSR that are increasingly being promoted by civil society and other groups. However, they are not without problems. Both the codes and the issues raised by them are discussed in the following chapter. However, for the time being they at least present small islands of effort for better environmental and social practices in sectors that have so far been notoriously informal.

[5] http://www.irft.org/projects.html

CREATING PRODUCER NETWORKS

Quite another kind of mainstreaming is under way in the rural areas, where small and medium-sized producers have struggled to eke out a living. Drawing the Indian rural population into greater participation in the economy both as producers and consumers is a significant challenge. Several government programmes are aimed at just this with uneven success. There has been the presence of a few fast-moving consumer goods (FMCGs) engaging in social investment for developing markets. A fillip to this process has come by way of initiatives by both government and trade union bodies to seek a new partnership role for corporate engagement in rural India. Business interests could well be served by these initiatives in the long run.

EVOLUTION OF HLL INITIATIVES

The particular initiative, discussed here, came at the end of a winding process of private-sector engagement in three related but different directions. This private sector engagement had begun first, as a direct and immediate commercial engagement invited by a state government. Later, the corporate entity was drawn into a consultancy engagement for developing the marketing infrastructure in a government programme. Third, it provided 'responsible' consultancy inputs, without any immediate returns, but which had the potential to deliver long-term commercial benefits all around and to contribute significantly to the development of the region.

The purely commercial interaction of broadening the market began in the year 2000. The FMCG major Hindustan Lever Limited (HLL) started a direct-to-home marketing of its own products in Andhra Pradesh under Project Shakti. This also held out a promise of employment in the rural areas through linking women's self-help groups and HLL in the direct-to-home marketing exercise. The marketing was to be of HLL products, which were to be given to the members of self-help groups on a 'cash and carry' basis. The self-help groups or banks were to provide credit for this. Dalip Sehgal, Executive Director, New Ventures and Marketing services, reported[6] that Project Shakti was adding up to 15 per cent of HLL sales in rural Andhra Pradesh and that approximately 50 per cent of HLL sales in the

---

[6] K. T. Jagannathan, *The Hindu*, 15 May 2003.

state came from the rural areas. In 2003, Project Shakti was reported to have a reach of over 5000 villages in fifty-two districts of Andhra Pradesh, Karnataka, Gujarat, and Madhya Pradesh. The company has visions of scaling this up by 2010 to 11,000 Shakti entrepreneurs and covering some 1,00,000 villages.[7]

The typical Shakti entrepreneur, according to HLL, is a woman living in a small village. The entrepreneur conducts business worth approximately Rs 15,000 a month, which gives her income in excess of Rs 1000 per month.[8] Following this success, HLL is in the process of piloting I-shakti—an IT-based rural information service that would provide solutions to requirements in agriculture, vocational training, health/hygiene, etc.

In a second variant of this model, the intervention still provided immediate commercial benefits though in a slightly different way. HLL began to play a facilitator and consultancy role in helping state governments to build their own brand of products. This was a paid consultancy. In 2002 HLL launched the Vindhya Valley project,[9] for Madhya Pradesh in which the state-owned Khadi Board formed a partnership with HLL to enhance the government's DWCRA (Development of Women and Children in Rural Areas) programme. The objective was for HLL to bring about women's empowerment by bringing greater prosperity to village entrepreneurs engaged in agro processing and village industries through higher sales. This in turn was to be achieved through a combination of improvement in product quality and improvements in manufacturing, marketing, and distribution of products developed under the aegis of the DWCRA. The sales network had grown to such potential that the company was considering offering it as a medium for other products as well, through some sort of arrangement with non-competitive companies.

The product range at the time of the launch covered items like pickles, *masalas,* turmeric, chillies, *papads,* and honey with a proposal to include *agarbattis* as well under the brand name Vindhya Valley. HLL was to be paid for its marketing support by the state government. HLL was also to support the state in enhancing the distribution network of fair price shops

---

[7] HLL website 2003.

[8] Ibid.

[9] 'HLLs Project Shakti Gains Momentum', *The Hindu*, 15 May 2003; See HLL website http://www.hll.com/HLL/reachingout/communitydev.html#writeup.

that the state had (some 15,000 of them), by helping in establishing marketing links further into the hinterland.

This model was also solicited by the state of Andhra Pradesh when chief minister, Chandrababu Naidu, asked HLL to facilitate the buy back of Rs 25 crore worth from the DWCRA in his state and strengthen its distribution through the existing public distribution system (PDS) and other systems to reach untouched areas.

This was the backdrop to a totally newer type of engagement under way. This case is as important for the outcomes achieved as it is for the public–private and trade union partnerships that were formed to create those outcomes Here the lead party included the government, a trade union group of women (SEWA), a not-for-profit firm, and international consultants and organizations. It was also unusual in the special space that SEWA held in this partnership.

Two case studies highlight this corporate engagement and its processes, and the following is based on the report of the Grassroots Trading Network (GTN).[10] The first case study is that of a partnership between several organizations and institutions. These include India's well-known Self-Employed Women's Association (SEWA), which is a labour union of self-employed women in the informal sector. SEWA has a membership of 7,00,000 in seven states across the country with a majority of them (5,30,000 members) being in Gujarat. SEWA assists its members in both agricultural and non-agricultural trades and engages in providing a host of services including micro-finance, banking, education, health care, and watershed management.

Another organization which was part of the partnership was an offshoot of SEWA. The SEWA Gram Mahila Haat (SGMH) was created in 1999, with support from the Gujarat government. This aimed at supporting SEWA's membership in the agricultural sector, eliminating exploitive middlemen and providing direct technical, financial, and marketing assistance to agricultural producers.

[10] Grassroots Trading Network Report, August 2004, Launching a Rural Distribution Network in India in Partnership with SEWA Gram Mahila Haat, the Agricultural Marketing Organization of Self-Employed Women's Association (SEWA) and Hindustan Lever Ltd. August 2004, and Grassroots Trading Network Report. July 2004. Linking Small and Marginal Indian Farmers to Corporate Buyers in Partnership with Sewa Gram Mahila Haat—the Agricultural Marketing Organization of Self-Employed Women's Association (SEWA) and ITC Ltd.

It was with the lead of SEWA, the World Bank and the Planning Commission that a global roundtable of Grassroots Producer Organizations (GPOs) was held in 2002 to address the perceived needs of GPOs in the new globalized scenario.[11] One of the needs so identified was to have an organization that could assist GPOs in entering new markets. The Government of India and SEWA commissioned the international management consulting firm, Accenture Development Partnership to develop the business plan. The Grassroots Trading Network (GTN), a private non-profit firm, was established under the sponsorhip of the Government of India and SEWA to develop the network of GPOs and work to address their challenges.

The GTN was formed in 2004. Its mission is described as being there to support, strengthen, and expand market opportunities for GPOs with a particular focus on women. This vision of the GTN is based on the now well-known ideological approach expressed by C.K. Prahlad, professor of business administration.[12] The approach views the global market, measured in terms of purchasing power parity as a pyramid, with four billion people at the bottom, (drawn mainly from rural and slum populations) with per capita incomes of less than UK £1500 a year. It urges 'governments, businesses, and NGOs to develop new strategies to make individuals in the bottom tier active market participants'.

The GTN and Digital Partners initiated the connection with the Indian subsidiary of the global conglomerate Unilever to help it establish SEWA's own Rural Distribution Network (RUDI). HLL was to provide the design and other management inputs free of cost. Its interest (if any) to use this network immediately for marketing its own products, was held in abeyance.

RUDI targets the betterment of a number of constituencies including small and marginal farmers, rural women, rural consumers, below poverty line (BPL) families, and SEWA producer members. It does this through strategies for procurement and employment which will benefit all these

[11] I am grateful to Rashid Kidwai, CEO of GTN, for appraising me of this initiative and providing this background information. 'Grassroot Trading Network—Linking Poor Producers to Markets—Overview', 2005. Permission to draw on the two reports sited here is also appreciated.

[12] GTN, Enhancing the Participation of Poor Producers in Global Markets: Launching a Rural Distribution Network in India in Partnership with SEWA Gram Mahila Haat, the Agricultural Marketing Organization of Self-Employed Women's Association (SEWA) and Hidustan Lever Limited, August 2004.

groups in different ways. Small and marginal farmers will be able to overcome disadvantages due to lack of scale of operations, lack of bargaining power, and exploitative credit arrangements by belonging to the RUDI network, which addresses all these issues of scale, distance, credit, and dignity. Employment will also be generated to fill the requirement of branding, sourcing, and sales of these products (see Annexure 5A for main objectives and strategies of RUDI).

This private, semi-private, and trade union engagement was estimated to give SEWA alone a Rs 76,00,00,000 turnover according to the GTN report. Additionally, for RUDI to function, SEWA would have to employ 10,000 women, apart from than its own members, for the rural distribution network in fourteen districts of Gujarat where this project is piloted. The GTN, which facilitated and developed this partnership hopes to expand its operations to other countries in Asia, Latin America, and Africa. The business model for this experiment is as given in Fig. 5.1.

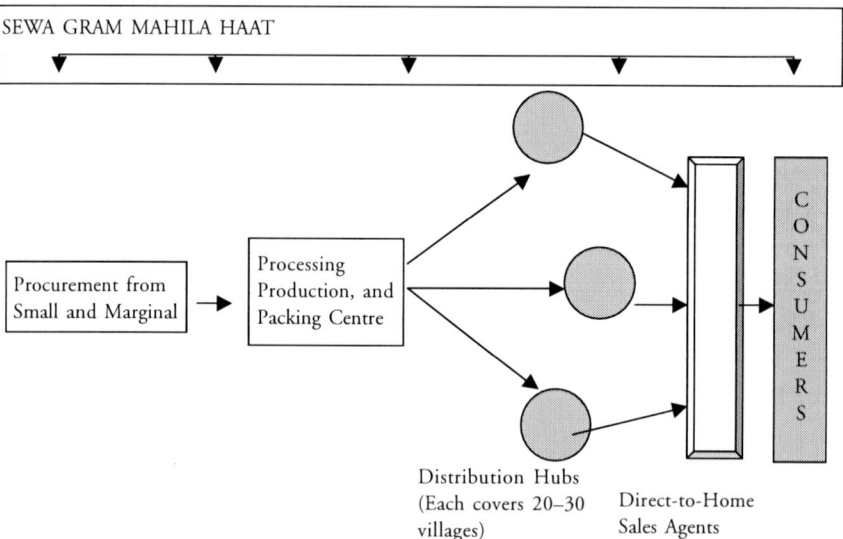

(*'One PPP Centre and three hubs are required for 84 villages. Additional PPP Centres and hubs will be created post-pilot after analysing the geographic distribution of SEWA members per district and clustering the villages'.*)

Source: GTN, 'Enhancing the Participation of Poor Producers in Global Markets', ibid., 2004.

Fig. 5.1: Business Model Snapshot

Providing free of cost inputs for this model has been part of the multi dimensional role of HLL. It has spanned inputs for designing the development of the project and its implementation. Key inputs here included market research for understanding consumption patterns, buying behaviour, satisfaction with products, etc. Other inputs included costing of the identified products for the enterprises, capacity building and training in business and production processes, specifying requirements of the processing, production, and packing (PPP) centres, giving exposure to HLL's own production and business processes and training in storage processing and packaging functions and quality control techniques as well. The training covered a visit to a similar engagement of HLL described previously, namely the Vindhya Valley Project in Madhya Pradesh where HLL was working with the state government and DWCRA groups on a similar initiative. This training in processes and systems of a business operation has not only been vital for SGMH staff, it has also been replicated to reach other SEWA members involved in the RUDI pilot.

Another expertise brought in by business is the development of the RUDI brand, which was done by EuroRSCG, the fifth largest advertising agency in the world. This also came free of cost and as a part of CSR efforts by the company. The RUDI-branded products are targeted to reach the rural hinterland with low literacy levels, and the campaign is designed especially for that market. The goal is, according to the GTN report, to provide direct-to-home marketing to the rural consumer. The consumers will have access to another range of products 'that have been hygienically processed using modern systems to deliver quality, purity, fair price, and right quantity'.

The results of this experiment are yet to emerge.

ITC

The GTN has been instrumental in putting together another similar exercise of partnership between the corporate sector (ITC) and the SGMH.[13] Unlike the HLL case cited in the preceding paragraphs, where capacity building was undertaken and other inputs given as a social investment for the future, the ITC case was slightly different. Here, through the efforts of the GTN,

[13] GTN Presentation, 'Linking Small and Marginal Farmers to Corporate Buyers in Partnership with Sewa Gram Mahila Haat, The Agricultural Marketing Organization of Self-Employed Women's Association (SEWA) and ITC Limited', Mumbai, July 2004.

the SGHM developed as the consolidator for one of India's largest agribusinesses and for providing sesame seed for ITC's export market. The ITC also provided the skills and other inputs described in the HLL model, but this was as a part of its business processes for the norms it needed to achieve. Nevertheless, it also introduced the consolidation and other standards and norms to a wide constituency, which had typically been left out of such developmental processes.

For the small and marginal farmers who constitute a part of the SGHM, a number of issues have kept this segment underproductive. This partnership addressed many of them. Additionally, they were exposed to global norms and training for the same, which would prepare them for other contracts. In the 2003 season, the ITC purchase of 250 tonnes of sesame seed from 1450 small and marginal farmers from Surendranagar district of Gujarat is estimated to have given the farmers Rs 2 per kg extra.[14] The GTN looks upon this as a model that can be replicated in other parts of the country.

The impact of this partnership will go beyond current experiments. In the wake of the success of this model, the potential of this engagement by the ITC for other agricultural product procurement was deliberated. Additionally, the ITC is also reported to be interested in entering into organic farming with the SGMH farmers. This has the requirement of land being free of banned pesticides and fertilizers for three years. Providing for the viability of this model while providing support to the farmers should be challenging.

That these changes will help companies targetting rural areas for sourcing and selling their products, is without doubt. Organizations like SEWA, on the other hand, are strong umbrella organizations that ensure that their members belonging to producer groups and workforce are protected. This is done by keeping open the option to decide how and by whom their producer outputs and networks can be used. SEWA has not excluded the potential of marketing HLL products but it will be on its own terms and at a time of its own reckoning, if at all.

Such organized group activity will help in standardizing and main-streaming producer groups. However, other issues are emerging.

Non-SEWA individuals or groups, also engaged in rural areas, may be vulnerable in the wake of these changes. There are some reports emerging

[14] Ibid.

that direct-to-home is also a method used by other small rural retailers.[15] This workforce also needs to be drawn into empowered groups of different kinds. There is some concern that those who belong to less empowered networks are having to compete with this model.

These are examples of how the grassroot producer groups can be linked to wider processes with benefit. Non-profit firms and corporates can bring to the table the information, management, marketing, branding, and skill enhancement role, with immediate and long-term benefit. However, there is a space for a facilitating and enabling role for the government to support the mainstreaming of those left out of such processes as well. The GTN is also turning out models of partnerships in new areas of assembling, distribution, and sales of cycles in a partnership between SEWA women and Hero Cycles.

[15] Amiya Kumar Bartia, 'Subhashini Nag versus Hindustan Lever Limited', *Social Change*, Vol. 35, March 2005, pp. 83–7.

CHAPTER 6

CIVIL SOCIETY ROAR
INDIA'S NGOs AND CSR

Societas Civilis (Civil Society) is a term whose antecedents can be traced back to Aristotelian antiquity. Kaviraj and Khilnani in a compelling book[1] on the topic have talked about the fresh emergence of this force worldwide. Today civil society stands revived, being championed across the globe as '*the* idea of the late twentieth century'.[2] In its influence over governments and business, civil society's role cannot be overestimated. Its connectedness with CSR issues comes from the vigilant eye that it keeps over the emerging power and influence of business. This is not an insignificant role, and as the chapter will demonstrate, the scrutiny has brought giant corporations to heel. However, to understand the full impact of that role there is a need to appreciate its complexity. That complexity lies significantly in the fact (among other things) that it is ideologically flexible, not necessarily being aligned with the right or the left of the political spectrum, has extra-democratic legitimacy, and engages with all manner of institutions in meeting its goals.

Civil society has, over the years, served a number of masters across the ideological spectrum. From working to redeem Marxist ideological purity and good governance from Marxist statism, to providing opposition to other authoritarian regimes that have appropriated civil society entitlements and violated civil society sentiments. It is now moving towards realizing what Kaviraj and Khilnani call 'the post-modern utopianism'.[3] A key part of that is the belief that market societies can be reinvented for even greater

[1] Sudipto Kaviraj and Sunil Khilnani (eds), *Civil Society: History and Possibilities*, Cambridge University Press, Cambridge, 2001.

[2] Ibid., p. 12. National Humanities Centre, *The Idea of a Civil Society*, Humanities Research Centre, Research Triangle Park, North Carolina, 1992.

[3] Kaviraj and Khilnani, *Civil Society*, pp. 12–33.

good, keeping in mind a changed vision of society. In that context, for many civil society groups, CSR is mostly yet another strategy to move towards that goal either through adversarial or collaborative efforts with business.

In its early avatar as a force primarily against the state (Hegelian formulations), civil society was viewed as a force deriving from the ineptness of legitimate political authority to play its roles. Working to regain various kinds of civility missing from the state (the state is supposed to be the embodiment of such civility), civil society moved to reclaim the voices of various constituencies whose entitlements were not represented. In doing this, it becomes 'state-like', playing many of the roles of the state and often being political and wresting 'legitimate authority' to some extent as well.

Kaviraj and Khilnani maintain that in post-modern society, civil society denotes something richer than 'constitutional representative democracy'. The strength and influence of civil society rest on this usurped state role. How representative are 'civil societies' is an issue that can and will be debated for some time. However, as of now its role is mostly 'as a supplement—and not a substitute (to government)—to address the perceived illegitimacies of this system'.[4] In the context of the emergent close alliance between corporates and government, the source of these illegitimacies is also seen in the eyes of civil society to expand to cover both.

Over the years we have come to recognize the power and influence of MNCs. That power has the potential of exceeding the financial power of many states. Almost as if to provide a balancing force, a new power is emerging. In 2002, the Edelman Public Relations poll revealed that the trust reposed in NGOs ran very high in Europe and the US, sometimes exceeding that of government or business. The survey showed 'superbrand NGOs' in Europe—namely Amnesty International, the World Wildlife Fund (WWF), and Greenpeace—outranked Microsoft, Ford, and Bayer as the three most trusted corporate brands in Europe. In the US, as far as trusted organizations went, the WWF was the highest ranked NGO with fourth place, just behind Nike the sportswear company.[5] These are symbols of the 'Third Force' after government and business.

---

[4] Ibid., p. 16.

[5] Guyde Jonquieres and Holly Yeager, 'Boost for Anti-Forum Groups', *Financial Times*, 31 Jan 2002.

THE GLOBAL INDIAN NGO

The globalization of NGOs is a factor in the force and strength of local NGOs everywhere and therefore are not without significance for developing countries like India as well. There are many indices of the trajectory of growth of NGOs. International non-government organizations, that is INGO (including those from developing countries), and internationally-oriented NGO secretariats (headquarters) have shown a steady trend of growth. Such data are maintained by the Union of International Associations. *The Yearbook of International Organisations: Guide to Civil Society Networks* shows that the international secretariats of civil society networks grew at a rate of 12.7 per cent between 1991 and 2001, from 15,937 to 17,968.[6] A majority of this growth has come from Europe and Central Asia. Indian international NGOs also marked a presence on this trajectory. From 150 such international secretariats in 1991, a modest rise to 165 in 2001 was registered, showing a growth of 10 per cent during this period.[7]

Organizational membership of INGOs has also grown considerably[8] globally, as well as in India. Such INGOs in India grew from 2044 organizations in 1991 to 3115 in 2001, showing an absolute growth of 52.4 per cent over the previous decade. During this period, the overall growth of INGOs was registered at 71.6 per cent.

The growth of internationalism among NGOs worldwide is becoming a key aspect of the power that NGOs can wield. The phenomenal percentage growth in all manner of links is indicative of the network that is developing. This could either represent the coalition of smaller NGOs with larger NGOs or the spawning of a large number of subsidiaries of the larger NGOs.[9] In the decade of the 1990s, for instance, international and internationally-oriented NGOs citing a financial link with another organization grew 34.4 per cent per annum, and those citing links with another organization for

---

[6] Helmut Anheier, Marlies Glasius and Mary Kaldor (eds), *Global Civil Society*, Oxford University Press, Oxford, pp. 318–23 (based on from Union of International Associations. *Yearbook of International Organisations: Guide to Civil Society Networks*, Brussels 1991 and 2001).

[7] Ibid., p. 319.

[8] Ibid., pp. 324–8. This refers to the number of organizations and not to membership which would be significantly higher per membership organization.

[9] Helmut Anheier *et al.* (ed.), 2002, ibid., pp. 329–30. Calculated from data here.

publications grew at 53.3 per cent per annum. Other forms of relations with another NGO grew between 10 and 14 per cent per annum.

The influence of Southern NGOs like those in India has grown over the years as well. One NGO newspaper commenting on the Rio conference in 1992 wrote, 'The Africans were watching, the Asians listening, the Latin Americans were talking, while the North Americans and Europeans were doing business'.[10] Northern NGOs have been accused of 'neo-imperialism' and one-way influence in exchange for resources.[11] NGOs of the South, however, are increasingly being drawn into the vortex of negotiations. They have exhibited the potential for lobbying and integrating their agenda into those of other groups, as well as maintaining an independent frame of reference where necessary. Between Vienna and Rio, UN conferences for human rights and environment, respectively, there were differences. The unity of Southern and Northern NGOs at Vienna in favour of limits to national sovereignty contrasted with Southern NGOs defence of sovereignty at the Rio Conference.

SIZING UP INDIA'S NGO SECTOR

While international registration makes it easy to track internationally operating Indian NGOs, information on the number and forms of Indian NGOs working in a national context is fragmented. Lack of registration of many organizations, and separate registration at state and centre levels have made it difficult to get an accurate picture of this sector.

The Government of India has been recognizing a role for the NGO sector in India right from the First Plan. However, it was from the Seventh Plan (1985–90) that this recognition was heightened. The voluntary sector found separate treatment in the Plan document. The segment on 'Rural Development of Poverty Alleviation Programmes—Involvement of Voluntary Agencies' outlined its roles and earmarked a sum of Rs 1500 crore, for voluntary organizations. Representatives were also made a part of high-level committees in departments to facilitate their inclusion into governance

---

[10] *Terra Viva*, 15 June 1992, in *Earth Summit: The NGO Archives*, in Ann Marie Clark, Elisabeth J. Friedman, and Kathryn Hochsteller, 'The Soverign Limits of Global Civil Society: A Comparison of NGO Participation in UN World Conferences on the Environment, Human Rights, and Women' *World Politics*, vol. 51, no. 1, 1998, pp. 1–35.

[11] Anheier *et al.*, *Global Civil Society*, p. 211.

processes. The Eighth Plan (1992–7) called for a collaborative relationship between government and NGOs.[12] Pronouncements of close engagement with NGOs were also made by the Congress government elected in 2004. The potential to define an expanded role for this sector was set.

A recent sample survey done in 2002 in selected Indian states[13] was used to extrapolate the presence of non-profit organizations in India. Both registered and non-registered NPOs (non-profit organizations) were together estimated to number some 12,00,000. About half of these NPOs were registered and the remainder unregistered. The organizations were typically small in terms of persons employed. However, this should not underestimate the total numbers engaged in such work. Employees were estimated as approximating 82 per cent of all central government employees and 25 per cent of all state and central government employees taken together.

The Government of India has also sought to draw together (June 2005) a subset of various perceived 'good and valid voluntary organizations' to make an indicative list of 16,430 organizations at the centre and in the various states, that have been funded by government or other donor organizations.[14]

The extent and source of funding to these organizations is difficult to determine for the sector as a whole. NPOs registering to receive foreign funds in India under the Foreign Contribution and Regulation Act since October 1999 up till the present was 21,000[15] with an additional 6000 NGOs registering for prior permission for receiving foreign grants under this Act. For a country as large as India, these data approximate the huge dimensions of this sector.

What has been the role that this sector has played in moulding corporate performance in India? There are at least two streams of such effort that occasionally converge but are largely separate approaches. One of these streams includes advocacy/activism efforts including those that find

[12] R. SooryaMoorthy and K.D. Gangrade, *NGOs in India: a Cross-sectional Study*, Greenwood Press, CT, 2001, pp. 48–9.

[13] Rajesh Tandon and S.S. Srivastava, 'Study on Indian Non-Profit Sector', Institute for Policy Studies, Johns Hopkins University, 2002, pp. 5, 9.

[14] Voluntary organizations data base—Planning Commission, updated as of June 2005. http://164.100.97.14/ngo/default.asp

[15] Manorajan Mohanty and Anil K. Singh, *Voluntarism and Government Policy, Programmes and Assistance*, Voluntary Action Network India (VANI), 2001.

expression through the mechanism of public interest litigation. The other comes from the collaborative efforts that NGOs are playing in terms of bringing changes more incrementally. There is an enormous landscape of both types of efforts in India that impinge on CSR. The profile of their actions helps understand how and what changes they seek to bring with respect to corporate behaviour in particular and development in general.

NGOs in India: Confronting for Change

NGOs in India, have a long record of taking the confrontational approach for leveraging change. For such confrontations that impact corporate action, a great deal of case study documentation is available. Adjudging the rights or wrongs of the movement/effort is not attempted here. Nor is it comprehensive in scope nor patterns of interaction. The lessons from case studies highlight key issues raised, the source of strength of NGOs, and the important processes followed. These are the conclusions that can be drawn from studies documented in great detail elsewhere and represent some of the formidable engagements taken on by civil society.[16]

The lessons here are of several types. To begin with: (a) there is an expansive scope of issues engulfing the state and the corporates; (b) the skilful leveraging of national and international networks to achieve the goals; (c) the different and multiple impacts achieved, and (d) the highly effective and volatile communication and branding processes in favour of objectives and against what is seen as corporate irresponsibility. These taken together multiply the strength of the individual campaign.

---

[16] Case referred to details are from the following cited works. The learnings extracted are not necessarily those of the authors. For case studies, see: Ranjita Mohanty, 'Save the Chilka Movement: Interrogating the State and the Market' and Neera Chandhoke, 'When the Voiceless Speak: A Case Study of Chhattisgarh Mukti Morcha' in Rajesh Tandon and Ranjita Mohanty, *Does Civil Society Matter? Governance in Contemporary India*, Sage Publications, N. Delhi, Thousand Oaks, London, 2003.

The information on soft drink and pesticide issue is taken from *Down to Earth*, WSF Special (Undated following the pesticide in bottled water and soft drinks controversy), Centre for Science and Environment, pp. 1–23 and *Civil Society*, vol. 1, no. 7, March 2004. Cover Story on the Cola Trial, pp. 8–14.

I. Barney, A.B. Ota, B. Pandey and R. Puranic, 'In Focus: Engaging Stakeholders: Lessons from Three Eastern Indian Business Case Studies', Resource Centre for the Social Dimensions of Business Practice at the Centre for Development Studies.

ENGULFING CORPORATES AND THE STATE

Civil society actions are increasingly targeting wider social developmental issues but are also narrowing the fight for rights-based issues. An equally visible trend is that the interrogation of corporates is sometimes an overflow from the interrogation of other stakeholders with whom corporates are seen to engage closely, typically the state. In the examples discussed in the following pages, both these traits are apparent. In the end the questions of responsibility extend to business as well and the concessions that it has received from the state. In this and other cases, corporate social responsibility has been called in to respond to an even wider canvas of responsibility, namely that of other stakeholders with whom it is seen to have engaged.

In the famous Chilka prawn culture fisheries case,[17] in 1986, the government in Orissa signed a deal with Tata Aquatic Farms Ltd. to lease 1400 hectares of land in Chilka for prawn culture in which the government had a 10 per cent share. Subsequent governments leveraged a 49 per cent stake in the deal.

Mohanty, in the case study, suggests mixed feelings that poor fisherman had about the deal. On the one hand, it was perceived as a threat to their traditional fishing techniques. Due to the property rights accorded to the corporates for fishing, it was also perceived as a threat to traditional entitlements to grazing grounds for fish, which were the source of their livelihood. On the other hand, there were hopes of employment generation and a market for their products. Promise of extensive technical and other services and a market for small-scale farmers and cooperatives was held out together with the hope of elevated socio-economic status.

Trust of either the state or corporates was, however, in short supply. Credible engagement process in such cases had not yet been institutionalized. The resistance groups worked for a 'solidarity confined to resistance against the Tata project'.

The immediate issue at hand was, however, the government action—the legality of the award, Chilka being a 'reserved wetland' and therefore not open for lease to any individual or company by the government under the Land Settlement Act. The protest, however, was against the corporate body as well.[18]

[17] Mohanty, Ranjita 2003: 'Save the Chilka Movement'.
[18] Ibid., p. 192.

In Chilka, the protest began when the state showed insensitivity to the people by putting their livelihood resources to commercial use. Moreover, shifting the responsibility for regulating the sphere from the state to the market further accentuated the dissatisfaction and apprehension among fishermen, who could not see the Tatas, governed by profit motive as they were, giving priority to their needs.

The state's inadequacies can sit heavy on the corporate partner as well. Moreover, flip-flop positions by the state are also considerations. In this case the union government put pressure on the state government to support the civil society protests. The corporates are increasingly having to concern themselves with the responsibility of other stakeholders with whom they are engaged in one way or the other.

Projecting similar issues and in the same state, but almost a decade apart, was the build up of opposition to the Utkal Aluminum International Limited (UAIL), approved by the state government in 1994. The Utkal Aluminum International Limited (UAIL) was a consortium of national and international companies prospecting the mining of bauxite reserves in southern Orissa. Independent reports have suggested that the major shareholders reflected a consistent and progressive attitude to their responsibilities. However, key issues of a very basic nature were raised in opposition to the project, reminiscent of the Chilka project. This opposition to the project contributed to delay in this project for a period of three years. The case study sums up the reasons for the delay succinctly.[19]

A lack of trust in large developmental projects was at the heart of the opposition to UAIL the government failed to meet its own legislative standards. It failed to follow the requirements of the land acquisition Act and inform local people of plans to develop the area. It also failed to follow the spirit of the Fifth Schedule and consult local government on all plans to develop the area. In addition, the way in which some local government employees interacted with local people was to the detriment of the project. Their 'bulldozer' mentality has not helped the UAIL cause.

In short, a collaborative process was being demanded. Civil society and the constituencies it represented wanted to be considered stakeholders as well.

It is not always the case that companies and corporates have to bear the burden of the fall-out of dissatisfaction with government. Examples are in evidence to show that it works in the reverse also. What began as a struggle

---

[19] Barney et al., ibid. 'In Focus: Engaging Stakeholders', pp. 6, 46.

for concessions by a company to labour ended up with the takeover of civic functions of the state by a civil society group. The struggle by the Chattisgarh Mines Shramik Sangh (CMSS) is a case in point.[20] The key issue here was better work conditions for contract labour, where the practice had been to pay lower than minimum wages, make erratic payments, and not provide health and safety conditions. Shankar Guha Niyogi who had come as an engineering apprentice to the Coke Oven Plant in the late 1960s initiated strikes to lobby for these changes. These were issues that neither management nor the unions representing mainly organized labour had cared to address.

After a protracted struggle, a federation of about twenty organizations called the Chattisgarh Mukti Morcha (CMM) was formed in the 1990s. The CMM had matured and several concessions were wrested from the company in the 1990s including a guarantee of twenty days work per month for contract labourers, 20 per cent of profits as bonus, and other facilites.[21]

What was interesting about this movement was that what started as an onslaught against the company for not meeting regulatory requirements became a demand for extra-regulatory concessions for the safety and well-being of the employees, and widened to encompass the support of many more organizations, and ended up with a broader mandate for action. The expanded mandate and actions not only sought to create mechanisms to address corruption in the government, but in other ways usurped the civic facilities-provider role of the government as well. In this connection, the controversial CMM undertook the distribution of ration cards, entitlements to government benefits for the handicapped, senior citizens, and widows, thus bypassing several of the government links prone to corruption in this sector. The CMM also ended up delivering many of the government functions including the setting up of schools, health facilities, and vocational training centres, releasing bonded labour, rehabilitating slum dwellers, addressing women's rights issues, and many more such initiatives. In other words, the CMM was not just addressing perceived 'illegitimacies' of business but also those of the state.

A more recent scenario and a different kind of civil society action was the controversy over pesticides and Pepsico and Coca-Cola. Unbelievable as it

[20] Neera Chandhoke 2003 ibid., pp. 198–242.
[21] Ibid., p. 214.

may appear now, the direction of attack was initially and principally on government's role. The effort was to bring higher standards of controls to packaged drinking water including those produced by branded companies such as PepsiCo and Coca-Cola. The non-governmental organization, Centre for Science and Environment (CSE), released its study which showed in its view '*legalized* pesticides in bottled water'. In other words, being legal it was still perceived by the NGO as having unacceptable levels of pesticide residue. This was followed by an examination for pesticides in the soft drink industry. This examination indicated that European standards of purity for water (of practically zero pesticide residue—.0001 milligram per litre for each substance) did not exist in India.

Several issues were brought to the surface and many of them had to do with role of government. Though it played out as an attack on the companies, the point was—as Sunita Narain, Director of CSE writes in an editorial.[22]

Even more startling we found that this human health impacting industry as being more or less unregulated. ... this issue is not about Pepsi and Coke or even pesticides in their soft drinks *per se.* It is about the functioning of effective mechanisms to manage industrial growth and its toxic fall-outs. From everything we see around us, it is clear to me that increased private sector participation will need more governance, not less. More importantly, we will need more democracy, not less. But government will have to be reengineered so that its regulatory role strengthens enormously. In this case, the norms for this industry are weak and meaningless. Government has more or less abdicated its role to safeguard public health.

It also emerged from this controversy that multinational companies will be scrutinized increasingly to meet the highest international norms and standards, regardless of mandated norms in India. Clearly this is a signpost for government to set out clarity of standard-setting process to constantly changing expectations and to ascertain what roles multi-stakeholder groups, including corporates, can play in this. Criticisms to the NGO attack are many and outlined in a following segment.

Leveraging Networks

In all of the civil society actions mentioned earlier, the point is emphasized that states and corporates are banded together for interrogation. There is

---

[22] Sunita Narain, Editorial, *Down to Earth*, WSF Special Issue, pp. 1, 2.

another learning in the way civil society functions against corporates. Civil society, as an organizational form, has very many dynamic characteristics that make possible its survival, despite its low financial resources in developing countries like India.[23]

The confidence and influence of corporate wealth is matched by the flexibility, commitment, increasing professionalism, and quick responses by CSOs (Civil Society Organizations) to what is perceived as a threat to their goals. But central to their increasing visibility is their ability to leverage the support of many constituencies. This has become strengthened manifold via recent acquisition and use of the communication revolution to its fullest extent.

The case of the Chilka movement mentioned earlier, was one of incorporating wider groups of various kinds to a joint struggle.[24] It was Meet the Students (MTS), with a radical ideology for social change, which galvanized the subterranean dissatisfaction and lack of trust with development projects. The students forum constituted at the provincial level, the Krantidarshi Yuva Sangha (KYS), which included non-students, also backed the resistance. Adding intellectuals to the group, the Chilka Suraksha Parisad began the work of mobilizing public opinion against the prawn culture project. Understanding its distance from local issues, the movement strategized to gain the support of the Chilka Matsyajibi Mahasangha, a mass organization of 122 revenue villages in Chilka to protect the interests of fishermen. An extension organization, The Chilka Bachao Andolan (CBA), was launched in 1992, which drew under its banner the farmers organization and an organization working for the rights of democratic peoples as well. This latter drew in international support when it campaigned that the Government of India must honour the Ramsar Convention, in which the Chilka lake had been declared an endangered wetland that needed to be protected. Together they were a formidable force.

A similar web of alliances worked in the opposition to the Utkal Aluminium International Limited (UAIL) and its consortium of national and international companies prospecting the mining of bauxite reserves in Southern Orissa.[25] The UAIL, by all accounts, has one of the best standards

---

[23] Tandon and Srivastava, Study on Indian Non-Profit Sector.

[24] Mohanty, Ranjita 2003, '*Save the Chilika Movement*', ibid.

[25] Barney *et al.*, ibid., 'In Focus: Engaging Stakeholders', pp. 6, 46.

for rehabilitation and resettlement, so much so that officials are reported to have concerns that these could be difficult for others to match. There were allegations that opposition to the project was at the instigation of a few and that most tribals were in favour of the project. Whatever the reason, four major NGOs, Agragamee, Ankuran, the Laxman Nayak Society, and the Weaker Section Integrated Development Agency (WSIDA), joined the struggle against the project and were sufficiently provocative to lead the government to deregister them in 1997. This led to further intensification of the resistance. Because of this opposition, the UAIL undertook a series of actions in 1998. A socio-economic assessment of the project's impact was undertaken, together with the formation of a rural development trust and the appointment of a CSR manager. Partly as a result of the delay and other frustrations and partly its own business corporate strategy, Tatas as a consortium partner withdrew.

Another partner in the consortium, Norsk, had three senior officials and UAIL Project Managers visit the site to better understand local issues. They were assaulted and 'encouraged' to sign a declaration against the project. Moreover, the criticism in Norway weighed heavily with the company and it was determined that the company did not want project progress at the cost of reputation.[26] Substantial constraint was advised by Norsk Hydro and other partners. The leadership at the top recognized the need to work closely with social issues. However, it realized that it did not have the systems or personnel to deal with these issues. There was also recognition that its own efforts and action in addressing the issues were not effectively communicated.

The case study highlights the fact that there resulted an 'entangled perception' of state and company and counsels that corporates should have an active role in monitoring and ensuring that other partners in the project fulfil their obligations and roles. In this context the company has, in its attempt at dialogue, quoted a Norway Amnesty perspective stating that while business was not expected to pay a full-fledged advocacy role, 'neutrality' was no longer an acceptable option, reflecting the fact that companies will be forced to play some role in getting other partners to act responsibly.

The Centre for Science and Environment (CSE), which researched and brought the issue of 'unacceptable' levels (in their view) of pesticides in

---

[26] Barney et al., ibid., pp. 41, 48, 49.

bottled water and soft drinks to public notice, has a list of partners spanning international organizations, local NGOs, and many others with whom it works on specific issues. The 'foreign' connection was brought up more than once as a cause for concern by those disagreeing with its approach and action. In this era of globalization, where the state, business, and every other constituency is well connected with the outside world, NGO groups cannot be far behind.

A special issue of the CSE magazine, *Down to Earth*, on the pesticides controversy issues was brought out for wider circulation at the World Social Forum. With a wide spectrum of participants at the forum, the issue was brought to the international centre stage of civil society awareness. The CSE's efforts, implications of its fight, and other aspects were replayed several times adding further to the dimensions that the debate took in public perception, multiplying several times the impact of the branding against the companies.

The Impact

Difficult as it is to list the full impact of such activism, from the NGO perspective, several insights are available. In the UAIL experience, apart from the reputation of the consortium, crude estimates indicate that the delays have resulted in the doubling of the initial planned investment to about US$450 million and a total loss of revenue of US $600 million if the project were not to start as per the further rescheduled date.[27] On the other side, the lessons learnt have refined the R&R guidelines which, if applied, could save costs for several other projects of the kind, not to mention benefit thousands of families caught in the displacement.

This kind of larger impact and snowballing of issues is particularly noticeable in the Coca-Cola, Pepsi pesticide controversy. The research effort by the CSE had begun as a campaign to establish that pesticide use in the country had gone out of control. As it played out, it once again brought into centre stage the regulatory role of the government, the role of the health ministry, of food standards, standards for municipal water, the use of caffeine in soft drinks, and of course the issue of national and international standards, all of which could have outmatched any corporate brief on the matter. It resulted in the notification of new standards for pesticide residues

[27] Ibid., p. 47.

in bottled water, and to examine which internationally established test methods would be used.[28] Moreover, the CSE's examination of ADI (Acceptable Daily Intake) showed that it is linked to nutrition, and since cold drinks do not offer nutrition and are not food, the CSE argues for a drink completely free of pesticides. The snowballing action brought to centre stage many of the issues that had remained undetermined so far. Equally, for a long period after the controversy broke, the companies suffered a loss in sales, estimated by various groups to be between 20 per cent and 40 per cent.

POWER COMMUNICATION

The networked power of civil society is only matched by civil society's ability to highlight a message and the tenacity to sustain a struggle. The impact of the Bhopal tragedy, almost twenty years after its occurrence, is an ongoing saga of efforts to get compensation for its victims. In this, international civil society associations are powerfully positioned. In 2003, Greenpeace activists highlighted the lingering issues of toxic clean-up still necessary. It did so by transporting (on Greenpeace ship *Artic Sunrise*) 250 kg of what the organization had determined to be toxic waste from Bhopal. This cargo was unloaded at the largest European Operation of Dow Chemical in the Dutch Town of Terneuzen.[29] In 2002 contaminated soil and water from Bhopal was also taken to the Dow Chemicals factory of Map Tha Phut Industrial Estate, Thailand, and to the Bombay premises of Dow.[30] Almost twenty years after the accident in 2004 a small group of survivors from Bhopal was presented at Dow's annual shareholders meeting in Midland, Michigan. Their presence was to support a resolution seeking full disclosure on the world's worst chemical disaster. The resolution was filed on behalf of Brethren Benefit Trust Inc., the holder of about 5000 Dow shares,[31] which perceived Dow as shirking its responsibility to survivors.

[28] *Down to Earth*, Special Issue p. 17.

[29] 'Greenpeace Gives Dow Chemical Taste of Bhopal Waste', Environmental News Service, 7 Jan. 2003.

[30] 'Greenpeace Preassures Dow for Environmental Clean-Up', Environmental News Service 12 March 2002.

[31] David Brinkerhoff, 'Bhopal Survivors Press US Company for Disclosure', Reuters, 18 May 2004.

The resolution was not passed but it had sufficient support to leave the door open for further resolutions.

Another India-related media campaign in the international swirl of activism has been that against the leather industry. The crusading communication of this campaign against international companies and their Indian partners and suppliers of leather was undertaken by PETA (People for the Ethical Treatment of Animals). PETA had made allegations against the company of the GAP brand regarding leather sourcing particularly from India. PETA argued that Indian slaughter houses do not conform to existing laws and that transportation of animals is done under inhuman conditions.[32]

This was supported by an information campaign capable of drawing international attention. A film was screened with narration by the famed American TV star Pamela Anderson Lee against GAP, one of the largest clothing retailers in the US whose policies extend to its subsidaries like Navy and Banana Republic. As M.M.Hashim, Chairman of the Council for Leather Exports (CLE), confirmed, the campaign has resulted in GAP cancelling orders worth $5 million from India. The company has decided to continue to source garments from garment factories in India but have the leather sourced from elsewhere. Alan Marks, GAP's vice-president for corporate communications explains, 'We thought it most prudent to have leather sourced in other countries than spend resources investigating the condition of tanneries.'

The campaign had the Indian government on the defensive, saying that the industry got most of its leather from animals that had died naturally or as a by-product of slaughter for meat. However, it is well recognized that the ban on cow slaughter in most states prevents the government from effectively regulating the conditions under which it is done.

The leather industry also suffered because of court restraints due to the lack of effluent treatment of waste water. The debate between pollution impact and loss of jobs impact is an old one. Arguments highlighting lost jobs were silenced by the then minister for social justice and empowerment Ms Maneka Gandhi, who retorted that in the process of saving 500 jobs.

... 5 million here are deprived of clean water.

[32] Vivian Fernandes, 'Cruelty to Animals Forces US Retailer to Boycott India Leather; Industry Dismayed', 28 April 2000. http://www.indiamarkets.com/imo/industry/leather/leatherfea1.asp

Since then a series of public interest litigations have resulted in court orders directing the containment of such pollution. The question as to how the small-scale sector can pay for this clean up will require innovative solutions.

Encouraged by the response that PETA received, it is poised to take up other companies like Flosheim shoes, Hush Puppies, Casual Corner, and Nordstroms that use Indian and Chinese leather. Here too companies will be asked to look at ethical practices beyond their immediate vicinity to the extended stakeholder chain as well.

Public Interest Litigation

Apart from social activism, as described above, legal and extra-legal norms in the social and environmental areas have been achieved in India through public interest litigations (PIL) and judicial activism. PILs are often seen by both governments and activists as an easier route to implementation of proposed goals. The PIL is of relatively recent origin in India, having emerged in the early 1980s, as compared to similar mechanisms in the West which appeared in the early 1950s. There are a number of aspects to PILs in India that have made them a relatively accessible instrument to bring to public notice grievances against the state or business. In India, the PIL allows any petitioner to file on behalf of public interest. It dispenses with formal court procedures, even allowing the petition to be written on a post card which would then be formalized. It can call on research to support its arguments. All this has allowed small voices to command huge attention, and has been interpreted by its supporters as delivering justice to the common person as opposed to justice for the elite alone.

The PIL in India, since its inception, has had a strong role in addressing social and environmental issues, arising out of industrial transformations in the country. Many of these PILs are directly aimed at regulating industry and its functioning, as subscribed by law, but others are directed at government to get it to play its regulatory role in containing industry excesses and defining the boundaries of what is in the public interest. Several of these battles have been in the area of environment. The UN Conference on the Human Environment held in Stockholm in 1972 was a landmark and it once and for all settled the debate between development and environment in favour of the latter. India at that time took the position that poverty was the polluter and that sovereignty was to be protected in this debate.

Environment, however, became the main focus—institutions, networks, and global agendas on environment emerged.

In the last ten years India, has seen several landmark judgments in PILs on environmental issues, many of which have had direct impact on industry. These highly visible cases include the PIL alleging that the yellowing and blackening of the Taj Mahal was due to industrial/refinery emissions, generator sets, etc. The Supreme Court in 1997 directed that 292 polluting industries deemed responsible change over to natural gas as an industrial fuel[33] and those not in a position to do this, stop functioning and relocate beyond the Trapezium zone. In 1996, one hundred and sixty-eight industries in Delhi identified as hazardous/noxious/heavy/large were directed to close down the same year,[34] allowing them to shift to other areas and receive the same incentives as new industry in new industrial estates but also indicating that rights and benefits be paid to workers.

Equally significant but less publicized issues were also dealt with through PILs. Between 1985 and 1989 a series of PILs by an NGO against the state of Uttar Pradesh[35] alleged that lime stone quarries were destroying the flaura and fauna of the Himalayan Valley, polluting the air and water and thereby posing a threat to the lives of people. The worst offenders within city limits of Mussorie were directed to close permanently by the court while others were to be examined by an expert committee. The Supreme Court subsequently allowed certain category A quarries outside the city limits to continue but only in some very selected cases.

Emerging out of these and other PILs like the Delhi Gas Leak, many socially sensitive but uncertain areas in law have been codified. It gave environment the 'polluter pays' principle, the strict liability principle—personal liability for deaths—the direction to set up a fund for potential victims, and environmental courts. Also, ruling on petitions, PILs have forced industries to undertake cleaning operations forthwith.

---

[33] See M.C. Mehta vs Union of India (1997)2SCC 353 in B.L. Wadhera, *Public Interest Litigation—A Handbook*, Universal Law Publishing Company, N. Delhi, 2003, p. 93.

[34] M.C. Mehta vs Union of India (1996)4SCC 750 in Wadhera, *Public Interest Litigation*, p. 88.

[35] Rural Litigation and Entitlement Kendra v State of Uttar Pradesh (1985)2 SCC 614, (1986) Supplementary SCC 517; (1987) supplementary SCC487; (1989) suppl (1) SCC 537; (1991) 3SCC 347; (1989) Supp(1) 504 AIR 1988 SC 2187, in Wadhera, *Public Interest Litigation*, p. 79.

It is less well known that PILs have also been used for creating preventive mechanisms for promoting environmental consciousness and awareness of the rights of citizens. These have indirect effects on the way corporates function. The constituency of those tracking responsibility issues will be broadened. Magasaysay Award winning lawyer, M.C. Mehta is well know for the remedial action he was able to set in motion to contain existing polluting trends. Less well known are his efforts for preventive measures through the PIL. In 1992, M.C. Mehta filed a plea for environmental promotion consciousness and sought direction from the court that cinema halls, radio, and television exhibit information regarding environmental protection, and that environment be made a compulsory subject in schools and colleges. The Supreme Court conceded all the above pleas, and directed that 'State [is] directed to enforce as a condition of license of all cinema halls, touring cinemas and video parlours duty to exhibit free of cost at least two slides/messages on environment in each show undertaken by them.' It also directed the state to make environment a compulsory subject at the school, college, and university levels for purposes of 'general growth of awareness', which could influence the way corporates and government handle environmental issues.[36] This directed the central government to instruct all educational institutions throughout India to have lessons relating to the protection and improvement of the natural environment in the first 10 classes, and to get textbooks written and distribute them free of cost.[37]

NGOs COLLABORATING FOR CHANGE

A strong adversarial role by NGOs in India in bringing to light government and corporate inadequacies or excesses is amply in evidence. However, there is another emerging role of the consultative NGO. In the context of the *confrontation, complimentarity, and collaboration*[38] roles that NGOs can play,

[36] M.C. Mehta vs Union of India, (1992)SCC 256, in Wadhera, *Public Interest litigation*, p. 84.

[37] M.C. Mehta vs Union of India, (1988)SCC 471, in Wadhera, *Public Interest litigation*, p. 83.

[38] Adil Najam, 'Nongovernmental Organizations as Policy Entrepreneurs: In Pursuit of Sustainable Development. Program for Non-Profit Organizations', Yale University *Working Paper* 231 and Institute for Social and Policy Studies, *Working Paper* no. 2231, 1996, pp. 23 and 13.

there is a space being created for the latter two types of roles as well. However, these distinctions cannot be too rigidly maintained—and there are mutant NGOs seeking to combine these different attributes. This has already emerged on the international scene. For instance, though we know well the Greenpeace–Shell conflict in the 'Brent Spar' issue, we know less about the partnership roles that Greenpeace has entered into with Shell for environmental purposes. Many of the international NGOs like Oxfam and Amnesty are looking at leveraging engagement with the corporate /business world and CSR as a way of achieving their developmental goals as well as their own business strategies.[39]

What is new in the NGO scene in India is a spate of NGOs playing the complementarity and collaboration roles for CSR. These are NGOs not necessarily linked to any one company. There are numerous NGOs in India, that support CSR implementation roles. However, organizations initiated as service providers exclusively for CSR developed in the late 1980s and 1990s. These are predominantly offshoots of organizations with more broad-based parent bodies from abroad. All the organizations come with a background of a clear social development mandate—poverty alleviation, serving the marginalized communities, or to essentially reform the culture of market and other social institutions to advance social justice, human rights, and sustainable development. The approach and specialized skills sets required for engaging with the corporate world have also led institutions to separate from parent bodies.

There are a number of prominent organizations among CSR-facilitating NGOs that have this kind of profile. Partners in Change (PIC), for instance, was promoted by a UK-based NGO—Action Aid—with headquarters in New Delhi. PIC, established in 1995, had its origin in the Corporate Partnership (CP) programme of Action Aid India.[40] Similarly, Business and Community Foundation (BCF) is an offshoot of PWBLF (now IBLF), a UK-based charity that started its operations in India in 1991, and with which it continues to have links. The BCF has been active in India since late 1995. The Centre for Social Markets (CSM) was established in 2000

[39] Bimal Kumar Arora, 'NGOs and Business Sector Relationships in the Context of Corporate Social Responsibility', MSc thesis on Management of NGOs, London School of Economics and Political Science Dissertation, Sept. 2003.

[40] Ibid.

and is an international organization with an India-based office. It describes itself as being dedicated to making markets work for the triple bottom line, namely, people, planet, and profit. The predominant focus of the Bharatiya Yuva Shakti Trust (BYST), inspired by the Prince of Wales Youth Business Trust, is corporate involvement in social development. Other than these major players in the field, there are a host of NGOs, that though not exclusively working on CSR also provide CSR capacity building and related services. Among these is the Charity Aid Foundation, which is a charitable trust, started in 1998, that provides financial services to corporates working on CSR. The services include fund-raising support. There are others providing training and other skills and information inputs to a whole range of institutions that may be linked to CSR in one way or the other. The Sampradhan Indian Centre for Philanthropy, is among them. Development Alternatives has developed an impressive menu of CSR resources and publications.

Organizations like PIC and BCF have acted as intermediaries in identifying and putting in place partnerships between corporates and other NGOS. Many of these latter have speciality areas of expertise. This has brought in a whole range of peripheral NGOs to work in the field of CSR. An exhaustive compilation of corporates in CSR, conducted by PIC in 2000, also profiles over twenty-five such NGOs that are working for forty-six major corporates on CSR initiatives.[41]

A broad range of services has been developed by organizations working exclusively on CSR. Partners for change, for instance, has a large menu of offerings including designing CSR; consultancy for implementing CSR policy, putting in place partnerships with NGOs that can work with corporates for specific business-modelled CSR (meaning that it will give business benefits as well); seminars for creating awareness on CSR among business, NGOs, and other stakeholders; and creating networks to integrate CSR into academic institutions, typically management institutes. Similarly, CSM purports to promote responsible entrepreneurship, ethics, and accountability among five key groups—business, investors, workers, consumers, and legislators. The CSMs inputs are offered to two constituencies:

---

[41] Harsh Shrivastava and Shankar Venkateswaran, *The Business of Social Responsibility*, Books for Change, Bangalore 2000. Has detailed treatment of business efforts for social responsibility and partnerships with NGOs. Also ibid.

diaspora and ethnic minorities engaged in business in the UK, and domestic/ indigenous business and stakeholders in India. Business and Community Foundation (BCF) inputs are available to its members, mainly multinationals and foreign companies and a few Indian companies, and primarily revolve around community development initiatives. Bharatiya Yuva Shakti Trust (BYST) plays a slightly different role in using the people resources of the corporates—skill, management, and entrepreneurial knowledge—for mentoring emerging entrepreneurs in the disadvantaged communities. The key learning from the services offered by these organizations is the variety of ways that corporates can engage in CSR. Development Alternatives offers training for the adoption and implementation of the Global Reporting Initiative (GRI), for general CSR awareness and implementation, for promoting the social codes adopted by industry association, and more.

There are, apart from these, also collective industry foundations and trusts as well as NGOs created by a group of companies in a given sector, (e.g. SVADES—Society for Village Development in the petrochemical areas in Vadodara). Foundations run by individual business itself, have been a traditional source of social development support and precede the organizations mentioned earlier.

Moreover, being foundations/trusts, they like other NGOs have been able to effectively leverage additional funds for their activities. In fact many of the foundations were able to leverage a large proportion of their development funds from outside.[42] The data from the early 1990s show that during this period, the Lalbhai group, Excel Company, and the Chandarias brought foundations funds ranging from only 1 to 11.6 per cent of the total funds required. The rest was leveraged from government, foreign donors and community contributions. As a strategy, the Tata's community development leverages substantial contribution for development projects from the community itself. This strategy for buy-ins and ownership are considered important for sustainability. This should not underestimate in any way the considerable resources directed to CSR by the Tata group of companies. Out of profits of Rs 7945 crore for 2004–05, the Group, through its companies and trusts, spent Rs 439 crore on CSR.[43]

---

[42] Pushpa Sundar, *Beyond Business: From Merchant Charity to Corporate Citizenship, Indian Business Philanthropy through the Ages*, Tata McGraw Hill, New Delhi, 2000.

[43] Tata Group Brochure 2004–05.

Non-profit organizations providing professionalized management of CSR are constantly expanding the scope of their operations and are developing a comfortable engagement with business. As they scour the social horizon, their mandate to understand, communicate, help institutionalize, facilitate, and track implementation of evolving CSR issues expands. The perception that disregard of social and environmental issues is a 'business risk' has led to growth of services in this area. Non-profit societies are meeting with competition from international consultancy groups as well in addressing these issues. The intermediation role of the adversarial NGOs will also be around till such time that grassroot constituencies can voice their own concerns more effectively.

QUESTIONING NGO ROLES

The 'confrontational' and 'collaborative' roles of NGOs in influencing CSR have been discussed in this section. These demarcating lines often tend to be fluid. Many of the cases cited here under the confrontational role of the NGOs, are meant to show how they have acted in promoting adherence to the law, and calling for a stronger regulatory role of the state where there were gaps in the law.

However, adversarial NGO activism has not been without criticism. There are many perspectives on this, much of which have to do with the roles of such NGOs in general rather than the specific issues they have raised. For one thing society has not developed a consensus on the 'voice' of activism as a trigger for change as opposed to the perspective of the silent majority (expressed through the electoral process). Activism takes place here and now, often has restricted perspectives, but is accepted as part of the democratic processes. On the other hand, electoral articulation takes years to come, is seen to be the essence of democracy, but is also the composite of many issues and therefore more blunted in its message. Critics see activist action as being incomplete and the perceptions that this leaves behind, intentionally or unintentionally, as being one sided.

There are other issues as well connected with this line of criticism. Globalization has brought the differences in cross-border ethics and norms to the forefront. There is also the question of bringing 'extra-legal' international norms to bear on business through the adversarial processes. The internationalization of NGOs has further heightened this trend of negotiating 'extra-legal' adherences in line with developed country norms. Critics point out that such adversarial activism has not always been in the national interest and have called into question the role of NGOs.

The role of the CSE in the cola controversy is instructive in this context. It is interesting that the CSE actually started with the intent of looking at pesticide in drinking water (supplied by government). This would have highlighted very wide ranging issues affecting most of the India's population. It would also have opened up the issue of clean supply of water for industry use as is done in developed countries. For whatever reason, the organization targeted another direction of action. The CSE was to say,

We were really looking at pesticides in drinking water but research on municipal water supply was too difficult, so bottled water it was.[44]

It must be said that in the process of the attack, many of the weaknesses in the regulatory role of government were also brought out in the pages of the CSE journal. In fact the plethora of regulations, bureaucratic inadequacies, and the lack of effective standards for the food industry were detailed. However, this got lost in the David versus Goliath form that the controversy took. The media exacerbated the situation and reactive and sometimes inaccurate statements from industry did not help either.

The intricacies of this controversy are many and ongoing.[45] Industry's grouse was that both packaged water and soft drinks did not violate Indian legal requirements at the time. Packaged drinking water met Indian legal requirements for 'safety' and was, at the time, almost fully harmonized with the international requirements of the WHO. Indian standards are continuously calibrated to the international WHO norms. Soft drinks, according to the then Minister of Health's initial statement in Parliament, met the 'safety' requirements in Indian law for water.

For industry, the controversy was also in part about the introduction of 'extra-legal' norms, benchmarked against developed country limits of 'safety'

[44] *Down to Earth*, World Social Forum Special, 'Pesticides in Food—Understanding Safety', Centre for Science and Environment, New Delhi (undated), p. 25.

[45] I am grateful to Parna Dasgupta, CIFTI (Confederation of Food Trade Industries) for discussions and for guiding me to the industry perspective. This section is mostly based on these discussions and on the 'Presentation to the Joint Parliamentary Committee on Pesticide Residues in and Safety Standards for SOFT Drinks, Fruit Juices and Other Beverages, where Water is the Main Constituent', FICCI.

by an NGO. This had to do with packaged water as well as soft drinks. One of the action points by the NGO was to highlight pesticide residue in excess of EU limits in twelve brands of soft drinks, as well as the lack of EU standards in Indian packaged water and in the water of the soft drinks The controversy ended with Indian norms for packaged water being fixed to EU limits within a very short period. Soft drinks were also, through a notification, required to meet EU water specifications. Through the notification, Indian norms became more stringent than the European limits, by being now more demanding in legislative intent. The European standard for water used in soft drinks is an aspirational code which serves more as a general guideline while the Indian norms have the status of falling within the purview of criminal legislation.

Both companies that were tainted by the controversy experienced a massive drop in sales for a prolonged period of time. Apart from the multinationals that were at the core of the controversy, there were reportedly 800 local manufacturers who are now subject to these norms. What this meant to local companies as opposed to the multinationals that have to meet these standards, and what it adds to consumer costs and to lost jobs, is yet to be fully understood. Additionally, industry was aggrieved that one of the most critical laws of the country got amended even as the government report clarified that the products were quite safe. There were additional concerns expressed that this controversy, linked as it was to sensitive food and agriculture issues, and to sudden change in standards would further hinder Indian's global competitiveness because of the lack of gradualism and calibration.

Another trajectory of NGO action has been to raise a voice against the lack of adherence to the law with respect to development projects, particularly those involving foreign investors. NGOs have largely been successful in this. However, even in the very rare cases where NGO action has been called into question as determined by court cases lost by NGOs, these have not necessarily been gains for the corporate world. Again, this has less to do with the 'rightness' of their cause, and more to do with the impact of the process.

For instance, raising development standards, post-liberalization, has led to a series of 'fast-track projects' in infrastructure. In the power sector, it is generally recognized that SEBs (State Electricity Boards) have for reasons of inefficiency, political expediency, as well as corruption not been able to deliver power. It has been estimated that there is need for investment of $US 100 billion in the next twelve years to meet this need. In line with these requirements, state and central governments in India have wooed foreign and private investments through a series of 'fast-track' projects. In the power sector, speed has been provided not just for getting clearances but also for creating conditions for favourable terms of investment, as well as through various tax concessions. The Cogentrix case is perhaps the most controversial and typical as to how new issues are opened up and where it leads to.[46]

The Cogentrix Energy, Inc., and China Light and Power International were to set up a US$1.3 billion investment in Karnataka for a 1000MW 'fast-track' power project. This was supposed to be a model project providing benefits of power at acceptable rates and delivering on all kinds of environmental standards. The new ethos of inviting such projects opened up a whole lot of processes circumventing earlier procedures and instead going through political avenues. A series of litigations followed by civil society groups (in collaboration at times with opposing political parties) and NGO-backed PILs alleging corruption. These included 'kickback' charges and 'environmental' charges. This was closely watched by other potential investors in the field. After over six years of litigation, the 'kickback' and other charges were dismissed at Supreme Court level in rather harsh terms. The judgement said that a criminal investigation could not be started on mere 'surmises' and 'conjectures' without any reasonable basis. The company leveraged this decision to secure even more unusual security conditions for itself, but eventually pulled out for several reasons including the long litigations. Had Congentrix stayed, the costs of these litigations would have been passed on to the consumer. Moreover, in the globalized context, the investments that India was wooing would either shy away or seek greater sureties, as many companies in the pipeline did, following the judgement in the Cogentrix case.

The NGO voice is here to stay, highlighting gaps in law, inadequate processes, regulatory systems, compliance and now, in the globalizing

---

[46] D. Fernandes and L. Saldanha, 'Deep Politics, Liberalisation and Corruption: The Mangalore Power Company Controversy', *Law, Social Justice and Global Development (LGD)*, 10 January 2000 or 2001.

context, the action to force the very highest international norms. In a developing country scenario, this can bring special pressures to bear. Clearly, both government and business have to be ready for a better appreciation of these roles and for a framework for incorporating these voices, replacing wherever possible collaborative processes for conflictual ones.

CHAPTER 7

EMBEDDING CSR IN INDIA

MULTI-STAKEHOLDERS: BENCHMARKING CORPORATE SOCIAL PERFORMANCE

By all accounts India is witnessing a plethora of initiatives in CSR today. Recent surveys in India have shown that overall upwards of 84 per cent of businesses in study samples are engaging in CSR practices of some kind.[1] But when it comes to institutionalization of CSR practices, it is a different story. That is to say, the managerial rigour applied to other business practices is marked by its general absence in the area of CSR. However, recent global trends have changed that somewhat, making it imperative for globally-linked business to act differently in its own business interests. A whole set of initiatives driven by economic imperatives has come through voluntary compliance. This is being called the business model of CSR. This model is as apparent in corporate India as it is at other levels of business like small and medium enterprises. The efforts in the latter segment in India come directly with the export linkages of the small-scale sector or sometimes indirectly through Indian corporate houses also linked to this sector.

In developed country democracies the integration and jostling for balance of values between political and economic organizations and civil society appear to be in a strong and continuous state of active engagement. Here, according to a MORI (Market and Opinion Research International) poll, the consideration of CSR issues in buying decisions, engagement in CSR by citizens, and actual buying on the basis of CSR was found to be present in varying degrees in Europe.[2] The highest congruence on these parameters

---

[1] Partners in Change, *Third Report on Corporate Social Responsibility in India, 2003*, p. 17.

[2] MORI poll 2000, Consumer Poll across 12 European Countries, cited in EU-India 'Corporate Social Responsibility: The Cross Cultural Perspective', 2001, pp. 18–19.

was reported to be in Denmark, where 67 per cent of consumers stated commitment to pay more for socially and environmentally responsible products. With global connectedness, the behaviour of developed country companies, transplanted to the new workplace and social realities of the less developed world, is also closely watched by consumers labour unions and civil society representatives in the home country. There is a case to be made that businesses racing to less developed countries understand that they are at reputational risk if they contribute to further deteriorating the social and environmental conditions existing there.

This has resulted in a continuous process of evolving a series of steps that integrate social concerns into business strategies by a number of groups. These voluntary efforts have come not just from the NGO sector, but also by professional accounting institutions, by governments, from bilateral and multilateral organizations, from foreign investors, and not least of all from business itself. Often, such influences come from a conglomeration of many such multi-stakeholder groups. In the globalization process many of these have relevance for India. A plethora of principles, guidelines, norms, codes, labelling, and reporting practices and more are released as a result. Introduced with different motives all hold the promise of some business benefit if they are adhered to.

Among business-driven initiatives, the giants of the outsourcing world such as Nike, Levi Strauss, and GAP have for over a decade been developing their own outsourcing codes. Equally, associations of business from different regions of the world have their own benchmarks for functioning. Examples of such principles are those emerging from the Caux Round Table, an organization of senior business leaders from Europe, Japan and the US, the Canadian Business for Social Responsibility, the Asia–Pacific Economic Corporation (APEC), the European Business Network, the International Chambers of Commerce, and many more such. A related category of business influences comes from the norms of functioning guided by the requirements of the foreign institutional investors who now see inadequate social and environmental standards as business risk. In a related category are the likes of Domino Funds, ASRI (the Association for Sustainable and Responsible Investing) with its SRI (Socially Responsible Investing), the Interfaith Centre on Corporate Responsibility, and the World Bank arm of business investments which has applications in India, namely the IFC (International Finance Corporation).

Among government-led initiatives are the examples of a series of OECD (Organization for Economic Cooperation and Development) led guidelines, principles, and conventions especially for MNCs operating abroad. The European Commission has been another active lead partner and the source of many initiatives in CSR since the late 1990s. Many of them are presaged on the European Union Social Policy.[3] Gaining recent global visibility is the emerging force of the UN Global Compact guidelines highlighting principles of business functioning.

Initiatives emerging from the NGO sector are as diverse as the NGOs themselves and the causes that they espouse. In order to get wider leverage, NGOs have been part of multi-stakeholder initiatives with themselves as the lead partners. Many such initiatives are industry-specific as for example in the case of forestry products, the Forestry Stewardship Council (FSC) has emerged as a labelling multi-stakeholder organization for forestry products. For marine products, the Marine Stewardship Council (MSC) seeks to promote sustainable marine fisheries, through standards and certification. This too is a multi-stakeholder group with one of the lead partners being Unilever. For transparency in government spending, a coalition of more than 130 NGOs bring various kinds of pressure under its banner of 'Publish what you Pay Campaign'.

The global retail business has been an important source for other codes originating in part through NGO networks in collaboration with business as in the case of Fairtrade or the Ethical Trading Initiative. Many of these are supported by governments though primary responsibility is taken by the organizations themselves. Alongside are the professional institutions that support the development of codes (Social Accountability International, Council of Economic Priorities, Sustainability). This whole segment is beginning to have a special relevance for India. This is not just through the demands of such codes in the SME enterprises directly but also through the demands that are made on corporates linked with such enterprises in the supply chain. Apart from the significance of the various kinds of norms, there is the significance of the formal commitment to ways of functioning.

---

[3] For a comprehensive round up of government initiatives for reporting, codes, and norms see Global Reporting Initiative, Government Initiative to Promote Corporate Sustainability Reporting Roundtable, Paris, 18 June 2001. Also see Jagdish Bhagwati, *In Defence of Globalization*, Oxford University Press, N. Delhi, 2004, pp. 122–34.

More importantly, such codes are accompanied by the requirement of having systems and processes in place to evaluate the performance that is being promised. The attempt to embed 'responsible' practices.

FILTERING IN: CODES AND STANDARDS

Here we look at four such social standards/norms of emerging significance for India: the SA 8000 standards, the Global Compact, the Global Reporting Initiative, and the IFC norms for investments in India. By no means the only ones to have a presence in India, these represent the different sources for such codes. These are also significant in terms of the visibility they have managed to command worldwide and for the reach at two ends of the enterprise spectrum, namely, the upper end of corporate houses, as well the other end formed by the SME. The significance of these commitments, codes, and guidelines for India is discussed in the following pages.

SA 8000

The US Council of Economic Priorities Accreditation Agency (CEPAA), now called Social Accountability International (SAI) was responsible for the development of SA 8000. It is based on the model of the quality and environmental auditing processes of the International Standards Organization of ISO 14000, and ISO 9000. Though voluntary, it is a certification standard for workplace practices and is based on International Labour Organization conventions, the United Nations Convention on the Rights of the Child, and the Universal Declaration of Human Rights. The SA 8000 proposes to be an international workplace performance standard calling in principles and covering issues and practices arising out of these conventions.[4] It includes performance on the following issues:

1. Child labour
2. Forced labour
3. Health and safety
4. Compensation
5. Working hours
6. Discrimination
7. Discipline

[4] Website of SAI *http://www.sa-intl.org/AboutSAI/FastFacts.htm*

8. Free association and collective bargaining
9. Management systems

The last of these is of special significance to the character of SA 8000 in institutionalizing CSR in the organizations that it engages with. It is also a management-led tool for overall standards in global manufacturing organizations.

The SA 8000, being a certification standard, has been able to bring in systems for the management of CSR by insisting as much on structures, processes, and practices as on setting and meeting requirements on the issues detailed. The processes are those of planning, accounting, auditing, and reporting of CSR as part of the complete package. There is also a focus on 'embeddedness' of CSR through structures in place for such interventions. Continuous review and improvement processes and key stakeholder engagements to develop the standards are some of the hallmarks of the system.

For India, as for all parts of the developing world, and for many parts of the developed world as well, the SMEs contribute a not insubstantial share of the GDP and also a considerable share of the employment generated. As pointed out, India's small-scale sector has in the last decade contributed in value anywhere from 30 to 36 per cent of all exports. In an export-led economy, the standards of SMEs with respect to labour and other issues have become important, driven by civil society and political imperatives. In this context, international SA 8000 certification has come to have a certain significance.

The certifying organization SAI was born in its current avatar in early 2000. By spring the same year the SAI had five auditing and testing firms accredited to conduct inspections. SAI certifications are made on a plant-by-plant basis. By late 2000, the SAI had certified sixty-one plants worldwide as being in compliance with the SA 8000 code, of which thirty-four were in China and one in Vietnam.[5]

The growth in the performance of SA 8000 is significant. As per the information available from the SAI in March 2005, SA 8000 certifications had been given in 44 countries, covering 50 industries, certifying 655 facilities, with 430,136 workers. India is one of the leading countries being accredited

---

[5] Douglas A. William, 'Who's Who In Codes-of-Conduct', *New Economic Information Service*, 2 Jan. 2001.

TABLE 7.1: Facilities Certified by SA 8000 by Country and Year

Country	31 March 2005		May 2004	
	Number of facilities	Per cent of total	Number of facilities	Per cent of total
Italy	192	29.3	97	24.3
China	94	14.4	53	13.3
India	93	14.2	47	11.8
Brazil	74	11.3	51	12.8
Pakistan	45	6.9	26	6.5

Source: SAI database.

TABLE 7.2: Workers Covered Under Facilities Certified by
SA 8000 by Country and Year[6]

Workers employed (by country) Country	31 March 2005		May 2004	
	Number of workers	Per cent of total	Number of workers	Per cent of total
China	79,075	18.4	41,766	16.2
India	70,721	16.4	23,073	8.9
Italy	62,666	14.6	50,609	19.6

Source: SAI database.

with SA 8000 certification.[7] China and India are well matched in terms of the SA 8000 coverage of workers employed in these facilities. Between May 2004 and March 2005, India has doubled the facilities with SA 8000 certifications and tripled the workers certified under this programme. On these parameters of the number of facilities certified and the number of workers covered, India is ranked third and second, respectively among nations receiving such certifications. Tables 7.1 and 7.2 show these trends.

Most of the certifications in India are of the apparel and accessories (mostly leather) industry. The removal of quotas in the WTO has opened up the industry everywhere and in India. In a competitive environment,

[6] Ibid SAI 8000.
[7] csr sa 8000 31 March 2005 (accessed on 25th May) and May 2004
http://www.sa-intl.org/Accreditation/SummaryStatistics.htm

for those who source, as well as for Indian exporters, business risk is seen to be tied to 'non-standard' factory and other environment concerns. A convergence of NGOs, foreign missions and government (various ministries) is taking place in order to facilitate those standards. India is no exception to the process. There has been an active engagement in this direction by all these stakeholders here as well.

A case in point of such convergences can be seen in the consultative workshops for textile industry, various government bodies, and the GTZ (German Technical Co-operation). In the information describing the 2004 Tripur consultative workshop, the Textiles Committee, Government of India describes itself as 'having come a long way from the role of an inspection agency, to become a facilitator for quality improvement in Indian textile and clothing industry'. Being competitive in the global marketplace also means being environmentally and socially acceptable. This has put special needs on this industry with its links to a huge contingent of SMEs. Though still largely driven by environmental issues, social factors are beginning to find a place. The Government of India has recognized the need to facilitate this process and this has led to the joint efforts of the Ozone Cell in the Ministry Of Environment and Forests, the Textiles Committee, and the GTZ, the Technical Cell of the German Technical Co-operation in promoting SA 8000 together with ISO 9000 and ISO 14000. The SAI reported in 2002 that, twenty-six meetings in different Indian cities are being convened under the aegis of this group to create awareness of SA 8000, ISO 14000, and ISO 9000 primarily for the SMEs in the decentralized sectors and to provide the findings of industry pollution studies in this segment and the possibility of provision of alternatives. The Textile Committee, Government of India, has offered its facilitative role and already over 300 textile and clothing companies in India have availed the services of this committee in the implementation of ISO 9000, ISO 14000, and SA 8000 standards.

There are innumerable such codes, labelling practices, and norms in business practices that have come to India from the outside via the globalization process. These are, however, not without problems particularly in the social sectors. While they can forge some inroads into social standards, via business, these are really a proxy for the failure to bring these standards of development internally. The broad sweep of what these practices seek to achieve must eventually come from commitment and action from within

India. Other than that these measures, though important in the interim, will not cover the scope of changes that are required and are prone to various kinds of problems. Interestingly 2006 has seen an initiative emerging by the Government of India to get the Bureau of Indian Standards develop Indian certifications on social responsibility indigeneously with multi-stakeholder participation. The motive and expectations are that, shifting the focus to voluntary certification would be a way to ease out of inspector raj.

A key issue in such practices is the increased costs on the local producer. Many of the initiatives in place are however, heavily supported by western buyers, customers, foreign and local governments, and NGOs in the interim period. Associated with this process is the concern that foreign sourcing companies in India, particularly those that are cost sharing in embedding such systems, are likely to deepen a few alliances and seek to institutionalize practices there, rather than seek a spread of suppliers. It is quite likely that in the process many small suppliers, otherwise engaged, together with those employed directly and indirectly through their families would witness a downturn in their fortunes pegged to international buyers, at least in the short run.

Another issue to contend with as a result of the institutionalization processes from outside, is the unequal processes and gyrations in globalization itself. This can lead to even more costs to the producer through exclusion. For example, on the sidelines of Cancun, in a session organized by an Indian NGO, Consumer Unity and Trust Society (CUTS), the noted professor Mustafizur Rahman from the Centre for Policy Dialogue[8] highlighted a fascinating conflict threatening Bangladesh's exports of garments to the United States. Massive investments had been made into Bangladesh EPZs (export promoting zones) by the Japanese and Koreans for modernizing garment exports, primarily exported to the USA. These zones were devoid of trade union activities. The American buyers on the other hand, with a strong AFLCIO (American Federation of Labour and Congress of Industrial Organizations) lobby were concerned about the CSR norms of collective bargaining behind their imports. All parties postured withdrawal, the US threatening withdrawal of the general system of preferences for Bangladesh

---

[8] I am grateful to Professor Rehman for information on this case, 14 August 2005.

and the Koreans wanting to approach the courts for the altered conditions of their investments. As of August 2005, the Bangladesh government was reported as coming to terms with the situation. Training programmes were conducted for workers in the special economic zones with goals of inculcating awareness of rights and also training on responsibilities, so that unions can play a matured role and not succumb to politicization from outside forces.

Another key issue is the plethora of codes that come to many suppliers from buyers abroad. Each will come with its own perspective of what issues are significant, depending on the industry segment, the country of origin, and the influence of those driving the process (civil society groups and government). Rationalization across codes is yet to take place. Companies complain that they have to show compliance to multiple codes.

There is increasing focus over the monitoring and verification challenges of adopted codes. Not only foreign companies operating in India with various codes of their own, but also NGOs supporting various codes are happy to say that they look at the adoption of codes as a process rather than an end product of compliance (although that is the aim). This can span efforts starting from mere disclosure of inadequacies, to identification of action points, first steps to address these, and accounting and managerial practices to capture these changes. In the interim between the first and last steps, the companies are said to belong to the category of 'fairly traded'. For interested consumers of products supposedly made according to these norms, transparency about these facts will need to be forthcoming. Interestingly, foreign companies that have grown out of the European 'fair trade movement' include erstwhile activists in the US, those who have emerged through workers' struggles in developed countries, etc. and are to be found among exporters from India. In some way their business stands apart, either by virtue of redistributing their profits with producer partners, strengthening cooperatives, or commitment to environment-friendly products like organic cotton. These companies are also being interrogated and nudged into more transparency regarding their efforts by other NGOs,[9] who have listed and identified the former's shortcomings.

An altogether different matter is the concern of companies that take on codes that they will be singled out for closer scrutiny and thereby negative

[9] Clean Clothes Campaign, 'Alternative' or 'Ethical Clothes', 2005 (available on http://www.cleanclothes.org/companies/04-04-alternative-ethical-clothes-review.htm).

attention.[10] On the other hand, non-export based companies may not be exposed to these norms. A recent ILO[11] study, however, has suggested that local suppliers in India, who implement codes for their export requirements, have already in place institutionalized embedded systems for implementing these codes.

The Prem Group is a manufacturer-exporter with a 100 per cent cotton garment stitching factory supplying exclusively to Mabrouc SA. Mabrouc requires all its suppliers to be SA 8000 certified. The Prem Group started in 1984 with a production capacity of 0.5 million units per year. With the Indian market growing steadily, the Prem Group in 1999 also supplies Mabrouc with products for the Indian market. The Prem Group, while benefiting from the expanded orders, had to go into vertical integration of companies in order to meet these requirements.

UN Global Compact

Running parallel to these process of 'business models' of CSR, there have been efforts to integrate CSR in India's corporate world through other forces. The UN efforts to get agreement on certain basic principles from the corporate world is one of the high-profile initiatives. Following the World Economic Forum in Davos in 1999, UN Secretary-General Kofi Annan, in consultation with multi-stakeholder groups including the International Chambers of Commerce, International Confederation of Trade Unions, International Employers Organization and NGOs in the areas of human rights and environment, issued the nine principles of a Global Agenda. It urged multinationals and other companies to be part of the Global Compact supporting this agenda. These nine principles were subsequently extended to ten. The UN Global Compact describes its efforts as follows:[12]

The Global Compact's ten principles in the areas of human rights, labour, the environment and anti-corruption, enjoy universal consensus and are derived from:

---

[10] An excellent discussion of challenging issues is brought out in the research by the monitoring and verification working group New Economics Foundation and CIIR 1997, 'Open Trading and Options for Effective Monitoring or Corporate Codes of Conduct', 1997, p. 5.

[11] Nikolai Rogovsky and Emily Sims, 'Corporate Success through People: Making the International Labour Standards Work for you', Management and Corporate Citizen Programme, Job Creation and Enterprise Development Department, 2002, ILO.

[12] *www.unglobalcompact.org*

- The Universal Declaration of Human Rights
- The International Labour Organization's Declaration on Fundamental Principles and Rights at Work.
- The Rio Declaration on Environment and Development
- The United Nations Convention against Corruption

The Global Compact asks companies to embrace, support and enact, within their sphere of influence, a set of core values in the areas of human rights, labour standards, the environment, and anti-corruption:

Human Rights

- *Principle 1*: Businesses should support and respect the protection of internationally proclaimed human rights; and
- *Principle 2*: Make sure that they are not complicit in human rights abuses.

Labour Standards

- *Principle 3*: Businesses should uphold the freedom of association and the effective recognition of the right to collective bargaining;
- *Principle 4:* The elimination of all forms of forced and compulsory labour;
- *Principle 5*: The effective abolition of child labour; and
- *Principle 6*: The elimination of discrimination in respect of employment and occupation.

Environment

- *Principle 7*: Businesses should support a precautionary approach to environmental challenges;
- *Principle 8*: Undertake initiatives to promote greater environmental responsibility; and
- *Principle 9*: Encourage the development and diffusion of environmentally-friendly technologies.

Anti-Corruption

- *Principle 10*: Businesses should work against all forms of corruption, including extortion and bribery.

While recognizing the important and new role that the UN can play in advocacy, there is legitimate discomfort among non-business stakeholders that due to the totally voluntary nature of the principles, corporate members will use the branding of the UN without any substantive changes in favour of the principles. Though there are specific guidelines as to how members can take this participation forward, adherence to them is not compulsory. It can fully be expected that lack of sincerity towards the principles will create civil society demands for disclosure.

In addition to observing the commitments of the framework of the Global Compact, a company may wish to actively support the principles and broad United Nation's goals by initiating and participating in projects in partnerships with the United Nations (Annexure 7A).

A number of companies/ institutions in India formed the Global Compact Society on 24 November 2003. The Indian Global Compact Society boasts of the second largest country membership of the Global Compact taken as a whole. As of March 2003 there were 717 companies subscribing to the Global Compact internationally. The single largest group of companies in this was from Spain (118) followed by India and the Philippines with 92 companies each.

Recent data from the UN show that after a hesitant start, the Indian chapter spurted ahead, but it has shown only small gains in recent years in terms of membership. The membership figures in India for the Global Compact over the years are as follows: 3 for the year 2000, 54 for 2001, 20 for 2002, 8 for 2003, 7 for 2004, 2 for 2005.[13] In the initial years the Society had a predominance of public-sector companies. The first fifty-four members were also heavily drawn from public-sector companies.[14] This was partly due to the role played by the Chairman of Scope, Dr Uddesh Kohli, who was among the two persons from India who were invited to attend the first meeting of the Compact (the other being a senior representative of the Tatas). Currently in 2005, both public- and private-sector companies are represented, with a preponderance of the latter.

Though several companies in India listed under the Compact website are known for CSR practices of various kinds, the required posting of case studies on the UN website and examples of their work, projects, and communication on projects has not matched the membership.[15] In order to assess performance on this, a recent compilation was made for the Global Compact meeting held in 2005 in Barcelona. This indicated that only 38

[13] The Global Compact. Ibid.

[14] Ibid.

[15] Interview with Dr Uddesh Kohli who is the focal point for the Global Compact in India, September 2005.

per cent of Indian companies on the Global Compact website were complying with the requirement of communication on projects (that is 37 out of 97 companies), with another 12 in process (Annexure 7B). However, the Global Compact in India in comparison to other countries is much more institutionalized in the sense of constituting a legal body, with a secretariat support. The Compact has plans to decentralize focal points of contact as a way of drawing in more membership as well as encouraging better voluntary compliance.

Global Reporting Initiative

The Global Reporting Initiative (GRI) is another effort by an independent, multi-firm body, which has gained a modest membership worldwide and a few high profile recruits in India. The GRI has what is known as the 'triple bottom line' (TBL) approach, which emphasizes the need for reporting on non-financial parameters of a company's performance. The triple bottom line refers to what is popularly called the 'people, plant, and profit' approach, including as it does the need to report on the financial, environmental, and social aspects of a company's operation. Companies following its guidelines have to report their performance on these three parameters. The GRI helps provide a framework for financial, environmental, and social reporting on several indicators. As in the case of SA 8000, this reporting framework is increasingly getting the endorsement of governments worldwide.

As of May 2005, 665 companies were registered as subscribing to the GRI guidelines worldwide.[16] Among these, seven companies were from India. Subscribing to the GRI guidelines formalizes the system of tracking company performance not just on financial matters but also on non-financial matters. It provides a framework for social and environmental issues, and has norms of disclosure. These are small beginnings but a focused part of the institutionalization process. The companies in India that have registered as subscribing to these guidelines and reporting on them are as follows:

---

[16] See GRI website http://globalreporting.org/guidelines/reports/searchResults.asp? Name=&Country=%3D62&subSector=%3C%3E-1&ReportType=%3C%3E%27NonGRI %27&Submit=Search

Name of company	Product
Dr Reddy's Laboratories	Health-care products
Ford India	Automotive
ITC Limited	Other
Jubilant Organosys	Chemicals
Paharpur Business Centre	Commercial services
Tata Motors	Automotive
The Tata Iron & Steel Company Limited	Metals products

Consultancy services are available in India for developing structures and processes for these specialized codes/norms/reporting practices as well as to embed more generalized approaches for institutionalizaton of CSR. Many of these follow and use the tools of financial accounting practices. These can be customized to the CSR requirements in different sectors. Typically, this starts with the identification of policy and approach followed by the identification of indicators to capture its presence in the institutionalization of company practices, followed by benchmarking, auditing, verification, certification, and reporting. Each of these processes can in turn have levels of standards of excellence. Policy, issues, and standards expected by business and society are constantly evolving, indicating the scope for constant improvement. Challenges for internalising issues like ethics,[17] which is the framework under which norms develop, are ever present and require changes in world-views. While these cannot be mandated by law, there is some unbundelling of ethics through various compliance imperatives outside of law that is emerging. This is addressed in the following pages.

IFC

Selected CSR compliance requirements are increasingly gaining presence on account of international investors. Demonstrating such compliance leads to further formalization and embedding of such norms. Typical of investor-driven CSR is that of the International Finance Corporation (IFC), which is the private-sector arm of the World Bank Group. Its mandate is to support

[17] Dipankar Gupta, *Ethics Incorporated Top Priority and Bottom Line*. KPMG, Harper Collins, India, 2004.

poverty reduction in member countries through increased private-sector investments with an eye on minimal social fallout. The IFC is the largest multilateral organization providing loans and equity to private companies in developing countries. The IFC-held portfolio in India is one of the largest worldwide and stands at US $1.2 billion. Out of this, infrastructure has a 14 per cent share, oil and gas 7 per cent, manufacturing 37 per cent, finance 33 per cent, and IT 9 per cent. The South Asia Region Office has most of the forty enterprises it currently supports in India.

The requirement of integration of CSR issues in the IFC is reflected in a number of ways. These include the IFC's approach, the menu of social and environmental issues to be considered for prospective customers, the requirement of integration of these aspects through all phases of the project cycle, measurement of sustainability of such integration, exclusion of projects considered risky socially and environmentally, and facilitative set-up for customers to meet these requirements.

As far as the approach is concerned, this is reflected in the way that IFC views risk. Its enterprise risk management, includes not just credit risk, financial risk, and operational risk but also strategic risk. This latter includes environmental, social, and reputational risk. Following this design by the IFC in analysing risk, twelve international commercial banks adopted this approach in 2003 and twelve others followed suit in 2004.[18]

Policy statements and guidelines outline the kinds of expectations from customers. While the environmental aspects have now become familiar, the social aspects include wide issues like those relating to safeguarding cultural property in IFC-financed projects, involuntary settlement issues, and impact on indigenous peoples.

The processes to be followed at the IFC require the integration of these at almost all stages of the project cycle. Environmental and social aspects are to be considered right from early review, through post-disbursement supervision.[19] There are also requirements of public consultation for categories of projects deemed to be particularly risky with respect to the environmental and social issues.

In early 2001, the IFC developed a framework for measuring sustainability of environmental and social clauses introduced in IFC projects. This has

---

[18] *IFC Annual Report 2004*, vol. 2, pp. 11–12.

[19] IFC Environment and Social Review Procedure on IFC website.

also led to further streamlining of existing standards and reporting practices,[20] and to processes and structures for embedding CSR in projects supported.

Like any investment business, the IFC has a list of social exclusion screens indicating what kinds of business investments it will not finance. This screen is fairly extensive including a rejection of projects that are not only environmentally risky but also deemed to be socially avoidable (see Annexure 7C). These include exclusion of business that engages in production of trade in weapons, alcoholic beverages, gambling casinos, etc.

The Development Corporation assists in various ways to address the social and environmental issues through the proposal, and implementation stages of IFC projects. The IFC office in Delhi steers and provides support to address and mitigate the social and environmental aspects of individual projects. The office, among other things, encourages clients to see the business model of these initiatives, showing how following environmental and social requirements helps the business case as well. It also assists in identifying consultants and NGO partners who can work with the companies to enable them to meet the requirements, provides and leverages other funds available to the clients, and does the monitoring and evaluation of this during project phases.

The IFC accords special focus to SMEs as being a significant part of market economies. In line with this overall emphasis, this office has also been looking at the value chain and SMEs connected with the businesses that are being supported in Asia and India. Embedding workplace and extra-workplace practices, relating to HIV/AIDS is another area that is encouraged to be undertaken and is driven to the worldwide attention and resources given to this area.

The Indian companies are reported to be positive about taking on these challenges. Fulfilling these environmental and social requirements is of course a condition of investment support. Additionally, companies are said to view meeting these challenges as a branding exercise as well. The resource commitment for such efforts, however, is considerable and often comes as a surprise according to the IFC office in India. The corporates are expected to contribute two-thirds of the costs for mitigation of adverse social and environmental impacts, while the IFC contributes approximately one-third.

---

[20] IFC, Measuring Sustainability: A Framework for Private Sector Investments 2003—A Framework for the Analysis of Environmental, Social and Corporate Governance Performance, IFC, USA, 2003.

Some resources can be raised by the IFC through donor organizations and in the case of AIDS this can contribute as much as 50 per cent of the costs estimated for interventions.

INTERNAL APPROACHES

Outside of external forces driving the institutionalization of CSR, institutionalizing CSR is generally acknowledged as being fairly weak in India. The single most comprehensive insight comes out of the occasional CSR survey of corporate India conducted by PIC in collaboration with IMRB, the market research organization. Of the several areas covered in the 2003 survey of CSR by PIC, issues relating to institutionalization of CSR in India find a special focus.[21]

CSR practitioners like to look to the existence of a written CSR policy as a vital sign of commitment and follow-up action in this area. It appears that only 17 per cent of companies surveyed have a written CSR policy according to the 2003 survey; this however is up from 11 per cent in the comparable previous survey in 2000. The upward trend was apparent across different types of companies in India—private companies, multinational companies (MNCs) and public sector undertakings (PSUs). The higher values for engagement were particularly marked in the case of PSUs in India, where written policies existed in 48 per cent of the cases. It was also the finding of this survey that the translation of a policy into action was more likely to take place in areas like labour and environment.

Evidence of embedding CSR into company structures is less encouraging. The assigning of an individual to take care of CSR (evidenced in 16 per cent of companies surveyed), or anchoring CSR in a given department (27 per cent of companies) was infrequent. CSR was mostly an activity driven from the top. It is a matter of considerable anguish (and not just in India) that the CSR principles structures and processes take significant effort to travel to middle management. It is certainly not the case that this does not happen. In fact, a not insignificant percentage of company policy (11 per cent for Indian companies; 44 per cent for MNCs in India and 24 per cent for PSUs) originated from company employees below the level of the CEO, CMD/MD.

[21] PIC, 'Third Report on Corporate Social Responsibility', 2003.

National-level business associations are also providing guidelines and codes of conduct for broader issues. The Confederation of Indian Industries (CII) has brought out a code for its membership (see Chapter 3), which encourages this.

There are of course, examples of institutionalizing CSR in India by individual companies, much before the external influences became part of India. Here again what the Tatas do becomes a benchmark for others to follow. Tata steel and the Tata group of companies have been in the forefront of institutionalizing CSR practices from very early on. The institutionalization process leads from the high priority given to issues of values, which drives the company.[22] The Tata Council for Community Initiatives (TCCI) is a focal point of that institutionalization across and above the individual Tata companies. The policy at Council level, is carried through an Executive Committee and Secretariat, through Regional groups, and Local Area Networks. The common direction is indicated at the policy level, and each company has the flexibility to develop interactively under this aegis.

Key aspects of the process include a commitment to a minimum programme. The approach to the programme is one of service, building community and the quality of life, facilitating sustainable networks, building through conflict resolution, evolving and changing at individual, team and company levels, performance-orientedness, being a facilitator, getting into a whole new way of being, continuous improvement and self-reliance, encouraging cultural change in public attitudes and government, perceiving this as a process of self-development.

What sets this group of companies apart is not just the clarity of vision and emphasis on core values. There is also great emphasis on internalizing this. Ratan Tata, Group Chairman, spoke on this issue in an interview in 2002.

Business, as I have seen it, places one great demand on you: it needs you to self-impose a framework of ethics, values, fairness and objectivity on yourself at all times. It is easy not to do this; you cannot impose it on yourself forcibly because it has to become an integral part of you. What has to go through your mind at the time of every decision, or most decisions, is: does this stand the test of public scrutiny...? As you think the decision through, you have to automatically feel that this is wrong, incorrect, or unfair...[23]

[22] Tata Sons, Tata Council for Community Initiatives, Guidelines for Community Development, 2000.

[23] See Tata website on Ethics http://www.tata.com/0_our_commitment/corporate_governance/overview.htm

In the context of new global levels of codes/ labelling and guidelines, Tata steel has come into prominence once again. Its recent acceptance of the SA 8000 certification will open up labour standards even to contractors who supply labour to Tatas. Similarly, the GRI standards discussed earlier have two of the Tata group companies subscribing and reporting as per this framework. Besides, senior leadership from the Tatas is also represented on the board of the GRI. The GRI is increasingly being supported by world governments for popularizing its use for reporting as per the triple bottom line.

Many of the institutionalization processes described in this chapter have emerged out of the global swirl of changes. These business-driven models relating to compliance to norms on labour and environment and society issues cannot be underestimated. They are at this time small steps in a huge and inevitable direction. If examples from other countries are any indication of what the future portends, one can expect greater engagement by the Government of India in facilitating and encouraging these processes, as has already begun to happen.

CHAPTER 8

GOVERNMENTS' GROOMING FOR CSR
GLOBAL AND INDIAN RESPONSE

Do governments have any role at all to play with respect to promoting CSR? For a country like India, recently out of the throes of a command-type economy, such a proposition is likely to be anathema to the business world. It conjures up visions of control and constraint to operate competitively in a global world.

Yet, in the advanced capitalist countries of the world, governments are playing rather extensive roles in a variety of initiatives to encourage CSR. The context and circumstances of CSR have influenced this engagement. There are also incipient signs of change in India as well.

THE GLOBAL CONTEXT

Inviting corporate initiatives in social development has not, until recently, had uniform reception even from nations in the developed world.[1] In France, Belgium, and Germany, countries with heavy taxes and strong emphasis on public sector, governments are expected and continue to play a strong role in development. Here there is much more discomfort, if not suspicion, of the role that corporates can play in social development through CSR. The UK and USA have exhibited much more flexibility and demand more from business. These countries have also pursued reduced tax regimes for business. They have also been countries aggressively promoting business engagement in CSR and public–private partnerships of various kinds.

There is another important context that has also influenced the government's role in CSR. One of the key features of twenty-first century capitalism can be described as its capacity to recreate not just the economic

[1] EU-India CSR, FICCI, 'Corporate Social Responsoibility: The Cross Cultural Perspective', 2001.

environment but the social environment at an unprecedented pace. In this, governments have begun to recognize the role of multi-stakeholder groups to address changes under way. In their view the 'consultation society' has emerged as the right and proper way to effectively bring about change. There is a strong push for 'participatory democracy' in addition to a representative one. The European Union and indeed many of the developed countries are known to fund and support the representative groups of many constituencies to play an important role in parliamentary processes and government policy. These new roles of civil society have compelled government to respond in various ways as well.

One of the demands of these civil society constituencies has been for close government scrutiny of issues of corporate responsibility, particularly in the dealings of companies outside their respective countries. The feeling about this is that companies must observe the higher home country norms, wherever they are, irrespective of laws (or lack of them) and other regulatory requirements where they operate. Two major streams of this kind of effort are clearly visible. One has been with respect to multinationals or the transnational corporations and their dealings in other countries. The other has to do with the cross-border production processes, which link transnational business with less regulated SMEs in the developing world.

Another trigger for government call for CSR has come from the fact that major economic changes have created other kinds of requirements of governments. The management of government roles to meet these challenges has been found wanting. For this corporate expertise is sought for addressing many national-level issues.

There is also recognition that the business model of CSR does not cover all contingencies where CSR is called for. These are situations where there is new awareness of 'costs' to society emanating out of business performance. An interesting argument has been made to highlight the limits of the business case for corporate responsibility on the basis of the experience in the UK.[2] Sustainability, it argues, is rarely in the immediate interest of business, which continues to be guided by the financial fourth quarter, bottom line. For instance, 'sustainable forest management is almost always

---

[2] Roger Cowe and Jonathon Porritt, *Government's Business—Enabling Corporate Sustainability*, Forum for Future, London, 2002, pp. 13, 19, 33.

less profitable than unsustainable exploitation'. Similarly, for all the talk about long-term investments, only 3 per cent of fund managers cited social and environmental issues[3] as criteria for investment. Ethical investments for all their growth are only a small part of total investments. Enquiries about ethical corporations by young entrants, if ever voiced, normally end when candidates become employees. Consumers for all their talk about ethical business (all surveys have shown), will often buy cheapest. NGOs for all their commitment have limitations of upscaling operations or targeting unfunded requirements.

However questions about balancing social costs are articulated. 'Sustainably harvested wood costs more but is less expensive than wood from destruction of forests.' The promise of higher standards of living, and jobs for many run parallel with inadequate social security, health, and education provisions and so on. It is to answer these queries to their constituencies that governments have begun to see a new role for themselves and others as well, including that of their corporate allies.

In developed countries, government intervention in CSR has taken many forms. Broadly it has aimed at facilitating business engagement in corporate responsibility and not to scare it away. In effect, though, the interventions have included finely nuanced options. These range from voluntarism on the one hand to more persuasive and incentivized opportunities on the other, followed by guidelines bordering on compulsion. The slow encroachment of norms into legislation is a natural evolution in a quickly changing world. But by and large the approach for CSR by governments so far has been to manage the changed scenarios by engaging as much with corporates as with other stakeholder groups in this process.

Developing countries like India have also begun to respond to these changes. As many of the examples in earlier chapters have shown, there is an emerging government- private sector engagement to meet the demands of civil society here and elsewhere. However, the developed countries have been at this endeavour for a long time. It is important to point out that such roles have been extensive and expanding on an almost monthly basis. Selected milestones in government roles in CSR, as well as those with some relevance for India are discussed.

---

[3] Ibid., pp. 13, 19, 33.

Institutionalizing Government Development Policy and CSR

Across the developed world, a number of institutional arrangements have been put in place for a government role in CSR. These have emerged to address specifically national as well as international requirements relating to CSR. Many of the former have direct relevance for India in terms of the facilitative roles government can play for encouraging CSR. The following are examples worldwide of some of the policies, mechanisms, and initiatives taken by governments for CSR.

The United Kingdom has been at the forefront of government initiatives in CSR. Little known to the developing world, in the spring of 2000, the then new Labour government in the United Kingdom, appointed the world's first Minister for Corporate Social Responsibility, Kim Howells. The post was positioned in the Department of Trade and Industry (DTI).[4] Within the DTI, it was the 'Social Exclusion Unit's Policy Action Team' looking at inner-city rejuvenation which spearheaded the campaign for a minister for CSR. On taking office, Mr Howells issued a report of case studies in CSR, highlighting the business role in CSR and affirming his government's view that CSR is a key component of mainstream competitiveness as well.

It was also stated that the goal would be to ensure fiscal and regulatory frameworks to encourage CSR rather than stifle it, and to evolve areas of partnership for business and government in the priority areas outlined by the nation. Subsequent to this date there have been over sixty government initiatives of relevance to CSR in the UK.[5]

Structural mechanisms were also in place to facilitate government engagement. At parliamentary level, there were two all-party groups on corporate citizenship.[6] The All Party Parliamentary Group on Corporate Social Responsibility, and the All Party Parliamentary Group on Socially Responsible Investment.

The Ethical Trading Initiative, a multi-stakeholder group of retailers, NGOs, and trade unions, is supported by the international development wing of the British government (DFID) to evolve and implement practical

---

[4] Ibid., p. 12.

[5] Center for Social Markets, Corporate Citizenship—Challenging 'Business–as-Usual', Center for Social Markets, London, Kolkata, 2001, p. 5 (also see www.societyandbusiness.gov.uk).

[6] Ibid., p. 2.

ways of ensuring international norms in their supply chain across the globe. India, as one of the key player in this sourcing chain, is also one of their countries of operation.

The CSR Minister was not alone in outlining what the government needs to do or the priority to be given to institutionalizing CSR in the government. Two organizations outside of government produced a catchingly titled report, ' "Good morning Minister, here is your job description"— The Government mandate for Corporate Social Responsibility'. This contained recommendations arising out of a survey of expectations from the CSR Minister.[7] The two organizations producing the report were the New Economics Foundation, which describes itself as an independent think tank, working with a wide network of NGOs, public-sector bodies and business, and Business in the Community, which is described as a business-led movement of over 700 companies including 70 per cent of the FTSE 500 companies. The survey was of experts in the field from business and industry leaders, NGOs, media, CSR practitioners and others.

As far as government engagement for CSR was concerned, the survey not only confirmed the need for the role, but asked for an enhanced profile for the Minister (considered at that time to be a junior minister) in charge of CSR. Specifically, overwhelmingly (83 per cent) of those surveyed urged that the Minister be dedicated full time. Most surveyed also recommended (60 per cent) that there should be an independent CSR unit within government with its own budget and dedicated staff. They also suggested strongly (69 per cent) that the Minister report to a higher ranked member than the one he reported to being in the DTI. A significant number (43 per cent) asked for direct reporting to the Prime Minister.

In terms of developing mechanisms, other European countries have taken steps for enhancing the government role in CSR.[8] At the European level there was a call at the Lisbon Summit in 2000 by heads of state, for CSR as an important link for reaching the 'strategic goal for a knowledge-based and highly competitive, as well as socially inclusive Europe'.

---

[7] New Economics Foundation and Business in the Community 'Good Morning Minister, here is your job description—the government mandate for Corporate Social Responsibility', June 2001.

[8] The Copenhagen Centre, '*It Simply Works Better—Campaign Report on European CSR Excellence 2002–2003*', The Copenhagen Centre, 2005, pp. 3, 46–7.

Many countries have taken the lead in providing high-level focus to CSR. For instance, in June 2002 France appointed France's first Minister on Sustainable Development.

Sweden & Norway led similar initiatives. In March 2002, the Swedish Partnership for Global Responsibility was launched by three ministers— the Ministers of Trade, Foreign Affairs, and International Development Corporation. This invited business to join the partnership. This would entail public commitment to the OECD guidelines and the UN Global Compact as a way of boosting its credibility.

Consultative Processes

Multi-stakeholder groups have contributed to government intervention in CSR. On the other hand, governments have also been instrumental in creating conditions for the development of multi-stakeholder groups, including that of business. Their combined inputs guide the paths forward in various ways. All across Europe this approach is apparent. The UK Ethical Trading Initiative has already been mentioned. The Norwegian Ministry of Foreign Affairs set up a consultative body in 1997 including employers association, and government employees, trade unions and NGOs for looking at human rights overseas.[9]

The Netherlands Government has a strong consultative process for CSR. One of the two main advisory bodies on social and economic issues, *Sociaal-Economische Raad* (SER) is a body set up by government in 1950 under the Industrial Organization Act. It is a tripartite body of trade union federations, national employers associations and independent members. In response to a government query, the SER developed the Corporate Social Responsibility: Advisory Report.[10] The response of the government to this report outlines the Dutch government strategy for CSR.

One of the most significant aspects of the government's response is its overwhelming endorsement of the SER report, which can be seen to be the result of the European promotion of what SER calls a 'consultation economy'. The surprise lies in some of its recommendations and achievements. In the debate on compulsion versus voluntarism for CSR, both

---

[9] Ibid., pp. 81–2.

[10] *Sociaal-Economische Raad, Corporate Social Responsibility: A Dutch Approach*, Koninklijke Van Gorcum: The Netherlands, 2001, p. 7.

government and SER favoured the latter. This led to decentralized decision making and decisions on cost-neutral reduction in working hours and wage moderation. Interestingly, what would appear as difficult to achieve was arrived at through the 1996 agreement addressing issues of 'Flexibility and Security' head on. This led the way for Dutch dismissal of the protection law as described in the SER report. 'Basically it exchanges a relaxation of the statutory protection against dismissal under regular employment contracts for an improvement in the rights of temporary workers. It therefore exemplifies the value of following the "win-win" strategies.'[11]

However, it cannot be overemphasized that CSR must be viewed as straddling a continuum from pure voluntarism to encouraged engagement and legislation. The government stance is that CSR is a response to structural changes and 'there is also every reason for the government to continue to respond to this, flexibly and in many different forms'.[12]

The Dutch government's approach, also detailed in the report,[13] outlines what it will do at local, regional, national, and international levels. (Annexure 8A).

In Germany the state has played a key role historically as manager and provider of social services. In 1999, the German Parliament appointed a study commission[14] made up of a broad coalition of political parties to report on the 'Future of Civic Activities'. The key finding released in 2002 was to point out the important role companies had to play, and the support that the commission would provide to such endeavours.

Legislatives and Directives

Nudging CSR in place also occurs by means of directives that stop short of legislation. These may become laws as well. They begin by pointing at the direction of desired change. Their intentions are thinly veiled. The last decade has seen many such directives impinging on CSR whose scope though is extremely wide, but yet a few directions can be indicated.

The UK government's review of company law resulted in a White Paper in July 2002 (which was to form the basis of a new companies bill) which encouraged corporates to look at long-term positions wherever they were in

---

[11] SER, 2001, pp. 8–9.
[12] Ibid., p. 108.
[13] Ibid., pp. 100–11.
[14] Copenhagen Centre, 2002–03 ibid., 'It Simply Works Better', pp. 60–1.

the shareholders' interests. It also maintained that large companies, while setting out the Operations and Financial Review should consider reporting on social and environmental issues to allow their shareholders to better assess the company's performance.[15] Though the tone was voluntary, as the report suggests, 'Ultimately the directors may need to defend their process behind the reporting before the courts'![16]

In 2001, the Prime Minister in Britain 'challenged' all FTSE 350 companies to report on environmental performance by the end of 2001.[17] In keeping with the approach of the European Commission, the UK government's review of company law had to have multi-stakeholder examination of all social, economic, and environmental implications of company law.

The Pensions Act amendment in 2000 required the fund trustees to report on the extent of CSR in their investment decisions, without necessarily including them as mandatory for investment. There are several other legislative measures like the climate change levy in 2002, the increased land fill tax, the community investment tax credit to get business into disadvantaged communities, which pointed to government initiatives for the direction of CSR in the UK.[18] In 1999, the Turnbull report required company directors to include a consideration of environmental reputation and business probity in their risk management strategies.

Belgium's Social Label Law is another example of some of the ambiguities sought to be straddled. While the law is aimed at promoting socially-responsible production (produced with respect to four fundamental social rights, secured by eight basic ILO conventions), the label is a voluntary scheme. It is not a condition for selling products in the Belgian market.[19]

France was the first country to require publicly-listed companies to bring out their triple bottom line reports with guidance as to how to do it.

Government CSR

Apart from such mechanisms in place, it is noteworthy that a portion of the role of government in CSR was often directed towards itself. It was

---

[15] Cowe and Porritt, *Government's Business*, p. 9.

[16] Ibid., p. 9.

[17] Center for Social Markets, *Corporate Citizenship*, p. 3.

[18] Cowe and Porritt, *Government's Business*, p. 8.

[19] The Copenhagen Centre, 'It Simply Works Better', p. 23.

quite clear that multi-stakeholder engagements would come up with such suggestions. In fact this is a theme that is addressed in many countries.

The UK survey cited earlier actually recommended that in addition to encouraging CSR among private business, government should turn its gaze upon itself. For the governmental role in the UK survey, there was strong recommendation (70 per cent) that the government should itself submit to good CSR practices as well. It was suggested that policy coherence between departments should be promoted and in things like procurement government should 'lead by example'.[20]

Italy has also been in the forefront of bringing CSR to government processes. In 2001, an ambitious proposal was put forward by Tuscany's public authorities. It required that all public procurements be done from SA 8000 certified companies (that is a fairly rigorous workplace certification in accordance with international labour and human rights norms). Eventually, this was not committed to *in toto*, but even in reduced form it provided the framework for substantial outcomes. The restatement committed that, rather than requiring that all supplier companies be certified, companies with such certifications would be given priority in public procurements. To facilitate this process, Tuscany authorities pledged to pay a portion (half in this case) of the consulting and verification costs of the company.[21] This strategy by the government to promote social and other certification standards can be found elsewhere as well.

In the Netherlands, the SER, the multi-stakeholder advisory group, had also made a strong case for government CSR, which is worth noting in detail.[22]

The government as a market party: The government also acts as a market party itself. It is an employer, procurer and contractor. In this role, the government will benefit from conducting itself in accordance with the principles of corporate social responsibility. For the government, too, responsibility does not end with its statutory commitments. Initiatives such as the 'sustainable procurement' and 'innovative tendering' are examples of government policies designed specifically to modernise government procurement and contracting policy.

---

[20] New Economics Foundation and Business in the Community, 'Good Morning Minister'.

[21] The Copenhagen Centre, 'It Simply Works Better', p. 66.

[22] SER, *Corporate Social Responsiobility*, p. 112. The government planned to formulate a guide for socially responsible procurement and contracting.

Similarly in Belgium, social clauses, requiring the cosideration of the social and ethical performance of supplier companies are increasingly being added to municipal tenders.[23]

Convergence of values of what is considered ethical is of course, at the heart of many issues globally. Within developed countries this consideration can be equally compelling, but the outcomes suggest that global commitments set the agenda. An interesting dilemma presented itself in Sweden[24] with respect to government CSR. In 2002, the government asked for state-owned national pension funds to take ethical concerns into investment decisions. The 'ethical' values were to be those of Sweden's National Parliament. The usual negative screens used for ethical investments for private-sector industry are often linked to business in 'undesirable' areas like weapons production, tobacco, nuclear energy. However, in the Swedish government case these were all considered legal and 'ethical' as per the criteria defined earlier. Sweden's international commitments often pointed in another direction. Managing these, the official position is for 'active engagement' to improve social performance. Similarly, the government has also been called into question for the investment portfolio of their Petroleum Fund involved in companies producing landmines, ammunition, and tobacco, and engaged in gambling.

Incentivizing CSR for Social Policy

A great deal of effort has been forthcoming in these countries, on a facilitative role by government for CSR. This includes, among other things, putting in place mechanisms at various levels of government for encouraging CSR, creating awareness and guidance for CSR reporting on social, economic and environment issues, awareness of OECD and other accepted guidelines for business functioning; it also includes case study initiation and presentation and compilation, and increasing emphasis on understanding both local laws and international commitments that are sometimes in contrast to one another. In many countries there is financial and non-financial support for understanding and skills to meet reporting standards. Innovative partnerships between government and the private sector have emerged on many of the issues of social concerns, which has relevance for India as well.

---

[23] The Copenhagen Centre, 'It Simply Works Better', p. 55.
[24] Ibid., pp. 82–3.

Creating Employability

Governments in the developed countries have played a significant role in drawing business commitment in various types of CSR engagement for employment-related issues. These can be instructive for India.

All over Europe the state is faced with 'employability' issues. Denmark is a country known for securing generous social security benefits. From the beneficiaries' point of view, living standards assured by the state, minimize some of the sting of unemployment. However, the state was expected to provide, not least of all social security payments. Additionally, other problems were also noticed from the state's perspective. Securing minimum living standards was not sufficient to ward off 'exclusions' of other kinds. These included health, substance abuse, etc. exclusions due to long-time rupture from the labour market, which now demanded new skills. Creating employability for the unemployed was considered a challenge in the 1990s. With active financial and non-financial commitments by the state, the business world was drawn in to address these issues. This kind of engagement in Denmark has been described as moving away from a welfare-state model to a new form of network-based governance.[25]

In fact, legislation was put in place for public/private and other stakeholder groups to facilitate this process. As per the Act on Legal Protection and Administration in Social Matters passed in Parliament effective from 1 January 1999, all local authorities in Denmark are obligated to have Local Co-ordination Committees—a multi-stakeholder bodies including local representatives from the Muncipal Council, the Danish Employers' Federation, the Danish Confederation of Trade Unions, the Confederation of Civil Servants, the Organization of General Practitioners, the National Labour Market Authority, and the Council of Organization for the Disabled. This was to ensure that local social and labour market challenges were addressed from a number of angles. This was preceded in 1994 by 'Our Common Concern Campaign' to engage the private sector for tackling some of Denmark's social problems. This led to a very conducive environment for multi-stakeholder collaboration. Ninety-three per cent of the 149 coordination committees expressed 'satisfactory or very satisfactory' cooperation and over 60 per cent expressed improvement of relations with other partners.[26]

---

[25] Ibid., p. 28.

The Ministry of Employment appointed the National Network (which includes 5 regional business networks covering 400 companies and 14 business executives) as advisory members to address the challenges of unemployment. However, government plays an important role. They are not only more 'flexible' with the kind of employability that is offered to business, but the local coordination committee also trains for employability. One of the committees reported that about 25 per cent so trained had got job offers.

The government also plays another role. For 'sheltered jobs'—that is to say jobs for the long-term unemployed, refugees, and immigrants—the government allow persons with reduced working capacity to apply for part of their salary from the government. While business gives them a chance of employment, any inadequacies in terms of skill are compensated by government subsidy to employ these persons. Business efforts are in the willingness to be so engaged in wider social concerns.

'Unemployed' issues are also coming up in another way in other European countries.[27] Ireland, with technically full employment, is faced with dwindling worker availability. The labour shortage is sought to be overcome in innovative ways. The Irish government decided to develop a linkage programme for reintegrating 'offenders' into society. The state's probation and welfare office linked with business networks, for both training and job placement. Approximately two years after the inception of this programme in 2000, approximately 1125 referrals were made to this programme, of which about half were placed in full-time employment and the rest in training schemes. The experience of business is reflected in the feedback for more such employees. The feedback is also that these employees are not foreseen to be targeted for redundancy.

Developing Entrepreneurship

Worldwide, in Europe as a whole, and for Portugal specifically, SMEs are a significant aspect of business. However, survival rates are known to be at the 50 per cent mark only. Portugal's response to remedy this has lessons for India. The government is in active partnership with business in developing these enterprises linked to their business. If the European Union's experience

[26] Ibid., pp. 27–9.
[27] Ibid., pp. 57–9.

is anything to go by, survival rates have risen upto 80 per cent after such interventions.

Portugal has responded by creating 'business incubators' in the initiative by the name of Social Employment Market (MSE) set up in 1996.[28] The MSE is the outcome of collaboration between eight ministries and ten business associations. This constitutes a public–private partnership to support the development of small business through the creation of 'insertion' business. This provides guidance for business plans, to run, administer, and develop the business.

Government/business partnership in a related field is to be found in Italy. Access to credit for the disadvantaged in Italy was very low. Alternative private usury serviced this need at very high costs. In 1996, the problem resulted in a national law, compelling regional authorities to take an active role in preventing usury. Together with public authorities, a multi-stakeholder group, including a church-based voluntary organization of great antiquity (750 years) and a private bank and its foundation, worked for an innovative solution. In Tuscany this worked successfully and is described as not being a 'charity' solution. A key part of this was the support to prepare loan applications, which was done by the retired employees of the bank, in collaboration with the voluntary organization with deep connections in the community. The loan fund was put up by a pool of local banks, to be disbursed at low interest rates recoverable over a five year period. The regional government authorities played a catalyst role in guaranteeing the loan awarded by the pool of banks. Over 50 per cent of the loan applications were financed, securing a 95 per cent recovery.

CONTEXTS FOR INDIA

Nothing on the scale mentioned above, with respect to apex-level government facilitating CSR, is apparent in India. A national vision and acceptance of the role that the private sector can play in development is yet to fully emerge. However, trends by the Government of India for facilitating CSR in the private sector can be discerned and the direction is unmistakeable.

[28] Ibid., pp. 74–5, 80–3.

The push comes from both internal and external forces and they are often interlinked. Some of the externally-driven government initiatives for CSR come via the forces of globalization as alluded to in the earlier chapters. Multilateral organizations have found the national commitments on the Millinieum Development Goals, as a space through which initiatives can emerge. Other initiatives have emerged from the role played by state governments in encouraging private-sector participation for development of the state. Finally, there are the CSR models of the public-sector companies, which with considerable presence in the economy, lead by example. A cursory glance at the spread of such initiatives will outline these emerging trends.

Facilitating the SME Links

A third of India's exports comes from the SMEs. The small-scale and informal sector is increasingly coming under pressure to meet environmental and social standards. The government of India as facilitating their competitiveness through supporting efforts in this area. This is done through a combination of awareness generation of various codes and norms required of SMEs. An earlier chapter has referred to the joint efforts of the Ozone Cell in the Ministry of Environment and Forests, the Textiles Committee, and the GTZ—the Technical Cell of the German Technical Cooperation—in promoting SA 8000 together with ISO 9000 and ISO 14000 in SMEs nationally in the clothing industry. These efforts also bring the much-needed convergence between ministries for achieving this. Similar interventions are being promoted in other areas through government bodies like APEDA, and the Ministry of Small-scale Industry for the agricultural sector.

Revamping Infrastructure

Other government interventions come at city and state levels. This is typical of the examples of public–private partnerships in education and IT education, which have been detailed in earlier chapters. Here the governments' role has come in different ways. In some cases, it has meant an openness to engage with private-sector CSR initiatives of mutual interest to the private sector and government. In another case, a series of public–private initiatives for development in Bangalore, Karnataka, have become a landmark of sorts, for revamping of civic facilities and other services.[29] The significance of this intervention (albeit not without hurdles) and its processes have given us examples of critical inputs required for success. In the case of Bangalore, there was the political stamp of approval at the highest level, with commitment to the project by the then Chief Minister of Karnataka. The legislative space was cleared for public–private partnership. This was done through a legislative order of 1999 under which the Bangalore Agenda Task Force (BATF) was constituted. There was a clear mandate for different stakeholder groups including the private sector for a public involvement at the advisory, resource generation, and implementation levels. The key terms of reference were outlined as follows: 'The Task Force will consider ways and means to upgrade Bangalore's infrastructure and systems, raise resources for its development and secure greater involvement of citizens, corporate, industry, and institutions in the orderly development of the City with enhanced quality of life of its residents.'

There were governance system challenges of multiplicity of institutions, weak financial positions, lack of accountability to consumers, etc, This had created a breakdown of services by the government. The BATF provided managerial and design inputs, critical financial support, and engagement with senior members of government for implementation. Contributions came from the Adhaar Trust of Nandan and Rohini Nilekani, CEO, Infosys, which seeded many innovations from the BATF office. The results were remarkable[30] both in terms of process changes in government functioning and results achieved on different fronts. The study[31] on the self-assessment scheme for property tax demonstrates how a combination of flexibilities and incentives and disincentives led 'Bangalore to became the first city in India to adopt a comprehensive, unit area method based property tax self-assessment scheme'. This led to the doubling of its property tax collection to Rs 200 crore and also managed to put an increased tax regime in place largely through a customer-friendly process. It also managed the inclusion of slums in the tax net at a differntial and minimal rate.[32]

[29] Ramesh Ramanathan, 'BATF—By the People and For the People', *Praxis Journal on Management*, December 2004; S. Raghunath and Chiranjib Sen, 'Public Private Partnership in Policy Innovation and Implementation: Reflections On The Self-Assessment Scheme for Property Tax of The Bangalore Muncipal Corporation', Indian Institute of Management, Bangalore, 2003.

[30] Ramnathan 'BATF'; Raghunath and Sen, *Public Private Partnership.*

[31] Raghunath and Sen, *Public Private Partnership*, p. 12.

[32] Ibid.

There were other notable achievements as well. The Bangalore Development Authority revived itself and became financially vibrant. The police and the city cooperation introduced new innovations with benefit to the consumers. Considerable as these achievements were, the full impact of this experiment was to be diminished without the continuity of policy in the new leadership elected in the state. Broadbased support for this process is yet to develop, and recent events from the state in 2005 indicate that issues of poor infrastructure and services are back on the front burner.

Millennium Development Goals

It is only very recently that at the apex levels of government, new global initiatives have drawn government support for a wider spectrum of development initiatives in partnership with the business world. With poverty reduction on the global agenda, and in light of the Millennium Development Goals (MDG) to be achieved by 2015, a series of efforts are under way to secure the inputs of private sector in development via the national governments. One of these initiatives is the UN Commission on Private Sector and Development started in 2003. The Secretary General in announcing the Commission pointed out the need to engage the private sector in development:

Our experience has shown that a large part of the work for development is about preparing the ground for sufficient private sector activity to provide the jobs and income needed to build a more equitable and prosperous society. Yet the UN has only sporadically tapped the power that can be drawn from engaging the private sector in the work of development.

A series of initiatives were unleashed worldwide to carry this forward. In India, the Commission's launch was done in December 2004 with the release of the Commission's Report, *Unleashing Entrepreneurship. Making Business Work for the Poor.* The launch was moved by two principles. The first principle was that of co-ownership and commitment by different sectors including government and private sector to be engaged in this endeavour. This was secured with the launch by private-sector representation in collaboration with the Government of India and UN agencies. The second principle was to get thinking and quick action started in this direction of business and government engagement for poverty reduction.

This sub-regional inauguration was launched by the business chamber, CII. The CII was also engaged under its India Partnership Forum, with government in exploring pilot initiatives for public–private–community partnerships for the achievement of the Millennium Development Goals. The Planning Commission is described as a partner in this process. This is an ambitious endeavour to address the development issues in an entire district. In this case it was Dungarpur district in Rajasthan, which is one of the poorest tribal districts of the country. It remains to be seen how this initiative unfolds and what the lessons are for private-sector engagement in development endorsed at national level.

Emerging on the horizon, is another kind of partnership initiative which is IT driven. This has emerged as a national alliance under the title 'Mission 2007: Every Village a Knowledge Centre Programme'. The key partners are NASSCOM Foundation, Microsoft Corporation India, and the International Crops Research Institute for the Semi-Arid Tropics (ICRISAT). This aims at reaching 6,00,000 villages by 2007 through IT. The cost of the project is estimated at Rs 6500 crore.[33] The Government of India has indicated strong support and is already a part of this alliance. This is expected to bring a sea change of connectivity not just for rural India but for the nation as a whole.

The public-sector companies in India despite diminution of influence still command a huge presence since liberalization. This includes many core-sector industries in India. The public sector should ideally be the exemplar of social responsibility demonstration. In many ways it has been. The PSUs, are of course, protected from the vagaries of market forces in many ways. However, in terms of scale of operations PSUs have an amazing array of interventions beyond the law. They are among the largest companies in India, and as such these industries provide challenges for CSR. Being the lead sector in many core energy and extractive industries sectors (that is coal, petroleum, aluminium, zinc), major environmental, health, and safety and resettlement issues, among others, have to be addressed. As primary employers in the organized sector, labour, reservation, and social services issues have also to be tackled. The PSUs are also moving away from traditional social responsibility interventions to new areas and types of interventions in collaboration with NGOs and other groups, with a focus on sustainability.

[33] *Business Line*, New Delhi, 12 July 2005.

There is a change in approach by government to the private sector in terms of drawing nuanced inputs from the private sector for development. Government has its work cut out to imbibe the culture to handle this and also play a facilitative and transparent role for CSR.

CHAPTER 9

LOOKING AHEAD

Following Independence in 1947, India chose a mixed economy model for its development. For over four decades after Independence, the State was the dominant driver, and India endeavoured to build under its munificence. Today, many nations across the globe are facing kaleidoscopic rearrangements of the roles of government, business, and civil society. It has been no different for India. The scope of expectations from business has expanded in many ways. An important survey cited here shows that different stakeholders in India are in favour of corporates doing, not just business, but also contributing to bringing about societal transformations. Business has inclined in that direction as a response to signals from the marketplace. In the process, there have been many development-sector initiatives, taken up by business both individually and in partnership with government. This book is in part been about these engagements.

Business engagement in such efforts, through CSR, have been of different kinds and have emerged differently. These efforts have sometimes been preventive, in that they have taken precautionary steps, being mindful of immediate potential negative impacts; at other times these efforts have been curative in taking corrective action where transgressions have been highlighted. At still other times, efforts have been promotive, by way of proactively engaging in changes beneficial to society at large in a long-term sense.

In this book I have analysed examples of all three kinds of engagement. Where business has been acting in the preventive and promotive modes, business interest has been seen to be served as well in the process. In a way there is a new embeddedness of the social, the political, and the economic for a more robust rendering of the full potential of the nation.

In the chapters of this book, specific streams of such engagement are discussed. Much of this is propelled by globalization. For the IT industry a sound infrastructure in education and IT is imperative. The IT industry in India is experimenting with initiatives in adding value and often building anew in various segments of school education. The initiatives of some of the major IT companies in India have been discussed.

Drawing large parts of the small-scale sector into the needs of global markets has created another vehicle for CSR. Enabling the mainstreaming of the marginalized in the rural economy, as employees, producers, and consumers, is yet another innovative effort described here. The requirement for social norms in workplace and other practices has propelled voluntary compliance from hitherto untouched sectors. They have been models for meeting developmental challenges, of speedy engagement, of bridging information and transaction gaps, while working to economic goals and targets. They provide new models for governance—of public–private partnerships, of trade-union-initiated private-sector partnerships for development, of NGO–corporate partnerships. In the vast landscape which is India, these are, however, still very small endeavours and mostly impact best those who have the capacity to be drawn into these processes but are on the fringes. There will continue to be many outside who must benefit from public safety nets, designed to prepare them to participate in these processes.

This book has also been about actors other than business, who have also driven these processes. Particularly important is the role of civil society in India discussed in a separate chapter. Developed countries have increasingly been playing a role in facilitating CSR. Their lessons for India, and the latter's own incipient forays through PPP are the subject of a chapter. It is in the context of the experience of the altered roles of business, government, and civil society that one can address what the future portends for CSR.

CORPORATE/BUSINESS SECTOR

The new roles being played by business are accepted with some caution. This caution is extended often to the public-private partnerships for development. Some of the criticism of the partnership approach is born out of concerns that such partnerships will open up areas of legitimate responsibility of government in social service delivery to privatization processes. The thing to remember here is that not all partnerships are cost-recovery processes, nor are they all pilanthrophic. There are nuanced ways in which corporate participation can be developed, retaining various levels of controls by the state and with various kinds of monetary and non-monetary incentives as well. However there are many gap areas where corporates can expand their contributions.

- The business model of CSR, while supporting important social infrastructure development and mainstreaming activities, cannot stop there. Business will have to take wider perspectives and engage with government to ensure the latter's role in providing adequate safety nets/ mechanisms to address those beneficiaries who cannot easily be part of this process.

- Corporate engagement in CSR sometimes carries the hallmark of good management practices. However, even here credible measurement and evaluation of what their development initiatives are able to achieve is only slowly emerging. This will become more imperative as reporting on CSR will increasingly have to lean towards accurate corporate communication and not advertising.

- There is another related concern. Leadership at the top recognizes the need to internalize environment and social risk as part of business strategy. This message still has to strongly reach all levels of management through different mechanisms and instruments. At another level there are efforts for an early awareness of this. This is through efforts to support Business school initiatives to expand their curriculum to include such an understanding.

- There is increasing and active engagement between business and government in areas as disparate as education, health, environment, credit, disaster management, and more. How the challenges of the clash of work cultures are overcome and how deliveries are made in quality, timeliness, and speed need to be examined closely for guidance. On the other side, there is the increasing involvement by the business sector with civil society for meeting CSR goals. Civil society groups complain of the non-sustainability and short-term nature of corporate inputs. Innovative ways to ensure sustainability will be a challenge.

GOVERNMENT

Government is the most important agent for addressing development issues. Government has the resources, infrastructure and, most important, legitimacy to do so. In India, as in other countries, we are seeing a large number of private–public partnerships being promoted in the development sector through CSR-type engagements. As government sets the direction for such changes, there will be several expectations to be met to fulfill this new role.

- India needs more enabling and less encumbering government. It also needs to be one that can match the transparency, flexibility, focus, convergence, and accountability required of it. In short, one would be looking for signs of an approach, a framework, and systems in place to handle this. Business chambers profiled here have addressed the issue of the role of individual personalities in government, which makes successful partnerships possible (or not possible) for development. Even in the case where business efforts are forthcoming in relief and rehabilitation, in the context of disaster situations, it is individual efforts of excellent civil administrators that make the partnerships work effectively. If government is to really act in partnership with business in this area, there will have to emerge a focus on systems in government which can deliver equally well, beyond the efforts of individuals. This will call for a revamping of its roles to take ownership of its legitimate space for partnership.

  There is very little information about the success of public–private partnerships at the highest level of bureaucracy. Such efforts are being solicited, as they have at the prime ministerial levels of almost every government in India since Independence. The marketing of success and learning from failures has yet to reach the critical mass to encourage more such engagements.

- Government in India, still commands a close second place in the economy in terms of capital formation, and is the prime employer of the organized labour force in the country. While compliance-driven CSR reporting is easily seen in major public-sector companies, other areas of social-sector benchmarking have yet to emerge. As a major procurement agency of goods and services, government ministries and departments can play a huge role and lead by example in encouraging CSR practices. Moreover, it can create markets for environmental and social products, thereby encouraging the direction of changes it deems necessary.

- Government in other countries is playing an important facilitative role in CSR, as described in one chapter in this book. Various ministries of the state and central government of India, are of course engaging in their independent efforts. In current years, there have been various kinds of international certification requirements, which have drawn the support of many ministries. An example is the Textiles Ministry in supporting and subsidizing certain certification requirements with social clauses as described here. There are other huge efforts at partnerships in value-added corporate efforts in education. In the Health Ministry there have been public- /private-sector initiatives for social marketing of Family Planning for a long time. Communication on this can encourage other initiatives.

- A single point of endorsement and facilitation of private-sector roles through CSR can give such efforts the filip of a national campaign, achieving quicker and more broad-based results. Equally facilitative mechanisms at several decentralized levels need to be in place to effectively respond to such initiatives.

- Government's role will not be less but different in many ways. With business models of CSR, government will have to ensure safety-net provisions for mainstreaming those left out of such processes. It will need to continue to be regulatory, and monitor its own processes as well, when it is in partnership with business for such initiatives. Fear that the business models of CSR can diminish to entry points for monopolistic practices for social-sector services needs to be addressed.

CIVIL SOCIETY

- The NGO sector is nowhere of a uniform genre. Civil society groups have taken a lead in being the third force in many 'consultative' economies of the developed world. In a globalized world, India's NGOs too are linked, as are business and governments to global processes that are analysed in this book. To really address civil society constituencies at home, the call to 'act local and think global' may have to be reversed and that would produce new challenges.

- A vast majority of people in India are not linked to processes that others benefit from, like education, health, employment, and credit. As business and industry get into this development space through CSR efforts, they have to, and increasingly will, rely on the intermediation of civil society. Credible organizations with skill and managerial abilities to upscale efforts are in constant demand. Civil society groups themselves will be called to work in transparent, accountable, and efficient ways to deliver to commitments. Managerial inputs provided by corporates working in partnership with civil society groups are already in evidence. Increasing demands for professionalization of civil society can be expected.

- Another aspect of the embedding of CSR is the plethora of codes, norms, and standards that are mushrooming. Some of these have been brought by civil society groups. Some rationalization across codes will also be apparent to reduce the burden of different expectations and in this civil society as well as other groups will have to play a role.

- Civil society approaches are diverse and it would not be unusual to find these groups on different sides of a given issue. Civil society groups are also prone to the ad hocism evident among corporates. They too would benefit from exercising effort to understand long-term perspectives in the context of their own ideological roles.

These are key aspects of the individual and combined constituencies driving CSR in India, which should be strengthened. A deeply felt recognition of the embeddedness of business and society and the symbiotic relationship between the two will lead to more enriched contributions. Gandhiji's call for trusteeship is a call for such awareness. The full implications of his thought will no doubt be centre-stage to many debates in the future. This will be particularly so in terms of the implications it has for India in the context of technology, globalization, employment, work conditions, and the roles of the state, civil society and corporates.

In India today, companies like those of the Tatas, the Narayana Murthys, and the Azim Premjis, are simultaneously on the world radar of business and of CSR as well. That which sets them apart in this are their constant efforts to address these societal issues, to chart out alternative and innovative paths of social development, to initiate and engage in them, and to display through example that there is a society out there of which they consider themselves an integral part. This integration of roles is something which government, industry, and civil society will also need to grow with to meet the impending challenges that lie in our path of great transformations underway.

ANNEXURES

2A. ETHOS OF GIVING

References to social giving can be found across major religions of the world. References to giving and social hierarchies as reflected in Sanskritic literature are abundant. Examples highlighted by scholars in the field are given

Transitory Nature of Wealth

'A generous person must give something in charity to a needy person.
He ought to see the long path of virtue.
Riches rotate like the wheels of a chariot and go to others'
(Rigveda 10.117–5 quoted in K.D. Divedi[1])

Intrinsic Value of Wealth, and its Moral Equivalencies

'The result of (having studied) the Veda is the fire sacrifice;
the result of (having) wealth is (the possibility) of giving and enjoying (wealth);
the result of (having) a wife is (the possibility) of sexual enjoyment and (of getting) sons;
the result of learning is (one's own) morality and virtuous conduct.
(Mahabharata[2])

Necessity of Giving at All Times

When fate is favourable we should give gifts, for then Lord Vishnu will fill our coffers again
We should give freely when fate is adverse for then all is (bound to be) lost.
(SSB, SSR quoted in Sternbach)

---

[1] Rigveda 10.117.5 quoted in K.D. Divedi 1984 Niti-Shiksha, Dharmraj Printing Press.
[2] Sternbach: Ludwick 1974 Mahasubharita-Samgraha Vol 1 pp. 34–5 Vishveshvaranand Vedic Research Institute, Hoshiarpur.

Rewards of Recognition and Fame

Sanskrit scholar, historian of religion and social anthropologist, Marcel Mauss captured the ethos of the Gift across cultures.[3] Key sources for this treatise was from the Anusasana Parva (Mahabharatha), where Bhisma responds to Yudhister's queries on gifts. Very many aspects of giving including the nature of giving, its rewards, its motives, its appropriateness etc are in these texts. The links of this ethos for modulating action and connecting to social systems, to the environment etc. is unmistakable. Excerpts from the translation of this text are given below.

Rewards of Recognition and Fame[4]

'By making gifts one acquires great fame in consequence of one's high achievements'

By making gifts of water and other drinks, one acquires eternal fame in consequence of one's high achievements'

'By giving away scents and garlands, one acquires fame that spreads over a large area.'

'The man who causes a tank to be dug becomes entitled to the respect and worship of the three worlds;'

'By planting trees one acquires fame in the world of men and auspicious rewards in the world hereafter. Such a man is applauded and reverenced in the world of the Pitris. Such a man's name does not perish even when he becomes a citizen of the world of deities.'

'The ruler who gives gifts of standing crop, or with animals or valuable land with minerals underneath and every kind of wealth above, wins inexhaustible regions of felicity in the next world (such a person 'is highly honoured and applauded by all righteous men.');

Equivalencies and Benefits of Environmental Giving

'A piece of land that is agreeable to the sight, fertile, situated in the midst of delightful scenes adorned with diverse kinds of metals, and inhabited by all sorts of creatures, is regarded as the foremost of sports. A particular portion of such land should be selected for digging a tank. . . . (with a view of drawing water for the benefit of all creatures). The man who causes a tank to be dug becomes entitled to the respect and worship of the three worlds. A tank full of water is as agreeable and beneficial as the house of a friend. It is gratifying to Surya (Sun God)himself. It also contributes to growth, to the deities. It is the foremost of all things that leads to fame (with respect to the person who causes it to be

---

[3] Marcel Mauss—Forms and Functions of Exchange in Archaic Societies–The Gift. W.W. Norton and Company. New York.

[4] Krishna Dwaipayana Vyasa 1981 Mahabharata–Anusasana Parva Part II, Vol XI. Translated by Kisan Mohan Ganguli–56, 57, 58, 60, 72 Munishram Manohar Publisher Pvt. Ltd. N. Delhi. Anusasana Parva (Mahabharata) Translation pp-56, 57, 58, 60, 60, 72.

excavated)'... 'Tanks, again are regarded as constituting the excellent beauty of a country. ... The merits earned by such an act of providing water is said have the equivalence of major sacrifices which few could afford. (p. 60).

The wise have said that that man reaps the merit of an Agnihotri sacrifice in whose tank water is held in the season of the rains. The high reward in the world that is reaped by the person who makes a gift of a thousand kines won by that man in whose tankwater is held in the season of autumn. The person in whose tank water occurs in the cold season acquires the merit of one who performs a sacrifice with plentiful gifts of gold. The person in whose tank water occurs in the season of dew, wins ,the wise have said, the merits of Agnishtoma sacrifice. That man in whose tank water occurs in the season of summer acquires, the rishis say, the merits that attach to the horse sacrifice.'

'The man who plants trees rescues the ancestors and descendants of both his paternal and maternal lines. Do thou, therefore, plant trees.... The trees that a man plants become the planters's children. ...Departing from this world, such a man ascends to Heaven. ...

The planter of trees is rescued in the next world by the trees he plants like the children rescuing their own father.' And on the planting of trees. (Anusasana Parva (Mahabharata 60–61)...

Reproductive Giving

As Mauss explains economy theology from his study of gift..[5]

"the thing given brings return in this life and in the other. It may automatically bring the donor an equivalent return –it is not lost to him, but reproductive; or else the donor finds the thing itself again, but with increase. Food given away means that food will return to the donor in this world; it also means food for him in the other world and in his series of reincarnations. Water, wells and springs given away are insurance against thirst; the clothes, the sunshades, the gold, the sandals for protection against the burning earth, return to you in this life and in the other."

There is further explanation of how this 'economic theology works'. The land you give away produces crops for another person and enhances your own interests in both worlds and in future incarnations. 'As the crescent moon grows from day to day so the gift of land once made increases at every harvest'. Land gives crops, rents and taxes, minerals and cattle. A gift made of it enriches both donor and recipient with the same produce. In Mauss's words –' Such economic theology is developed at great length in the rolling periods of the innumerable cantos, and neither the codes nor the epics tire of the subject".

[5] Ian Cunnison. 1967. The Gift-Forms and Functions of Exchange in Archaic Societies –Marcel Mauss. W.W. Norton & Company:NY pp. 53–81

However such benefit models of giving was considered somewhat less worthy motivation of giving than the disinterested giving of the rajasik category.

Highest of All Gifts

Though the discourse on gifts and giving is heavy with the benefits it will bring, in response to Yudhister's query as to which is the best gift of all, Bhisma responds that though rewards are attributed to many gifts the most 'distinguished gift' is disinterested giving done in the spirit of humanity.

'Assurance to all creatures of love and affection and abstention from every kind of injury, acts of kindness and favour done to a person in distress, gifts of articles made unto one that solicits with thirst and agreeble to the solicitor's wishes, and whatever gifts are made without the giver's ever thinking of them as gifts made by him, constitute, O chief of Bharata's race , the highest and best of gifts. Anusasana Parva (Mahabharata p. 60)

Bonded Gifts

Referring[6] to other Indian sacred literature (Gautama, and Manu), Marcell Mauss draws on sensitivities surrounding gifts. He highlights the links between the ethos, and motives with which gifts are made and how it can alter existing social arrangements. The need to be cautious about receiving is emphasized. 'The gift is something that must be given, that must be received and that is at the same time, dangerous to accept.' And again 'the recipient is in a state of dependence upon the donor. Mauss draws on the literature to show circumstances in which gifts are accepted with reluctance because they alter the existing social arrangements. This is done through the receipt of gifts together with the denial of receiving them OR the conducting of ritual purification in order to alter damaging effects of these gifts.

---

[6] Marcel Mauss. Forms and Functions of Exchange in Archaic societies- The Gift. WW Norton and Company. New York pp 58.

2B. Fundamental Principles of Trusteeship
Original Draft With Comments by Gandhiji (in block letters) and Professor Dantwala (in italics)

Comments		Original Draft
I have added *Instead of transforming*	(1)	Trusteeship provides a means of transforming the present capitalist order of society into an egalitarian one. It gives no quarter to capitalism but gives the present owning class a chance of *reforming* itself. It is based on the faith that human nature is never beyond redemption.
(1) *In the original 'may be necessary for the service'. Who would determine the necessity?* (2) *Option is suggested in brackets* OPTION WILL DO.	(2)	It does not recognize any right of private ownership of property except so far as it may be permitted(deemed harmless) by society (social organization).
	(3)	It does not exclude legislative regulation of ownership and use of wealth.
NO HARM IN REMOVING THIS	(4)	[I suggest deletion of this clause because 'safe-guarding of property-rights' will lend itself to misinterpretation. Besides point 3 includes the essence of this point.]
In place of 'irrespective of' ALTERATION MAY BE MADE	(5)	Thus under the State-regulated trusteeship, an individual will not be free to hold or use his wealth for selfish satisfaction or *in disregard of* the interests of society.
I have added this. THIS IS UNNECESSARY. HAS BEEN INCLUDED UNDER CLAUSE 2.	(6)	The owner will be duty bound to manage his property for the service of society. As a trustee, he will be entitled only to a statutory commission for his labours. This cannot be exorbitant.
I have added *The ideal aim being the obliteration of the difference.*	(7)	Just as it is proposed to fix a decent minimum living wage, even so a limit should be fixed for the maximum income that could be allowed to any person in society. The difference between such minimum and maximum

(cont)

Comments		Original Draft
		income should be reasonable and equitable, so much so that the tendency would be towards obliteration of the difference.
THE DELETION WILL NOT AFFECT THE MEANING. IF RETAINED, THE REVISION WOULD BE UNACCEPTABLE.	(8)	Suggest deletion of this clause. If it is to be retained, suggest the word 'trustee' in place of the present owners of wealth' and the addition of the following clause—'subject to the overriding necessity of conforming to the principles of social justice mentioned above' (or the ethics of the new economic order).

Source: Social Responsibility of Business, IIC 1966.

3A. The Research and Action Agenda on Child Labour on the Sports Goods Industry[1]
The Sportsgoods Manufacturers and Exporters Association

OPERATION EDUCATION

1. Although the survey report on child labour in the sports goods industry, commissioned by the ILO , is not yet published, the preliminary findings do indicate that there are some children stitching footballs full time in the industry. (If figures are available by the time of the WFSGI meeting at Munich, then these will be added at the end of this paper.)

    Suffice it to say at this juncture that the Indian sports goods exporting industry along with the whole of the global community is totally committed to send these children to school and at the same time try to create conditions where they do not work on a regular basis after school also.

2. The preliminary findings also indicated that a significant number of children do stitch or help to stitch footballs after returning from school. The ILO has suggested that although this is child work as opposed to child labour, yet they feel that child work causes children to drop out of school at a young age, due to the dual burden of studying and working. The exporters would therefore like to tackle this problem also. They will be suggesting norms for child work after school so that stitching does not interfere with education.

3. The sports goods exporters believe that the basic problem of child labour is caused by poverty, which in turn is caused by lack of education.

4. The sports goods exporters of Jalandhar propose to set up a FOUNDATION FOR PROMOTION OF EDUCATION AND MONITORING OF CHILD STITCHING.

[1] FICCI/ILO/OPEC, 'Child Labour in the Sports Goods Industry', 1999, conducted by V.V. Giri National Labour Institute, Noida, India, pp. 77–8.

Exporters will join the Foundation on a voluntary basis. All members of the Foundation will pay a monthly contribution equal to 0.25 of the value of their football exports. They will be requesting the Apex Chambers- NGOs-Government and Trade Unions to join as partners in this foundation and also if possible to contribute to this noble cause

Overseas customers of Indian exporters will also be welcome to contribute if they so wish.

5. The Sports Goods Manufacturers and Exporters Association will also be partners in this Foundation through its members(those who export footballs) and directly as a partner to work for the goals of the Foundation.

The Foundation would commence work with effect from 1ˢᵗ January, 1999.

1. The World Federation of Sporting Goods Industries will also be requested to join hands. They will publish the names of those Indian exporters who are members of the Foundation. They will also publish the names of the importing companies who pledge to only buy from these Indian companies who are members of the Foundation.

2. Indian exporter members of the Foundation will, in addition to giving financial contributions as above, pledge:

    a) That they will not allow their sub-contractors to recruit any stitcher under the age of 14, either directly or indirectly.

    b) That they will ensure that the contractors will pay the fair agreed wage to the stitchers for stitching balls.

    c) That any child under the age of 14 who is currently stitching balls and not attending school, be persuaded to go to school without causing loss of income to the family (Foundation will train ladies of the household any/or any child above 14).

    d) They will fix an age below which no stitching whatsoever be done by a child even if he/she is going to school.

    e) They will suggest suitable maximum hours of work for school going children.

    f) They will fix a sensible time scale to implement and execute these objectives, along with shorter-term goals e.g., a two year period to achieve, split into 4 six monthly goals.

6. The role of the Foundation will be to promote education and to monitor that children are phased out of the stitching of balls as quickly as possible without causing economic hardship to the families concerned. Inter-alia it will:

a) Work in conjunction with the local and central government agencies to Promote education in Jalandhar and the surrounding villages.

Punjab government is very keen to open more schools in the villages and the

Foundation can hopefully provide the impetus and the financial assistance, especially since Apex Chambers, NGOs, Government and Trade Unions will be involved.

b) The Foundation will conduct a survey to see why children are not going to school i.e. is it:

i.   Lack of facilities/schools.

ii. Lack of money to finance children at a school

iii. Lack of motivation to go to school.

c) The Foundation will register all sub-contractors in the industry along with their addresses. They will also register each and every stitcher along with his address. They will perhaps even issue identity cards if necessary. Members will have to keep stiticher-wise records of balls stitched so that these can be checked, monitored and audited by the Foundation at any time. The international agencies who we hope will be partners in the Foundation will be requested to deeply involve in this aspect.

United Nations Development Programme

Confederation of Indian Industry

SOCIAL CODE FOR BUSINESS

In recent years, the concept of Corporate Social Responsibility has emerged as an increasingly important feature of the business philosophy. No longer is business seen as basing its decisions solely on economic criteria. Businesses are now expected to consider the ethical, moral and social impact of their actions and decisions. A corporate that is sensitive to the surroundings and to the needs and aspirations of the community in which it operates not only creates goodwill and a strong market for its business, but also helps support a sustainable neighbourhood. We list here a set of principles and standards for good corporate citizenship for voluntary adoption. Concern, understanding and responsibility are the essence of this set of principles.

* The Company affirms the interdependence of its enterprise with the well being and self-reliance of the community. This can be done by adopting an Article of Association on Corporate Social Responsibility (CSR) that advocates harmonising of economic progress with social and environmental considerations.

* The Company has a specific written policy statement on CSR (social & environmental) which is in the public domain.

* The Company has an explicit strategy on social and environmental issues that can be seen in the form of an Annual Work Plan mainstreamed with its business process.

* The Company has included CSR as part of its corporate communications including newsletters and there is reporting on CSR in the Company's Annual Report.

* The Company has a senior executive under the CEO responsible for CSR and managerial level officers tasked specifically with social and environment work. The CEO reviews the CSR programmes twice in a year.

* The Company ensures equal access to employment and promotion opportunities across gender and cultures through policies and programmes.

* The Company has allocated specific resources for CSR activities and has monitoring systems to track implementation process and impact.

* The Company demonstrates its CSR by providing an enabling environment for employees to volunteer that includes recognition and accounting for volunteer time.

* The Company is committed to document its learning experiences in terms of human achievements, contribution to the community, the learning for all stakeholders for sharing with local governments and development agencies.

* The Company is also known for the partnerships it builds with various development players in the field to synergise all available opportunities to bring about holistic development of the local community.

* The Companies to expand the scope of learning from each other in their role of being good corporate citizens by way of exchanging data, views, implementation procedures and even exchange of expert personnel whenever necessary.

United Nations Development Programme
55 Lodi Estate New Delhi 110 003 India
Phone : 91-11-462 8877 Fax : 91-11-462 7612
Internet: www.undp.org.in e-mail: fo.ind@undp.org
Internet: www.un.org.in

Confederation of Indian Industry
23, Institutional area, Lodi Road, New Delhi-110003
Phone : 91-11-4629994-7, 4626164
Fax : 91-11-4626149, 4633168 e-mail:cnco@ciionline.org
internet : www.ciionline.com

*FICCI-CARE Gujarat Rehabilitation Project[2]

*FINANCIAL RESOURCES MOBILIZED FOR RECONSTRUCTION = RS 57.44 CRORE

Approaches

- Rapid Appraisal—To Rehabilitation Strategy.
- Emergency Relief—To Short-Term and Long-term Rehabilitation
- Multi-stakeholder model—Community, Government, NGOs, and Corporates
- Close monitoring and evaluation.

Emergency Relief

Essential temporary shelter, food, blankets, cloth, plastic sheeting, floor mats, kerosene lamps, cooking sets and medicines, also medical teams for treatment of injured and sick. Temporary family structures and temporary community infrastructures (schools, health posts, panchayat offices, etc.)

Short- and Long-term Rehabilitation

Reconstruction Related

- Constructed 4999 houses in 23 villages. In addition, 15 Schools, 12 Panchayats, 11 Community Centres, 21 Anganwadis and 5 Sub-Health Centres.
- Water Supply in 21, Sewage line in 11 villages and Roads in 3 villages.
- Livelihood Security through reconstruction activities
- On-the-job skills training in new earthquake resistance construction techniques.
- Technical and financial assistance for income generating activities eg. Small-scale building components.
- Block making Centres (with Resources and assistance).
- Ten Training Guilds—one for each group of 8–10 villages both for providing trained

---

[2] Information from FICCI Socio-Economic Development Foundation, 2005.

* Finances raised from Indian and global corporates and the government of India. Corporates also provided technical (earthquake resistant engineering and design) and managerial inputs consistently over a period of two years.

services (masonry, plumbing, electrical repair, carpentry, welding RCC, centring, and block making). Also 2000 persons trained in this who were not part of the guilds.
- Training and production centres for women (for processing, handmade paper products, leather goods, bead work and other activities).

Agriculture and Water

- Seeds and tools to 1632 farming families.
- Training in organic farming practices to 14 villages.
- Demonstration drip irrigation for 30 villages.
- Distribution of 1200 irrigation kits.
- Repair of 54 water-harvesting systems serving 10,5400 farming families in 47 villages.

Agriculture

- One hundred and twenty three farm ponds.
- Earthern bunds for 525 hectares of small and marginal farmers.
- Agricultural inputs to 3083 households.
- 7000 acres of tillage for 740 farmers.
- Kitchen gardens developed for 1441 households.
- Four seed banks in four clusters of villages.
- 3920 horticulture grafts distributed through women's groups and planted in 53 villages.
- Ten fodder banks for 3500 households.
- Sixteen Animal health camps.
- Fifty awareness programmes on water conservation and community participation.
- Eight exposure trips to successful watershed experiments in Rajasthan and Gujarat.
- Thirteen Village Development Committees and 68 Self-help Groups have been formed across thirty villages.
- Four Training Programmes for project's NGO partners on social technical aspects of watershed, livelihood and documentation, respectively.
- Demonstration and training cell for vermin-compost to improve farm productivity and/or to augment farm incomes.
- Ninety-six rooftop rainwater-harvesting structures in 30 villages with capacity of harvesting approximately 5000 litres per roof top.
- Expansion of drinking water systems in 6 villages.
- Repair of Damaged drinking water sources. The repair of 32 common wells serving 3500 families in 30 villages.

Off-Farm Livelihood Enhancement

- Setting up of a Business Resource Centre—offers business development services to artisans—through enterprise management, technology, market information and linkages and product development. One thousand artisans have been trained in these services (range includes textiles, metal ware, terracotta pottery and hand made paper). Coverage is to be extended to 3000 such artisans.

- The Development of an Artisan-owned Society—Kachchi Hast Kala Maha Mandal—which has over 500 artisan members. The society has facilitated artisan product sales of approximately Rs 29.4 lakh through its linkages with local national and international marketing channels.

Other

- Setting up of a community level disaster mitigation fund. Persons from 900 households in Anhar and Rapar blocks have been organized into 60 self-help groups.
- Additional project facilitated insurance coverage (life health and assets). In Anjar and Rapar blocks 7,500 women have been organized into 60 self-help groups federated into the community-based organization to manage the fund. Women also trained in how to claim their returns.

4A. Participatory and Multi-stakeholder Engagement in the Learning Guarantee Programme Azim Premji Foundation[1]

Key Foundation Mechanisms of the Learning Guarantee Programme.

- Voluntary Participation.
- Full multi-media communication about the programme.
- Support from the government via canvassing participation authorized and signed by the Commissioner for Public Instruction Karnataka.
- Orientation Programme for Block Education Officers and Block Resource Coordinators.
- School Development Monitoring Committee (SDMC) for every participating school comprising of parents, teachers and wider community members.
- Multi-stakeholder (government, foundation, parents, teachers, students, community) inputs to put in place a qualified and credible evaluation group for the programme.

[1] Based on Anjali Prayag, 'Premji's Passion' in Corporate Social Responsibility–How Companies are Delivering the Good, *Praxis Business Lines Journal on Management*, December 2004, pp. 18–30.

5A. Rural Distribution Network Objectives[1]

The major objectives of the Rural Distribution Network are:

- To improve the overall realization of small and marginal farmers by establishing a system to market their produce directly to consumers.
- To empower rural women through sustainable income generation activities.
- To bring affordable, hygienic, and quality goods—sourced from poor producers at a fair price—to rural consumers who are most often cheated on weight and quality.
- To eliminate the chain of middlemen for the socio-economic development of Below Poverty Line (BPL) families.
- To create a consciousness of a weight to price relationship among rural consumers.
- To help establish SGMH as a credible and effective arm of SEWA.

The Rural Distribution Network will:

- Procure agricultural commodities and cottage industry products from SEWA's rural producer members, and
- Employ SEWA members to:
  * Process and pack the goods.
  * Sell the finished products in villages using a direct to home distribution model, which is highly effective given low literacy in rural areas.
  * Implement the promotional campaign, delivering the message through personal contact channels such as folk songs and skits.

---

[1] Grassroots Trading Network. August 2004, ibid., and GTN 2004 'Linking Small and Marginal Indian Farmers to Corporate Buyers in Partnership with Sewa Gram Mahila Haat. The Agricultural Marketing Organization of Self-employed Women's Association

7A. Global Compact Commitment

A company wishing to subscribe to the Global Compact can do so by sending a letter from the Chief Executive Officer to the United Nations Secretary-General expressing support for the Global Compact and commitment to take the following actions:

Issue a clear statement of support for the Global Compact and its ten principles and to publicly advocate the Global Compact. This may include:

Informing employees, shareholders, customers and suppliers

Integrating the Global Compacy and ten principles into the Corporate Development training programme.

Incorporating the Global Compact principles in the company's mission statement.

Including the Global Compact commitment in the company's Annual Report and other public documents.

Issuing press releases to make the commitment public.

Provide once a year a concrete example of progress made or a lesson learnt in implementing the principles for posting in the Global Compact website. This letter is to be sent to :

Kofi Annan
Secretary- General
United Nation
New York, NY 10017
E-mail: globalcompact@un.org.

India Global Compact Companies

INDIAN COMPANIES LISTED IN UN GC (15 JULY 2005)

1. Abar Group
2. Air India
3. Apollo Hospitals
4. Artificial Limbs Mfg Corporation
5. Atlas Cycles (Haryana) Limited
6. Balmer Lawrie & Co. Ltd
7. Bharat Aluminium Company Limited
8. Bharat Heavy Electricals
9. BIOCON
10. Bongaigaon Refinery & Petrochemicals Limited
11. Cement Corporation of India
12. Central Cottage Industries Corporation of India Limited
13. Central Warehousing Corporation
14. Chennai Petroleum
15. Comat Technologies
16. Dena Bank
17. Divgi Warmer Pvt Ltd
18. Dredging Corporation of India
19. Engineering Projects (India) Limited
20. Engineers India Limited
21. Excel Industries Limited
22. Global Calcium Pvt Ltd
23. Global Synergetic Organisation
24. Heuback Colour Pvt Ltd
25. Hi-Tech Carbon
26. Hindalco Industries Limited
27. Hindustan Aeronautics Limited
28. Hindustan Lever Ltd

29. Hindustan Organic Chemicals Limited
30. Hindustan Paper Corporation Limited
31. Hindustan Sanitaryware & Industries Limited
32. Housing Development Finance Corporation
33. HSCC Hospital Services Consultancy Corporation Limited
34. Indian Aluminium Company Limited
35. Indian Farmers Fertilizers Cooperative
36. Indian Oil Corporation Limited
37. Indian Renewable Energy Development Agency Limited
38. Indo Gulf Corporation Limited
39. Infosys Technologies Limited
40. Infrastructure Development Finance Company Limited
41. Kolam Information Services Limited
42. Konkan Railway Corporation Limited
43. Kudremukh Iron Ore Company Limited
44. Mahanagar Telephone Nigam Limited
45. Mahindra & Mahindra Limited
46. Mazagon Dock Limited
47. Metalman Auto Pvt Ltd
48. Mineral Exploration Corporation Limited
49. Mishra Dhatu Nigam Limited
50. MMTC
51. National Buildings Construction Corporation Limited
52. National Mineral Development Corporation Limited
53. National Research Development Corporation
54. National Textile Corporation Limited
55. North Eastern Electric Power Corporation Limited
56. NTPC-National Thermal Power Corporation Limited
57. O/E/N India
58. Octaga Green Power & Sugar Ltd
59. Oil & Natural Gas Corporation
60. Oil India Limited
61. Paharpur Business Centre and Software Technology
62. Parijat Agencies
63. Power Finance Corporation Limited.
64. Priconser India Pvt. Limited
65. Psi
66. Punjab National Bank
67. Quadra Advisory Private Limited

68. Rallis India Limited
69. Rashtriya Chemicals and Fertilizers Limited
70. Renata Plastics
71. Satluj Jal Vidyut Nigam Ltd
72. Scooters India Limited
73. Semiconductor Complex Limited
74. TAL Manufacturing Solutions Limited
75. Tata Autocomp Systems Ltd
76. Tata Chemicals Limited
77. Tata Industries Limited
78. Tata International Ltd
79. Tata Metaliks Limited
80. Tata Motors Ltd
81. Tata Power Company Limited
82. Tata Steel Limited
83. Tata Tea Limited
84. Tata Autocomp Systems Limited
85. Telco Construction Equipment Company Limited
86. The Indian Hotels Company Limited
87. The Associated Cement Companies Ltd (ACC)
88. The Shipping Corporation of India Limited
89. The State Trading Corporation of India
90. Titan Industries Limited
91. Transnational Supply & Service
92. Twenty First Century Battery Limited
93. Unit Trust of India
94. Voltas Limited
95. Wadia Group
96. Water & Power Consultancy Services Limited
97. Winsome Textile Industries Limited

EXCLUSION LIST OF THE INTERNATIONAL FINANCE CORPORATION[1]

1. IFC does not finance the following projects:

   - Production or activities involving harmful or exploitative forms of forced labor*/ harmful child labor*
   - Production or trade in any product or activity deemed illegal under host country laws or regulations or international conventions and agreements.
   - Productions or trade in weapons or munitions.*
   - Production or trade in alcoholic beverages (excluding beer and wine)*
   - Production or trade in tobacco*
   - Gambling, casions and equivalent enterprises*
   - Trade in wildlife or wildlife products regulated under CITES*(Convention on International Trade in Endangered Species of Wild Fauna and Flora)
   - Production or trade in radioactive materials.*
   - Production or trade in or use of unbonded asbestos fibers*
   - Commercial logging operations or the purchase of logging equipment fior use in primary tropical moist forest (prohibited by the Forestry policy)*
   - Production or trade in products containing PCBs.*
   - Production or trade in pharmaceuticals subject to international phase outs or bans.*
   - Production or trade in ozone depleting substances subject to international phase out.
   - Drift net fishing in the marine environment using nets in excess of 2.5 km. In length.

A reasonableness test will be applied when the activities of the project company would have a significant development impact but the circumstances of the country require adjustment to the Exclusion List.

---

[1] The International Finance Corporation Procedure for Environmental and Social Review of Projects, 1998.

* all star market exclusions are further clarified in terms of definitions in the Procedure document

8A. LOCAL, REGIONAL, NATIONAL, AND INTERNATIONAL LEVELS OF ENGAGEMENT BY GOVERNMENT FOR CSR
DUTCH MODEL[1]

LOCAL LEVEL

CSR is most visible at the local level and government will support all partners individually and together, wherever they are initiated. Examples of existing support is

- *The subsidisation of the Society for Business Foundation—which provides for a growing network of the business case for CSR.*
- *Developing studies as part of the regional economic policy and cooperation between the government, Association of Muncipal Authorities, and Association of Provincial authorities-which would give insights of what can be done*
- *Preparing a tax legislation and voluntary work.*
- *Co-financing by central government as a reward for cooperation at the local level*
- *Organisational and Infrastructure support for Muncipal executives understanding informational requirements and developing networks*
- *Encourage contact with private citizens and private parties.*
- *Professionalisation of welfare institutions in collaboration with multistakeholder partnerships.*

NATIONAL LEVEL

- *Knowledge and information centre set up by the government on corporate social responsibility which will collect, analyse and disseminate general information.*
- *Outline a clear framework for reporting. The government will seek advice from the Council for Annual Reporting.*
- *The integration of corporate inputs into the Fourth National Environmental Plan*
- *The government as a market party. As an employer, procurer, contractor, the government is*

---

[1] Abstracted and summarized from SER, *Corporate Social Responsibility*, pp. 100–11.

into business in its own way, and needs to be ahead of legislation to set examples. 'Sustainable Procurement' and 'innovative tendering' have been designed for this purpose.- and the development of a guide for such procurement and contracting.

INTERNATIONAL LEVEL

- *Ireland, UK, Denmark and the Netherlands conduct talks regularly at the national level on CSR for informational purposes.*
- *In Feb 2001, bribery of foreign officials was made a penal offence, thus bringing critical areas of CSR into regulatory framework.*

INDEX

Accenture Development Partnership 8
Action Aid 112
Adhar Trust 153
Agragamee 105
All Party Parliamentary Group on Corporate
    Social Responsibility 142
American Federation of Labour and
    Congress of Industrial Organizations
    (AFLCIO) 127
Amnesty International 95, 112
Annan, Kofi 3, 129
Anukaran 105
APEDA 152
Apollo Hospitals 47
Ashok Leyland: initiative for environment
    protection 39
Asia-Pacific Economic Corporation (APEC)
    121
Assemblee' Permanente des Chambres De
    Metiers (APCM) 83
Association for Rural Economic
    Development (ARED) 84
Association for support of Ashalayam (ASA)
    84
Association for Sustainable Responsible
    Investing 121
Azim Premji Foundation 55, 56, 58–62
    Learning Guarantee Programme 62

B&O plc, small-scale sectors 82–3
Bangalore Agenda Task Force (BATF) 153
Bangalore Development Authority (BDA)
    154
Bayer 95
Belgium
initiative for CSR 148
Social Label Law 146
Bhagavadgita 23
Bharatiya Yuva Shakti Trust (BYST) 113,
    114

Bhave, Vinoba 22
Bhavishya Jyoti Scholarships (NIIT) 68–9
Bhopal gas tragedy 107
Birla Agricultural Farm 32
Birla Rural Development Association 32
Birla, G.D. 30–1
Birlas, initiative for education 32
Bombay Plan 30–1
BOOT (build, operate, own and transfer)
    67
Brent Spar issue 112
Brethren Benefit Trust Inc. 107
British Telecom (BT) 73–5, 78
    community development support 80
    outsourcing with CSR issues 76–7
Bureau of International Standards (BIS)
    127
Business and Community Foundation (BCF)
    112, 113–14
business chambers and associations 41–2
business process outsourcing (BPO) 72–4
    CSR, issues in India 76–7
    false accents, names and locations, 80
    job security and working conditions
        76–7, 80
    overtime/nightshifts 80
    unionization of employees 78–9

CC Shroff Self Help Centre 33
Canadian Business for Social Responsibility
    121
capitalism, 8, 11–12, 20, 21, 24, 26, 30
Capital Hospital, Bhubaneswar, Orissa 70
CARE 48–9
Caux Round Table 121
Centre for Corporate Sustainability 43
Centre for Disease Control and Prevention
    (CDC) 51
Centre for Indian Trade Unions (CITU) 77
Centre for Policy Dialogue 127

Centre for Science and Environment (CSE)
    103, 105–7, 116
Centre for Social Markets (CSM) 112
Confederation of Indian Industry (CII) 41,
    43, 46, 137, 155
    AIDS at the Workplace Programme 46
    disaster relief initiative 49–50
    Education and Literacy Committee 44
    Exim Award for Business Excellence 43
    India Partnership Forum 155
    initiative for health and education 46,
        47
Chandarias 114
Charity Aid Foundation 113
Chhattisgarh Mines Shramik Sangh (CMSS)
    102
Chhattisgarh Mukti Morcha (CMM) 102
child labour 44–5, 47
Chilka prawn culture fisheries case 100–1,
    104
China Light and Power International,
    Karnataka 118
Christian Aid Society 44
civil society and non-governmental
    organizations (NGOs) xx, xxii, xxiii, 1,
    11, 14, 85, 94ff, 121, 126, 127, 128,
    141, 144, 156, 159, 162–3
    in India
        collaborating for change 111–15
        confronting for change 99
        engulfing corporates and the state
            100–6
        leveraging networks 103–7
        power of communication 107–11
    corporate partnership 158
    global Indian NGOs 96–7
    questioning the role 115–9
    sizing up India's NGO sector 97–9
    to small and medium enterprises
        (SMEs) 84–6
Coca-Cola 102–3, 106, 116
codes and standards
    Global Reporting Initiative (GRI) 114,
        132–3, 138
    International Finance Corporation
        (IFC) 64, 121, 123, 133–6
    SA 8000 standards 123–9, 132, 138,
        147
    UN Global Compact 3–4, 122, 123,
        129–32, 144
Cogentrix Energy Inc., Karnataka 118

Coke Oven Plant 102
Computer Assisted Teaching and
    Rehabilitation project (NIIT) 68
Consumer Unity and Trust Society (CUTS)
    127
Corporate Free UN Alliance 3–4
corporate houses, corporate/business sector
    158–9
    ahead of government responsibilities
        36–41
corporate social responsibility (CSR)
    ahead of government responsibility 36–
        41
    ideology 2–8
    politics and markets 8–11
    research leading to CSR 43–6
    sociology of economics 11–14
    terminology 1–2
Costello, Tim 74
Council for Leather Exports (CLE) 108
Council of Economic Priorities
    Accreditation Agency (CEPAA), see
    Social Accountability International
    (SAI), United States of America
Council on Environmental Quality (CEQ)
    40–1

Dantwala, Professor M.L. 25
deception issue 80
Delhi Transport Corporation (DTC) 39
Denmark, Act on Legal Protection and
    Administration in Social Matters 149
Deshmukh, C.D. 11, 25
Development Alternatives 113
Development Corporation 135
development issues 1, 2, 16, 55
    policy debates on 30–3
    projects, implementation 48
Development of Women and Children in
    Rural Areas (DWCRA) 87, 88, 91
Diamond Workers Co-operative Society,
    Surat 84
Digital Partners 89
disaster relief and rehabilitation 48–50
Domino Funds 121
Dow Chemicals 107
Durkheim, Emile 12

Eklavya 44
employability issues 149–50
entrepreneurship 84, 150–1

environment management, corporate social
responsibility 38–41
Escorts Rural Development and Uplift
Division 33
ESOP options 69
Ethical Trading Initiative 122, 142
ethos of social giving 16
European Business Network 121
European Commission/European Union
122, 146
India Network for Corporate Social
Responsibility 82
European Foundation for Quality
Management 43
EuroRSCG 91
Excel Company 114
Excel Industries Vivekananda Research and
Training Institute, Kutch 33

Fair Trade E.V., Germany 84
fair trade movement 128
Federation of Indian Chambers of
Commerce and Industry (FICCI) 10,
29, 30, 42–6
CARE Gujarat Rehabilitation Project
(FCGRP) 48–9
Reproductive and Child Health (RCH)
Projects 47
Socio-Economic Foundation (FICCI-
SEDF) 41, 47
Ford 95
Forestry Stewardship Council (FSC) 122
Foundation of Pierre Abbot 84
Friedman, Milton 5–6, 14

Gandhi, M.K. xx, 15, 21, 29, 30, 32
concept of trusteeship 20–5, 28, 29,
163
view on economics of humanity 25–6
on property and entitlements 26–7
on role of state and business 28–9
Gandhi, Maneka 108
GAP 108, 121
German Technical Co-operation (GTZ)
126, 152
Germany, initiative for CSR 145
Ghosal, Sumantra 13
Global Agenda 129
Global Compact Society, India 131
global connectedness 6, 21, 33, 121
Global Corporate Citizenship 37

Global Leaders of Tomorrow (GLT) 46
Global Sustainable Development Facility
for a Corporate Partnership
Programme 3
globalization process xx, xxii, 1, 4, 7, 14, 25,
34–6, 43, 38, 45, 73, 96, 115, 118,
126–7, 152, 157, 163
Godrej, initiative for education 32
government(s) 16
and corporate houses collaboration 48–
50
development policy/initiative 142–4
grooming for CSR, global and India
response 139ff, 160–1
Grassroot Trading Netwok (GTN) 88, 89–
90, 91–3
Grassroots Producer Oragnizations (GPOs)
89
Greenpeace 95, 107, 112
guilds,
institutionalization of development
activities 18–20
morally embedded social responsibility
18
and state-governance partners 15–17

handicrafts and agriculture segment 45–6
Hashim, M.M. 108
Hero Cycles 93
Hewlett Packard India Limited 43
Hindustan Computers Limited (HCL) 77,
80
Hindustan Levers Limited (HLL),
initiatives 86–91, 92
IT-based rural information service 87
marketing 86
rural development 32
women's empowerment 87
Hitachi Foundation 37
Howells, Kim 142

incentives for corporate social initiatives 32,
42–3, 148–51, 159
India Expert Advisory Group for Polio
Eradication (IEAG) 51
Indian Marketing Research Bureau (IMRB)
136
Indian National Congress 31
Indian Sports Goods Manufacturers and
Exporters Association 45
Information Technology (IT)

creating the education base 54–5
information technology enabled services
    (ITES) 72
Infosys Technologies Limited 43, 55, 69–72,
    80, 153
    Infosys Foundation 69–72
    arts, support 71–2
    education initiative 70, 71
    health initiative 70, 71
    Library for Every Rural School Project
        71
    rural development initiative 70–1
    social support initiative 69
    partnership with the government 72
infrastructure, revamping 152–4
Interfaith Centre on Corporate
    Responsibility 121
International Association of Lions Club 52
International Chamber of Commerce 121,
    129
International Confederation of Trade
    Unions 129
International Crops Research Institute for
    Semi-Arid Tropics (ICRISAT) 72, 155
International Employers Organizations 129
International Labour Organization (ILO)
    45, 47, 76, 129
International Resources for Fairer Trade
    (IRFT) 85
International Standard Organization (ISO)
    123
ISO 9000 123, 126, 152
ISO 14000 123, 126, 152
IT Professionals Forum of India (ITPF) 79
Italy, initiative for corporate social
    responsibility (CSR) 147, 151
ITC Limited, initiative for agribusiness 91–
    3

Jayaprakash Narayan 11, 24–5
Jones, Melvil 52

Katha Information Technology and E-
    Commerce Schools (KITES) 80
Kidwai Cancer Institute, Bangalore,
    Karnataka 70
Kohli, Uddesh 131
Krantidarshi Yuva Sangha (KYS) 104

Lalbhai group 114
    initiative for education 32

Rural Development Fund 32
Laxman Nayak Society 105
legislatives and directives 145–6
Levi Strauss 121
liberalization 6, 45, 155
Lions Club of India xxii
    disaster relief, health and education 51–
        2
Lions International 50, 52
lost jobs and the CSR 73–5, 77

Madhukar, C.V. 60
Mahindra and Mahindra 80
Marine Stewardship Council (MSC) 122
marketing development 81ff
Marks, Alan 108
Maruti Udyog Limited 43
Mashruwala, K.G. 27
Mathai, John 30
Mauss, Marcell 13
Meet the Students (MTS) 104
Mehta, M.C. 111
Microsoft Corporation India 71, 72, 95,
    155
Millennium Development Goals (MDG)
    152, 154–6
Mission 2007: Every Village a Knowledge
    Centre 72
Mitra, Sugata 64
models and pilot projects for business 46–8
Modis, initiative for education 32
morality in business 25, 27–8
Multimedia Super Corridor Smart Schools
    68
multi-stake holders, benchmarking
    corporate social performance 120–3
Murthy, Narayana 69, 163
Murthy, Sudha 69

Naidu, Chandrababu 88
Narain, Sunita 103
Narottam Lalbhai Rural Development Fund
    (NLRDF) 32
NASSCOM Foundation 72, 155
National People' Congress, Ninth, Beijing,
    China 11
National Planning Committee 31
Netherlands
    initiative for CSR 144
    Sociaal Economische Raad (SER) 144–
        5, 147

Newata Mandal Village Project 33
NIIT
    Hole in the Wall programme 63, 64–6
    IT education and social development
        55–63
    Kindergarten to class 12 (K-12)
        programme 63, 66–9
    LEAD (learning, experience, adventure
        and discussion) 66
    partnership with the government 65,
        66–8
    Research and Cognitive Systems 64
Nike 95, 121
Nilekeni, Nandan and Rohini 153
Niyogi, Shankar Guha 102
non-governmental organizations (NGOs),
    see civil society and non-governmental
    organizations (NGOs)
Norsk Hydro 105
North American Alliance for Fair Economy
    (NAFE) 74
Norway, initiative for CSR 144
Norway Amnesty 105

Organization for Economic Cooperation
    and Development (OECD) 122, 144,
    148
outsourcing and offshoring 73–7
Oxfam 112

Pandhey, M.K. 77
Partners in Change (PIC) 112, 113, 136
partnership
    between business and government 32–3,
        58–9, 63, 65, 66–8
Pasquier, Bernard 64
People for the Ethical Treatment of Animals
    (PETA) 108–9
PepsiCo 102–3, 106, 116
PHD (Punjab, Haryana and Delhi)
    Chambers of Commerce and Industry
    disaster relief initiative 50
    social development initiative 41
philanthropy 32
Planning Commission 89, 155
polluter pays principle 110
Pollution Control Board (PCB) 39
Polyani, Karl 11
Population Foundation of India 47
Portugal, Social Employment Market
    (MSE) 151

Prahalad, C.K. 89
Pratham 44
Prem Group 129
Premji, Azim 56, 58, 163
Primary Health Care system 63
Prince of Wales Business Trust 113
private ownership of property 24–5, 27
    Gandhi on 25, 26–7
privatization process 158
public interest litigations (PIL), social
    activism through 109–11
public-private partnership xxi, 31, 32–3,
    34–5, 48, 51–3, 55, 58–9, 63, 65, 67–8,
    89, 139, 152–3, 155, 158–9
PWBLF 112

Rahman, Muzaffar 127
Rajiv Gandhi Foundation (RGF) 68
Rajiv Gandhi Mobile AIDS Counselling
    Services Project 47
Rescue models 48–53
Rotary India xxii, 50
    health initiative 51–2
    Polio Eradication Advocacy Taskforce
        51
Rotary International 51
Rural Development Foundation 41
Ruskin, John 21–2, 26–8
    on role of state and business 28
    Unto This Last 21, 28

Sainsbury 85
Sampradhan Indian Centre for Philanthropy
    113
Sarv Shiksha Abhiyan 68
    see also NIIT
Satyam Computer Services Limited 55
Scope 131
Sehgal, Dalip 86
Self-Employed Women's Association
    (SEWA) 88–9, 92–3
    Gram Mahila Haat (SGMH) 89, 91–2
    Rural Distribution Network (RUDI)
        89–91
Setalvad, J.C. 31
Shakti Project 86–7
Shastri, Lal Bahadur 11, 24
Shell 112
Shiksha India 46
Shinawatra, Thaksin 9
Shops and Establishments Act 79

Shroff, A.D. 31
Sifsa 47
Singh, Manmohan 10
Singhanias, initiative for education 32
small and medium enterprises (SMEs) 83–4,
    85, 122, 124, 126, 135, 140
Social Accountability International (SAI),
    United States of America 122, 123 –4
    see also SA 8000 standards
Social Development Council (SDC) 41
social development initiative 14, 15, 42, 58,
    63
Social Development Programmes 44
social norms, embedding 81–2
Socially Responsible Investing (SRI) 121
Society for Village Development (SVADES),
    Vadodara 114
sociology of economics 11–14
South Gujarat Diamond Workers
    Co-operative (SGDWA) 84
Spastic Society of Tamil Nadu 68
Sri Ram, Lala 32
Sustainability, United Kingdom 75, 122,
    140
Swami Shivananda Sanitary Charitable
    Hospital, Tamil Nadu 70
Swaminathan, M.S. 72
Sweden, initiative for CSR 144, 148
Swedish Partnership for Global
    Responsibility 144

Tata Aquatic Farms Limited 100
Tata Council for Community Initiatives
    (TCCI) 137
Tata Group of Companies, Tatas 36, 137,
    163
    commitment to community
        development 38, 114, 137–8
    education initiative 32
    labour welfare measures 37
    rural development 32
Tata Steel Mill 38, 43, 137
Tata Steel Rural Development Society 32
Tata, J.R.D. 10, 30, 31
Tata, Ratan 137–8
Thakurdas, Purshottamdas 30
Tolstoy, Leo 28
Triple Bottom Line (TBL) 43, 132, 138
trusteeship xx, 11, 15, 27, 28, 29, 163
    Hindu philosophy and 22–3

India's gift to the world 20–2
    mechanization with human face 26
    and values 24–5

UNICEF 52
Uniliver 122
United Kingdom
    initiative for CSR 140, 142–3, 146, 147
    Ethical Trading Initiative 144
United Nations (UN) 3–4, 129–31, 155
    Commission on Private Sector and
        Development 154
    Convention on the Rights of the Child
        123
    Development Project (UNDP) 3, 39
Universal Declaration of Human Rights 76,
    123, 130
Utkal Alumina International Limited
    (UAIL) 101, 104, 105, 106

Vajpayee, Atal Bihari 10
Vindhya Valley Project, Madhya Pradesh
    87, 91

Walchand Hirachand 30, 31
Weaker Section Integrated Development
    Agency (WSIDA) 105
Webb, Beatrice 38
World Health Organization (WHO) 51,
    116
Wipro Technologies
    Applying Thought in Schools 56–8, 63
    Community Learning Centres 59–61
    disaster relief initiative 62
    healthcare 63
    IT education and social development
        55–63
    partnership with the government 58–9,
        63
    Wipro Cares 62–3
World Bank 89, 121, 134
World Economic Forum, Davos 1999 3,
    46, 106, 129
World Federation of Sporting Goods
    Industry 45
World Trade Organizations (WTO) xxiii,
    125
World Wide Fund for Nature (WWF) 95

Young India Fellows (YIFs) 60